site-seeing

a visual approach to web usability

site-seeing

a visual approach to web usability

Luke Wroblewski

With contributions by Nan Goggin and Jennifer Gunji

Hungry Minds™

Best-Selling Books · Digital Downloads · e-Books · Answer Networks · e-Newsletters · Branded Web Sites · e-Learning
New York NY, Cleveland OH, Indianapolis IN

SITE SEEING: A VISUAL APPROACH TO WEB USABILITY

Published by
Hungry Minds, Inc.
909 Third Avenue
New York, NY 10022

Library of Congress Control Number: 2002103280

ISBN: 0-7645-3674-5

Printed in the United States of America

10 9 8 7 6 5 4 3 2 1

Production: 1K/RS/QW/QS/IN

Distributed in the United States by Hungry Minds, Inc.

Distributed by CDG Books Canada Inc. for Canada; by Transworld Publishers Limited in the United Kingdom; by IDG Norge Books for Norway; by IDG Sweden Books for Sweden; by IDG Books Australia Publishing Corporation Pty. Ltd. for Australia and New Zealand; by TransQuest Publishers Pte Ltd. for Singapore, Malaysia, Thailand, Indonesia, and Hong Kong; by Gotop Information Inc. for Taiwan; by ICG Muse, Inc. for Japan; by Intersoft for South Africa; by Eyrolles for France; by International Thomson Publishing for Germany, Austria, and Switzerland; by Distribuidora Cuspide for Argentina; by LR International for Brazil; by Galileo Libros for Chile; by Ediciones ZETA S.C.R. Ltda. for Peru; by WS Computer Publishing Corporation, Inc., for the Philippines; by Contemporanea de Ediciones for Venezuela; by Express Computer Distributors for the Caribbean and West Indies; by Micronesia Media Distributor, Inc. for Micronesia; by Chips Computadoras S.A. de C.V. for Mexico; by Editorial Norma de Panama S.A. for Panama; by American Bookshops for Finland.

For general information on Hungry Minds' products and services, please contact our Customer Care department within the U.S. at 800-762-2974, outside the U.S. at 317-572-3993 or fax 317-572-4002.

For sales inquiries and reseller information, including discounts, premium and bulk quantity sales, and foreign-language translations, please contact our Customer Care department at 800-434-3422, fax 317-572-4002 or write to Hungry Minds, Inc., Attn: Customer Care Department, 10475 Crosspoint Boulevard, Indianapolis, IN 46256.

For information on licensing foreign or domestic rights, please contact our Sub-Rights Customer Care department at 212-884-5000.

For information on using Hungry Minds' products and services in the classroom or for ordering examination copies, please contact our Educational Sales department at 800-434-2086 or fax 317-572-4005.

For press review copies, author interviews, or other publicity information, please contact our Public Relations department at 317-572-3168 or fax 317-572-4168.

For authorization to photocopy items for corporate, personal, or educational use, please contact Copyright Clearance Center, 222 Rosewood Drive, Danvers, MA 01923, or fax 978-750-4470.

 *is a trademark of Hungry Minds, Inc.*

site-seeing

a visual approach to web usability

Outline Contributors: Nan Goggin & Jennifer Gunji

Book Design: Jennifer Gunji

Book Layout: Jennifer "The Goonj" Gunji, Ryan "Raza" Ruel, & Jeff "Wiggy" Wegesin

Permissions: Luke Wroblewski

Editor: Kelly Ewing

Technical Editor: Kyle D. Bowen

Acquisitions Editor: Tom Heine

Editorial Manager: Rev Mengle

Indexer: Johnna Van Hoose

Cover Design: Anthony Bunyan

Cover Photo: ©Alexander Walter/Getty Images

Senior Vice President, Technical Publishing: Richard Swadley

Vice President and Publisher: Barry Pruett

Production Coordinator: Nancee Reeves

Publisher: Wiley

Luke Wroblewski currently heads the interface and new media design efforts at the National Center for Supercomputing Applications (NCSA), birthplace of the first readily available graphical Web browser, NCSA Mosaic. At NCSA, he has designed interface solutions for Hewlett-Packard, IBM, and Kellogg's, codeveloped the Open Portal Interface Environment (OPIE), and worked on numerous other Web interface design projects.

Luke is also the founder and creative director of LukeW Interface Designs (www.lukew.com) and has taught Sequential Design in Web Technologies and New Media courses at the University of Illinois. Luke's research on Web-based application interface designs has been published and presented at national and international conferences.

As an interface designer, Luke studies the theory that explains how people communicate, comprehend, collaborate, and create. His aim is to unify visual communication principles with disciplines that have traditionally not given visual design sufficient emphasis. Luke's work underscores a mutual understanding of visual and functional principles that stems from his interdisciplinary education: graphic design, human factors, and computer science.

PREFACE: LOOKING AT WEB USABILITY

Although Web usability is receiving lots of attention (possibly even more following the recent dot-com downturn), the focus remains mostly on "technical" guidelines. Web usability experts stress the disadvantages of frames and too many images on Web pages. They recommend cutting down on unnecessary words and writing in the nonlinear style of the Web (all valuable advice, of course). But less frequently do they highlight the importance of the visual presentation aspects of Web pages.

The Web is a communication medium that does most of its talking visually. What you see on a Web page tells you what you might find within the site, how to get to it, why it might interest you, and more - not to mention the instinctive emotional response (to the visual presentation) that shapes your Web experience from start to finish.

As a result, Web usability issues are communication issues, and easy-to-use sites are sites that communicate effectively (and quickly) with their audience.

In an effort to make you a better Web communicator, I have attempted to write a book that provides you with design considerations from each of the three areas that contribute to a superior Web user experience: technical (how the site is built), structural (how it is organized), and visual (how it appears to your audience). However, the focus is on the visual, which communicates quickly, intuitively, and convincingly.

The visual presentation of a Web site does much more than make a Web site "pretty." It organizes information in a manner indicative of its function, it engages and directs your audience, it creates distinct and appropriate personalities, it provides emotional impact and attachment, and more (see Introduction).

HOW TO USE THIS BOOK

Note that I purposefully use the words "design considerations" through-out this book. Though you might have been led to believe otherwise, there are few "rules" in Web design. Each site's unique goals and audi-ence set the guidelines to which you should adhere (see Chapter 1).

The design considerations presented here are just that: points and possi-ble solutions to consider when deciding what's best for your site design. You don't have to adhere to every consideration I present in every site you design. In fact, I recommend you don't.

Instead, I hope by learning about each consideration and why it is impor-tant in Web design, you become versed in the unique language of the Web. When it comes time to communicate to your audience, you can make use of your new vocabulary to craft eloquent and informative nar-ratives that engage and educate. In other words, the knowledge of Web design considerations presented in this book should empower you to cre-ate original yet appropriate solutions.

That said, I would like to emphasize that any one person's views on what makes a Web site successful are naturally biased. After all, we all have our own likes and dislikes (even online). But we are not designing sites for ourselves (well, sometimes we are), but rather for our end users. Therefore, you need to make use of user testing throughout the Web design process. Repeatedly test your Web solutions on your target audi-ence (or simply on outsiders) to confirm that you are making the right design decisions.

These tests don't have to be (and shouldn't be) long or expensive. Even a few quick questions here and there is often enough to discover problematic areas. Trust me, you will often be surprised by the issues these tests uncover, and the payoff will be evident rather quickly.

This methodology is not unique to Web design. Automobile manufacturers, mapmakers, book designers, and just about everyone involved in a design-oriented process follow a similar progression. For example, automobile designers need to make sure that the cars they design are usable (they meet the constraints of the road system and skills of users), comfortable (adequate room, for example), and have enough personality to distinguish them from the throngs of other cars available elsewhere. As a result, they have lots of design considerations that need to be adequately addressed in whatever solution they decide upon. How can I make this car's silhouette feel faster? Is this odometer readable at night? Being aware of these considerations does not limit their ability to design cars. Rather, it empowers them to come up with unique solutions, which are then tested and tested again to ensure that they are effective and appropriate.

It's exactly this process that I prescribe to you for designing Web pages.

THE EXAMPLES IN THIS BOOK

The Web sites you will find featured in these pages are gathered from all walks of Web life: from mega-corporation home pages to individual designer's personal projects, from educational resources to pure entertainment sites. This diversity is intentional and hopefully makes it clear that each site ultimately calls for a unique solution (and applications of the design considerations outlined in this book).

Although the majority of the examples within these pages are of sites beyond my control, I have also included several that I have designed and developed. (Thanks to everyone that participated in and made these projects happen.) In most cases, I chose these examples because I was very familiar with the goals, process, and audience of the project. Therefore, I felt better qualified to justify the design decisions that were made.

I don't claim that these (nor any other examples) in this book are flawless. All have room for improvement . However, they do serve to illustrate certain points within this book. After all, a book focusing on visual communication techniques needs lots of visual examples, right?

ACKNOWLEDGEMENTS

Thanking everyone involved in this project is bound to be an imperfect process. If I forget to mention anyone, please feel free to torment me for it.

First and foremost, I wish to thank Nan Goggin and Jennifer Gunji for their inspiration, insight, and time. The original content and ideas for this book are largely a result of our collaborative efforts and the contributions of Joseph Squier and Robb Springfield. I would like to especially thank Nan for bringing the project to Jennifer and me in the first place and shaping the direction this book would ultimately take. Her experience as an artist, designer, and design educator was invaluable to me when determining the focus of this book, and her assistance throughout my graduate education not only shaped my views on design, but also my growth as an individual. Thanks again, Nan.

My sincere thanks and admiration also go to the design team of this book led by Jennifer Gunji who was greatly helped by Nan Goggin, Ryan Ruel, and Jeff Wegesin. Her layouts and ideas breathe life into this book and fill it with a unique energy that is both exciting and elegant. I have nothing but the highest regard for her design skills and am honored that she was willing to participate on this project (which wasn't always fun and games).

I would also like to acknowledge all of the designers, usability experts, writers, and researchers from all disciplines that influenced my ideas and approach to Web design. In particular, the faculty at the University of Illinois at Urbana-Champaign: Esa Rantanen (Human Factors), Michael Twidale (Library and Information Sciences), Andreas Veneris and David Padua (Computer Science), and Robb Springfield and Joseph Squier (Art & Design). Special thanks go to Colleen Bushell (Graphic Design) for her guidance and assistance all the way from my undergraduate education to the present. Also, thanks to Donald Norman, Jakob Nielsen, Bruce Tognazzini, and Edward Tufte, whose talks and ideas often informed and provided lots of great examples.

Finally, sincere thanks to John Melchi and the rest of the staff at the National Center for Supercomputing Applications (NCSA) for dealing with my sometimes irregular hours as I wrote this book., as well as the original team that developed NCSA Mosaic (the world's first widely distributed graphical Web browser), which let the world finally "see" the

Web. Thanks also to Tom Heine and Kelly Ewing at Wiley & Sons for their continual support and assistance throughout this project and Vernon Area Public Library in Lincolnshire, IL, and Grainger Engineering Library in Champaign, IL, for providing me with quiet places where I could stare at the laptop screen. And last but most certainly not least, to my family and friends who not only put up with my continual absences and frustrations, but provided encouragement at all times.

Thanks and Enjoy,

Luke Wroblewski, April 2002

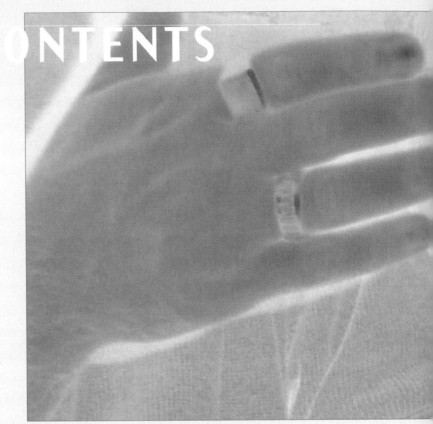

PART ONE

THINK BEFORE YOU... COMMUNICATE:
[THE PLANNING STAGES]

HOW TO . . . COMMUNICATE:
[THE THREE LEXICONS OF WEB USABILITY]

START COMMUNICATING:
[ONLINE, THAT IS!]

THINK

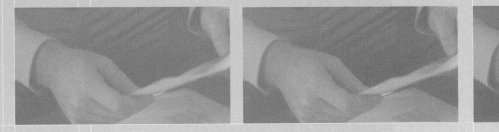

PART ONE

BEFORE YOU. . . COMMUNICATE:

THE PLANNING STAGES

The Web is a means to communicate, and whenever you're communicating, you need to know what you're saying, to whom, and how. Answering these questions up front will provide you with a roadmap to follow throughout the Web design process. If you make a wrong turn, you can always check your map and get back on course.

LEARNING TO SPEAK WEB

introduction

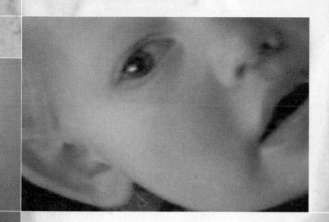

At birth, we have few ways to express ourselves: frequent crying, an occasional laugh. But as we mature, so does our ability to communicate. After many years of development, we become expressive and eloquent and can easily describe complex scenarios and information. The Web is no different. As a communication medium, the Web has gone through many stages of evolution. From its first "words" to its current complexity, the way the Web "speaks" to us has changed dramatically. However, the key to creating articulate Web sites remains the ability to communicate with our audience.

THE EVOLUTION OF THE WEB]

ᴺᴼ1 Simple Sharing
Allowed researchers to share information

ᴺᴼ2 Image & Table
The first graphical Web browsers made simple layouts possible

ᴺᴼ3 Design Intro
Visual designers unfamiliar with the Web began creating layouts for Web sites

ᴺᴼ4 Techno-Hype
Overindulgence in graphics and a use of new technologies for the sake of it characterized this era

ᴺᴼ5 Usability
A focus on the users and content of Web sites

ᴺᴼ6 Speaking Web
What this book is about

When we're young, even simple actions seem like grand feats. Our first steps are welcomed with great pride, and our first words signal an ability to make our ideas known to the world around us. Once we mature, however, few of us give talking and walking much thought. Instead, we use our grasp of language to convey complex narratives, and our firm footing to execute graceful athletic maneuvers. But, this maturity doesn't come quickly or easily. The lessons of adolescence and our early mistakes play a critical role in our evolution. They shape our understanding of the world around us and provide us with direction for our continued growth.

We are not alone in our progress: New technologies likewise go through a similar evolutionary process. To use Donald Norman's example from *The Invisible Computer (Mit Press, 1998)*, a person more or less needed a mechanic to operate one of the first automobiles. Simply turning on the engine was a multistep process involving fuel lines, spark settings, cranks, and more. Now, all a driver needs to know is "*turn the key, and off you go*". This simplicity did not come about instantaneously. It took years of mistakes and improvements for the automobile to evolve into the "mature" product it is today: a product centered on efficiency and ease-of-use rather than technological accomplishment.

At barely ten years old, the World Wide Web still has a long way to go before maturity. But due to the large amount of attention it has received, it is progressing rapidly. We can best see this progress by looking at the history of the Web in significant stages (distinguished by overall Web design trends). Thankfully, each successive stage has built upon the lessons learned in stages past. As a result, our knowledge of Web technologies and design principles has grown substantially, and Web sites

have progressively become easier to understand and use. This allows us to now make better, more informed decisions when we design and develop Web sites. With that goal in mind, let's see what we can learn from the stages of Web evolution that have brought us to where we are today.

stage ONE: THE SIMPLE SHARING ERA

stage TWO: THE IMAGE & TABLE ERA

stage THREE: THE DESIGN INTRO ERA

stage FOUR: THE TECHNO-HYPE ERA

stage FIVE: THE USABILITY ERA

stage SIX: SPEAKING WEB (WHAT THIS BOOK IS ABOUT)

The first four stages should be considered lessons in history and in how not to design Web sites. We'll just briefly touch on each of them to provide a frame of reference for our current situation. We'll spend considerably more time on stages five and six: the focus of this book.

The Simple Sharing Era: The World Wide Web was born at the CERN research facility in Switzerland. As envisioned by Tim Berners-Lee, the Web was to transfer information between people in an easy-to-access format. Because of this vision, the first Web pages consisted of text-based data and little more.

At this very early stage in its evolution, the Web was clearly not for everybody. It "spoke" in a language only its parents could understand (URI, http, and so on). Getting started took some know-how, and once you did, the experience was hardly user-friendly. But, researchers and academics, thoroughly impressed with how the Web allowed them to share data, were quick to embrace the new technology. They found enough value in the Web to make using it worthwhile. They formed a community that would gradually nurture and raise the Web.

AN IMAGE | TABLE ERA LAYOUT

The National Center for Supercomputing Applications (NCSA) home page from 1993 is an example of an early Web site from the Image/Table Era. The ability to incorporate both images and text within Web pages was an important milestone in Web evolution that attracted lots of people.

The Image/Table Era: As traffic on the Web began to grow, so did the demand for the ability to share more than just text. In response, the first graphical Web browser (Mosaic) was developed at the National Center for Supercomputing Applications (NCSA) in 1993, and with it came the

A DESIGN INTRO ERA LAYOUT

NCSA's home page from 1995 is exemplary of the kind of sites popular during the Design Intro Era. All the text on this site is contained within images, resulting in long download times and poor accessibility. Designers at the time were unfamiliar with the characteristics that made the Web a unique communication medium, and instead designed as they would for any other publishing technology.

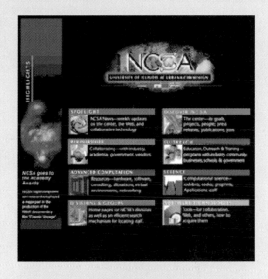

ability to view and include images as parts of Web pages. When these images were dropped into tables, the Web's first layouts were born. This development caused a lot more people to get interested, and Web sites began popping up everywhere. When the first commercial Web browser (Netscape Navigator) was released and distributed in 1994, people all over the world were suddenly aware of the World Wide Web. No longer only in the hands of technology enthusiasts, the Web now had to be accessible and understandable by people outside its early community of "parents." It had to learn to communicate with the rest of the world.

The Design Intro Era: It was now clear that the Web was no longer confined to academic circles. Corporations, entrepreneurs, and early devotees all rushed to put up Web sites. They brought in graphic designers to take full advantage of the layout possibilities now available online. While these designers knew a great deal about communicating through text and image, very few knew the vocabulary of the Web: a new and unique communication medium. Because of this ignorance, not enough attention was paid to the navigation, behavior, and structure of Web sites. Instead, most Web sites were characterized by an oversaturation of images and poor functionality. Designers created great presentations,

A TECHNO-HYPE ERA LAYOUT

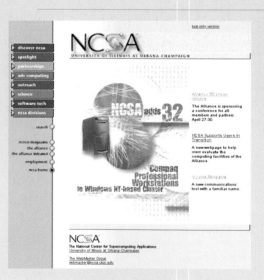

NCSA's 1997 home page consisted of an animated, multilevel navigation system coded as a Java applet. Though the applet looked "cool" and moved fluidly, it took a long time to download and was confusing to users. Technology was in charge, not usability.

but tended to fall short in interactivity and organization. They hadn't yet learned how to "speak" Web.

The Techno-Hype Era: Once images became commonplace on Web sites, designers and their clients looked for new ways to stand out from the crowd and get the attention of a continually growing Web audience. As it were, technology was more than willing to lend a hand. Embedded applications (applets and videos), add-ons to Web browsers for increased functionality (plug-ins), and new Web browsers (with advanced features) saturated the Web industry. Suddenly, if you were using the latest Web gimmick, you were at the forefront of Web design. Introductory animations created in Macromedia's Flash (a Web animation tool and browser plug-in) and navigation applets coded in Java (the programming language) were all the rage.

And while Web developers and designers paid lots of attention to glitz and glam, considerably less attention was paid to a site's content (substance) and ease of use. The Web was in its "teenage" years: It was only concerned with itself. Web site designers, like rebellious teenagers, thought they knew what was good for the Web better than anyone else. Consequently, sites were exciting and cool, but did little else for their audience.

THE USABILITY ERA
[SECTION TITLE]

It quickly became apparent that sites that only looked "cool" were not. Finding relevant information amidst a downpour of large graphics and gratuitous animations was no easy task. Add long download times and poor information organization to the mix, and it's not too difficult to see why something had to change. The Web had to grow up and accept some responsibility for its shortcomings. Visitors to Web sites were confused by needless glitz, and they often found themselves leaving a Web site

A USABILITY ERA LAYOUT

NCSA's 1999 home page has few large images (for a faster download) and focuses on providing the information visitors need up front and without effort.

without achieving their goals. On the advice of these frustrated users, Web sites began focusing on clarity, efficiency, and customer satisfaction. In others words, they focused on usability. Within a usable Web site, customers can accomplish their goals easily and leave happily.

With customer satisfaction in mind, usability professionals began taking a detailed look at what works and what doesn't work online. Taking an engineering approach to the problem, they performed rigorous user studies and interviews. From the data they acquired, they were able to generate a series of guidelines for Web site design and development. Many of these guidelines are based on "technical" factors (issues that can be generalized to mechanical solutions). For example, because the use of *frames* (Web pages divided into columns and rows of multiple Web pages) broke the unified model of the Web (bookmarking is not possible with frames, and so on), usability guidelines discouraged their use. Similarly, if a Web page contained links to large files, usability guidelines suggested indicating the file size near the link to warn users of a lengthy download time.

Though specific usability guidelines have helped many sites become much more useful and efficient, they're not the end-all solution to a successful Web experience. For example, quick download times are proven to be high on the list of user needs. If a page takes too long to load, users may become impatient and take their Web business elsewhere. For this reason, usability guidelines suggest that Web page elements that contribute to large page sizes (and thereby download time) should be minimized. Because images tend to have large file sizes, few images on a Web page might be considered "good" in terms of Web usability.

However, this guideline can be wrongly interpreted to mean that less visual elements provide a better Web experience. Such thinking could very well produce Web pages that download quickly, but only confuse users through poor layout and are as interesting as staring at the "Smith" page of a phone book.

The problem is not that Web usability guidelines discourage the use of frames, nonstandard Web interactions, too many images, and anything else that hinders content delivery. All of these are important considerations for designing a successful Web site and should not be ignored. Rather, the problem is that these same guidelines do not highlight the importance of visual communication principles (keep reading) for content delivery, interpretation, and presentation. A good Web experience consists of useful and usable content framed by the principles of visual communication to create meaning and understanding for an audience. Improving the overall experience for Web site visitors involves not only proper solutions to technical concerns (such as download time and accessibility), but also presentation, emotion, approachability, and more. It means advancing to the next stage of Web evolution.

[WHAT THIS BOOK IS ABOUT]
[SECTION TITLE]

We are now in a stage of Web evolution where it's clear that a good Web experience is the result of mutual collaboration between presentation, interaction, and organization considerations. Web designers need to consider how their sites are structured (organization), how they look (presentation) and how they respond to users (interaction) —in other words, how they communicate.

When a visitor comes to your Web site, they have only the presentation to tell them what you have to offer, and how they can make use of it. As a result, the presentation has a lot of responsibilities. (Both

WEB SITE CONSIDERATIONS

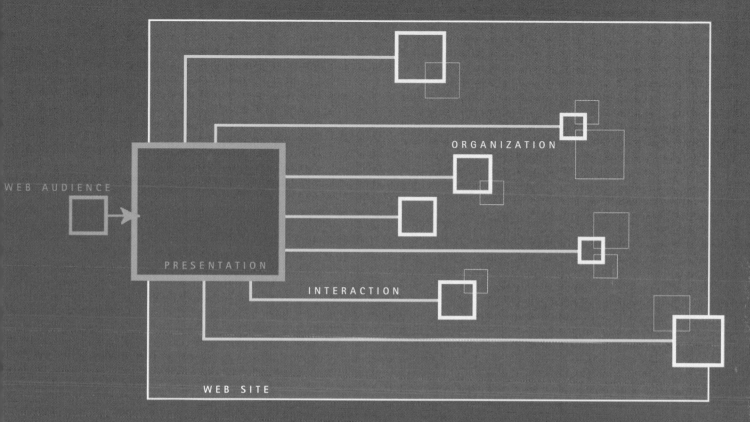

When designing a Web site, we need to consider three basic factors: presentation, organization, and interaction. **Presentation** is how your site appears to your audience, **organization** is the structure of your site, and **interaction** is how your site behaves in response to user actions. Because all interactions between your audience and your structure occur through the site's presentation, it must be understandable and engaging. If the presentation is not clear, your audience might not be able to make it to your content. If the presentation is not engaging, your audience might not be motivated to try.

THE ROLE OF PRESENTATION

AMONG OTHER THINGS, AN EFFECTIVE WEB SITE
PRESENTATION CAN HELP

Provide situational awareness

Provide clarity

Provide emotional impact

Engage and invite users

Explain organization

*Guide users through content
and sequences*

Maintain consistency

Educate users

Establish relationships between content

*Create emphasis and focus within Web
pages and sites*

Send the right message to an audience

*Give sites unique personalities
and distinction*

Establish a sense of place

organization and interaction are dependent on it.. A good presentation makes organizational systems understandable and clear, supports user goals and actions, effectively conveys the messages and ideas that we want to express to your audience, and more. (A poor presentation can do just the opposite, as evidenced by the techno-hype era.)

Effective Web site presentations aren't just flukes of evolution; they come from the proper use and understanding of visual communication principles. We use visual principles to communicate concepts to our audience: concepts about the behavior, structure, and purpose of our Web sites. The better at communicating we are, the easier it is for our audience to understand our messages and intentions, and the easier it is for them to use and appreciate our Web sites.

By introducing the fundamental principles of visual communication and then applying them to Web site interaction and organization, this book is designed to provide you with the skills necessary to enter the next stage of Web evolution: the skills to speak "Web". The book is divided into three sections reflective of how we convey information. Before attempting to communicate (visually or aurally), you need a solid understanding of what it is you want to say. Section 1 outlines a methodology for determining what you're trying to communicate and to whom. Once we know what we want to say, we need to know how to say it. The second section teaches you how to speak visually. It is in this section where I introduce the principles of visual communication and their role in Web usability. Finally, I start speaking "Web." Section 3 applies the lessons of Section 2 to the many elements of Web sites: page elements, navigation, home pages, and dynamic content design. By the end of Section 3, you'll be ready to make understandable and engaging Web presentations. You'll be fluent in the language of the Web!

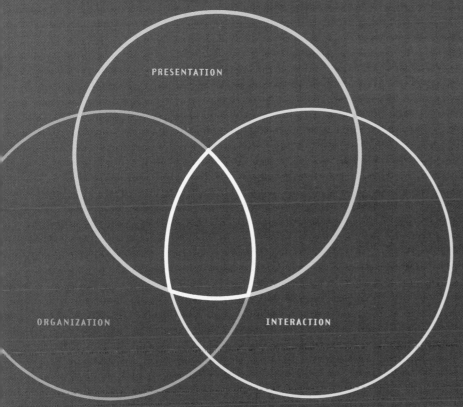

PRESENTATION

ORGANIZATION

INTERACTION

PRESENTATION

Presentation includes everything related to how a Web site communicates`: fonts, images, colors, and so on. The fields of sensorial, graphic, and information design provide the visual communication skills necessary to create a successful Web site presentation.

ORGANIZATION

Organization encompasses everything related to the structure of a Web site: information architecture, labeling systems, writing, and content decisions. Library and information sciences provide excellent references on organizing information.

INTERACTION

Interaction takes into account how users and systems behave. Human factors and engineering disciplines provide valuable resources for developing interaction models and technological solutions.

THIS BOOK AND THE BIG PICTURE

The key to a successful user experience is a combination of interaction, presentation, and organization considerations. This book goes into considerable detail about everything inside the blue circle including how the presentation can complement and enhance the organization and interaction of a Web site. Though we discuss the areas outside the blue area, other books discuss them in greater depth.

GETTING IT RIGHT

Note the orange area where these three considerations intersect. Not too big, is it? This area is reflective of just how difficult it is to get things right. On the Web, interaction, organization, and presentation are intertwined, and ceding one consideration for another is a surefire way to limit the success of your Web site.

chapter one

At some point in our lives, we all have been told to "think before you speak." Though this advice seems like good counsel and easy to do, the truth is, it is rarely utilized. Communication is such a natural part of our daily routines that when we have something to say, we do just that: Say it. Speaking comes so easily we don't need to think too long about what we really mean to say. The same is true for other relatively easy actions. Currently, putting up a Web page is an easy task for anyone with some time to spare and a willingness to learn. As a result, a lot of Web pages are thrown together just like sentences: quickly and without much forethought.

At some point in our lives, we all did think before speaking, and we still didn't get our message across. Perhaps the problem was that we only thought about the words we were using. In our day-to-day communication, words play a small role. We communicate in many more nonverbal ways. Body language helps give words meaning. Intonation can make all the difference in a phone conversation. In online chat rooms, *smilies* (also called emoticons) attempt to articulate our intentions ("Just kidding" or "I'm confused"). Words alone are often not enough. Visual, aural, and temporal cues enhance our understanding and interpretation of what is being said and often infuse words with the proper meaning. The more we know about how to provide and receive cues, the better we can communicate.

The Web has its own set of cues: image, text, interaction, organization, motion, and sound. Just as in conversation, words are just a small part of how you communicate on the Web[1]. To create effective Web presentations that "speak" to our audience, we must take all our nonverbal cues into consideration. On the Web, "thinking before we speak" means far more than simply understanding verbal communication; it means thinking about how image, text, organization, interaction, motion, and sound can work together to create successful presentations. This process can be thought of as learning the language of the Web. Because the Web is still relatively young, both Web designers and their audience are new to this language. On the other hand, we're familiar with the verbal language we speak every day of our lives. So it is often possible for us to understand what someone means regardless of what he or she actually said.

HOW WE COMMUNICATE

Through:

Language

Gestures

Facial Expressions

Intonations

Space

Time

Culture

Images

Actions

Silence

Inactivity

And More...

[1]Steve Krug, in his book Don't *Make Me Think: A Common Sense Approach to Web Usability*, lists one of his "rules" of usability as "Get rid of half the words on each page, then get rid of half of what's left."

But, the Web not only speaks in a new language, it speaks in many languages (image, interaction, and so on), so there is no accepted vernacular from which you can interpret intended meaning. As a result, miscommunication occurs on a regular basis. Most of us haven't yet learned to "speak Web."

The problem is often escalated, because many Web authors simply "start talking" instead of thinking through what they want to say, and how to say it in the Web's unique language. Speaking "Web" means thoroughly thinking through the organization and interaction of a Web site, and how it is presented to an audience. Because the Web is visually rich, the presentation of a Web site must communicate in many nonverbal ways. Not only does the written language used need to be clear and approachable, but so does the visual language.

Ultimately, the Web is a communication medium. Therefore, effective Web design is analogous to effective communication, and we can often think of Web usability issues as communication issues.

[KNOW WHAT TO SAY]
[SECTION TITLE]

No matter the medium of communication, there is always a message. But real communication cannot take place unless someone is there to interpret the message and give it meaning. When we don't think through the message we're sending, it can often come out the wrong way or be interpreted in a manner the author never intended. In other words, it can lose its intended meaning. When the author of a message thinks through the intended meaning, odds are much better that the receiver's interpretation will be a close match.

Yet, even thinking through intended meaning is often not enough to communicate effectively. Sometimes the same message can be interpreted in two shockingly distinct ways by two separate individuals. The best way to explain something to Carl is not necessarily clear to Chris. Carl might be a mathematician and think in a very logical and rational manner. Chris, on the other hand, might be a therapist and analyze your message emotionally, coming up with something totally unlike what Carl surmised. So, how can we communicate successfully?

How can we make sure that Chris and Carl both receive the same message, and that the message is indeed what we intended? The answer is really not as complex as you might think. Thinking through the main message that you need to communicate and how best to articulate it often does the trick. Basically, we need to be certain we are aware of who is saying what to whom.

SAY IT IN "WEB"

When you open a Web page for the first time, the first thing you may ask is, "What am I looking at? And what does it mean?" Each and every Web page has a message, whether intentional or not. The message is communicated through images, text, colors, sounds, motion, and so on and assembled on the other end by you, the user, into meaning. If the Web page author did not give enough consideration for the audience and message of their Web page, the viewer might be confused or upset and leave quickly for a Web page that "speaks their language." If Carl, the mathematician, is the intended audience, numbers might be the proper form of communication; however, the therapist, Chris, may not know how to interpret the numerical presentation.

In order for a Web site to be "usable," it must be understandable. It needs to communicate, and communicate effectively. The intended message of a Web site needs to match the interpreted message of the user. In other words, a user must be able to successfully interpret meaning from how the Web site author selected and organized the many Web site elements (image, text, and so on). Therefore, Chris and Carl might find different sites more usable and suitable to their needs. But when both of them are your audience, you need to make sure that neither is confused.

When creating a Web site that effectively communicates a message, you should begin by asking numerous questions — questions like "What is my Web site's goal?", "Who is my audience?", "Why are they likely to come to my site?", "How do they communicate?", and so on. The following sections take a detailed look at some of those questions, how best to ask those questions, and what their answers may tell you.

Our client? Oh, that's easy. He's Joe from widget.com. Not quite. Getting to know your clients involves a lot more than first names. Prior to designing a Web presence for your clients, you need to really understand your clients, what they do, what they want, and how they expect to get it done. (Though I use the term clients here, you could certainly be designing a site for yourself, or someone within your company.)

Getting to know your client involves some reading and a lot of talking, especially a lot of inquiring. When you design Web sites for clients, you're effectively developing a means of communication for that client. Your clients' presence in cyberspace is their virtual showroom, open 24 hours a day and available in every household. The Web sites will provide information, offer services, and give visitors an understanding of your clients and their business. So, before you can start "speaking" for your clients, you have to learn what they would say. An initial step to understanding your clients might involve reading their business collateral or brochures, examining their business and marketing plans, trying out their products, or researching current trends and issues in your clients' industries. You need to try to understand your clients' intentions and focus, as well as their constraints. It might even be beneficial to sit down with some employees of the firm and have them describe to you, in their own words, what they feel their company is about. Do not be afraid to ask lots of questions. Only by having a clear idea of your clients' goals can you speak for them. The most important answer to "Who is your client?" is understanding what your client does, for whom, and why. Keep this information at the tip of your tongue (or in the case of Web design, your mouse). When it comes time to communicate for your clients, make sure that this information remains in your forethoughts.

UNDERSTANDING YOUR CLIENTS' GOALS

Now that you know more about Joe's company than even he does, you need to understand why Joe's company needs to be on the Web. When designing or organizing for the Web, it is your job to understand your clients' intent and direction. You need to define the problem. Clients sometimes think in very broad loosely defined goals or are convinced that they need the same solution their competitor just implemented. During this discussion, you should try to identify the problem. Without directly referencing the Web, have your clients try to clearly identify their needs. For example, instead of saying, "We need a form with five input fields and two drop down menus...", it is better to understand your clients' need as "We need the ability for interested parties to send us their contact information, so we can..." Make certain that you have the problem clearly identified, or you may end up spending most of your time developing solutions to ancillary issues.

JUMPING THE GUN

Sometimes, in the rush to get a site up, important portions of the preplanning process are overlooked. When this happens, the result is often a mixed bag of content sewn together very loosely and called a "Web site." Deciding on a clear focus and set of goals for your Web site beforehand ensures that your final product meets the agenda of you and your audience.

In this Web site (to the left), potential customers are asked to complete a lengthy survey to initiate contact with the organization. The site's goal, to gather information from potential customers, could have been better met through a more approachable interface or series of interactions (perhaps involving more than just the Web). Instead, the site forces potential clients through an immense survey, which is unlikely to be filled in online.

The real question is "What need is the Web site going to solve?" Delivering information and technical support for a product? Providing educational tools for high school students? Promoting a musician's solo career? The designer needs to determine the best means for meeting their clients' needs. Believe it or not, this means can be different from what the clients think is necessary (see sidebar). This is why it is important to understand your clients' needs independent of the Web. When you start talking about Web site elements, you're already thinking about a possible solution. This is the time for thinking about problems. There will be plenty of time later for solutions.

UNDERSTAND YOUR AUDIENCE
[SECTION TITLE]

"Who is your audience?" isn't just one question. It's a series of questions that need to be answered so that a designer knows with whom he or she needs to be communicating. The answers to these questions will also help to provide a composite idea of some typical members of this audience. A composite idea will help establish the tone, personality, and attitude of a Web site and is formed by asking questions. What is the age of the audience we're trying to reach? What kind of experience do they have? How well do they know our client's firm? How experienced are they with the Web? What type of shared culture do they have as an audience? What are their objectives? The answer to these questions and others will help you determine the content needed within your Web site. More importantly, it will determine what content you do not need in your Web site.

WHO'S YOUR AUDIENCE?

Who is Williams-Sonoma's audience? Seems like cooks, but what kind of cooks? What value do they place on cooking? Clearly, Williams Sonoma customers take their cooking very seriously. As a result, they take the time to seek out specific cooking and baking products and appreciate the quality of such goods. From high-quality pots to top-of-the-line appliances, Williams-Sonoma provides a wide range of specific products for cooking and entertaining. The site had to capture a sense of elegance and simplicity that is reflective of the quality of the firm. High-quality images, refined design, and a clear and concise presentation of information begin to provide the user with a Web experience that meets the expectations and established qualities of the products sold.

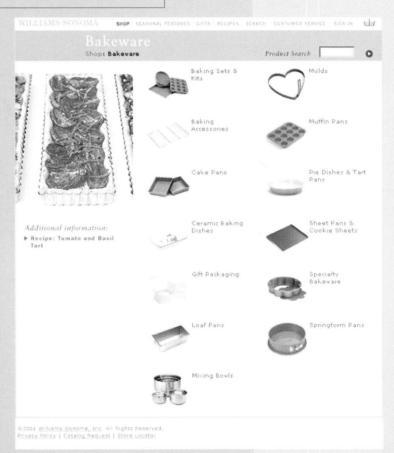

Perhaps the most important question regarding your audience is "What is their purpose for coming to your Web site?" Consider what they want to achieve, and how their needs can be met. Visitors come to Web sites with questions and expectations. For example, they expect to be able to find information on how to use your product, or they want to know who scored a touchdown in last night's football game.

By anticipating the types of questions users will bring to your site, you can design sites that meet and even exceed customer expectations. When your audience can achieve their goals quickly and easily, they will be content. That said, knowing and accounting for what your audience expects from your Web site doesn't guarantee a successful Web experience. You also need to understand how they expect it.

HOW THEY COMMUNICATE

How does your audience communicate? Perhaps your audience uses a certain lingo to communicate ideas between one another. Certainly, industry-specific connotations and phrases are shared by like-minded individuals. In the Williams-Sonoma example, distinctions are made with the conventions of thousands of cookbooks worldwide in mind. *Pan* here means cooking utensil, not to move a camera so as to follow a moving object, as it would on a cinematic-effects Web site. Knowing how your audience communicates, however, goes beyond the meanings associated with words. For example, what connotations do colors have? In the financial world, red is associated with negative trends, and investors instinctually interpret red text as bad news. Other concerns might be cultural. In the United States, mailboxes appear as rounded blue rectangles, whereas in Italy, they are often red squares (see image below). However, the image of an envelope with a stamp in the corner signifies mail for both cultures.

United States

Italia

France

Danmark

How does your audience like to receive information? Do they rely on images for an understanding of concepts, or are they more inclined to comprehend information presented in tabular form? Know what your audience finds useful and effective and present your information in that manner.

Another important point to consider here is the Web-specific requirements of your audience. Are they comfortable on the Web? What sorts of interactions do they typically engage in online? What have they come to expect from Web sites? It might be valuable to examine other sites in a similar area as your clients and see how their user base conducts itself online. Understanding how typical members of your audience communicate amongst each other online and in person will better allow you to communicate with them.

USING PROFILES AND SCENARIOS

Another technique commonly used to better comprehend an audience is the use of scenarios. A scenario is a sketch of why a typical audience member may use the site. It usually includes information such as the visitor's goal, the best way to realize that goal, and an ideal outcome for the site visit. Williams-Sonoma, for example, needed to consider a variety of scenarios: a visitor who needs to create a registry for an upcoming wedding; a visitor with an extensive knowledge of gourmet cooking utensils who is seeking a specific product within the Williams-Sonoma catalog; a visitor who is uncertain what gift to purchase for a friend and would like to casually browse the selection; a visitor who has been referred to the site and wants to understand Williams-Sonoma; and more.

DESIGNING FOR VARIETY

In order to accommodate the various needs of its audience, Williams-Sonoma presents visitors with several choices on its home page. If you're looking to buy a specific knife, you can jump right to the "Cutlery" section. If you need to buy a gift for mom, but don't have a specific idea, go to "Gift Ideas."

WILLIAMS-SONOMA *a place for cooks*

Shop
COOKWARE
ELECTRICS
FOOD
CUTLERY
AND MORE...

Gift Ideas

Recipes

Catalog Quick Shop

Wedding & Gift Registry

Within a scenario, it's common to create user profiles — that is, to specify the gender, status, employment, age, education, and so on of a fictional audience member. Profiles can even be based on information gathered from interviews with potential customers or from previous customer records. Profiles also often include the person's viewpoints and expectations. When designing Web sites, it's useful to refer back to your fictional audience member profiles and ask, "How would Amanda expect her information to appear?" or "Would this organization make sense to Mike?" Walking through the site as a typical audience member will allow you to map that user's needs to actions. Say that Amanda is a typical audience member of widget.com. Amanda needs to get in contact with her sales representative. She comes to the home page and...? Walk through the steps Amanda makes when she tries to find this information. What is she thinking about? What content descriptions would make sense to her? What does she expect to see? What does she believe is possible?

By developing several different scenarios, we're able to determine how a representative portion of the target audience expects your sites to appear and act. By asking many questions, we're able to accommodate the full range of interests likely to be part of your audience. This knowledge is important, because an understanding of the audience's needs should form the basis for your Web sites' content.

DETERMINING CONTENT

"Well, Joe gave us a bunch of documents, so we are just going to put those online and call it good." Though that seems like an easy way out, it's more than likely not a good solution. The majority of Web users come to the Web for one thing: content. A good way to make sure that you meet your audience's needs is to provide the content that they seek. When you've

determined who your audience is, let them determine what the content of the Web site should be. Even though Joe is paying the bill, you're not really designing a Web site for Joe. You are designing for Joe's audience. An easy way to see the difference is to look at how both your client and your audience perceive the same action[2]. Joe wants to sell his product. Joe's audience wants to make a purchase. Joe wants to reduce his costs by introducing services online. Joe's customers want to get their work done. Joe wants to provide information. Joe's audience wants to explore Joe's Web site to see what they can find. Fundamental differences

WHAT IS YOUR AUDIENCE LOOKING FOR?

The Macromedia site is a good example of audience determining content. Most visitors to Macromedia's Web site are software users interested in "what the Web can be." The majority of Macromedia's audience is interested in its software products. The navigation indicates this interest with categories such as products, support, resources, and showcase, all focusing on Macromedia's software. On each software page, there are lots of technical descriptions of the software, user feedback forums, support notes, and additional content all appropriate for users interested in Macromedia's products. Macromedia also has a "featured site" section where it showcases a site utilizing their software. Again, this site is a good example of audience determining content. Macromedia software users are interested in what others have done with the software, so they can better understand what is possible for them.

[2]A full discussion of this issue can by found in John Cato's *User-Centered Web Design* (2001).

between the client's viewpoint and their customer's can be seen just in the verbs used: sell/buy, provide/explore.

Content included in a Web site should meet the needs and expectations of your audience. If your audience does not need the content you are putting online, why is it there?

WRITING IT ALL DOWN
[S E C T I O N   T I T L E]

Now that you understand your client, their goals, and their audience, let this knowledge keep your project focused and on track. I recommend that you develop a short mission statement to help you. A *mission statement* should outline what the site needs to do and whom it needs to reach. In other words, the mission statement will detail the intended meaning of your message.

REFERRING BACK TO IT

Throughout the Web design process, it's a good idea to refer back to your mission statement to make sure that the work you're doing fulfills the goals of your client, and more importantly, meets the needs of your client's audience. It is also a good idea to develop a form of measure to evaluate how well the site you're designing fulfills the mission statement. This measure could be a series of user tests involving members of your client's intended audience, or it could be systematic checklist to make sure that all the needs outlined in the mission statement are being met.

A clear understanding of the purpose of the Web site will help the designer create a useful and effective site and a mission statement is an effective way of maintaining that objective. Now that you have a firm grasp of your message and your audience, you're ready to take a look at the steps needed to begin laying the foundation for your site.

A DOORWAY TO COMPUTING

Sample mission statement: The University of Illinois Computer Science Department

"The goal of the UIUC CS Department Web site is to communicate information about the department's current activities and available resources. The site design needs to reflect the department's position as a leading innovator in computer science research and education. In addition, current students, alumni, faculty, corporate sponsors, and the general public need a clear understanding of the information available within the site."

PLAYING FOR FANS

Sample mission statement: Robert Randolph.net

"The goal of the Robert Randolph site is to maintain and develop lasting relationships with fans of Robert's music. In addition to being visually and emotionally appealing and appropriate to Robert's fan base, the site should be a reliable source for current information on Robert's activities and provide consistently updated audio and visual stimuli that encourage repeated visits from fans."

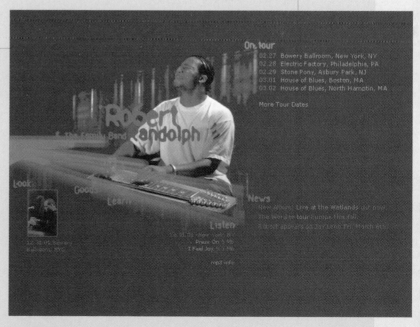

chapter two

Attempting to build anything without a plan will surely lead to lots of backtracking, lost time, and headaches. Not only can a plan keep you on track, it can also allow you to communicate your ideas to others and provide an excellent reference when it comes time to make design decisions. When we build a Web site, we need to think through the organization, navigation, personality, and limitations of our site. Ironing out these issues before jumping into the production stage can save us time and ensure that we end up with a site that "speaks" our audience's language.

[ORGANIZING YOUR SITE]
[S E C T I O N   T I T L E]

From libraries to books to sentences, we make sense of our surroundings through organization. We organize our houses into rooms and our cities into neighborhoods. No matter how full our homes get, or how big our cities grow, we can still find what we need in them, because they are organized in a manner we can understand. It would be quite difficult to find your way in a city that sometimes used numerical addresses, occasional color-coding, and an irregular system based on building height. The lack of a clear, consistent organization system would leave most people lost and confused.

But even in a city with a very perplexing organization system, we might still be able to find our way around using spatial clues. ("I remember passing by the red building earlier. If I turn right at this corner, I might get to where I am going.") Online, our audience has no such "last resort" to get them where they need to be. Though we refer to groups of Web pages as "sites," there are no physical landmarks to fall back on for guidance[1]. Worse still, Web users have few clues to tell them "where" a clicked hyperlink may take them. Links could lead to a different site or further down the page (in the case of inline links), or they could open a new Web browser window (quickly becoming a common practice with today's Web advertising) or begin downloading a large file. Given these possibilities and the lack of spatial cues on the Web, it is especially important that our organizational systems be well thought out and meaningful. They need to accurately outline the content of our sites in a manner appropriate to our audience.

SPACE-LESS SPACE

Unlike books and cities, the Web lacks any "real" physical structure. As a result, Web users are often landmark-less and unable to understand "where" they are within a site.

[1] A number of authors have discussed the lack of any real "space" on the Web, including Colleen Bushell (1995), Peter Morville & Louis Rosenfeld (1998), Patrick Lynch & Sarah Horton (1999), and Steve Krug (2000).

The manner in which your site is organized allows your audience to understand what they can expect to find within. It also provides them with an overall awareness of the big picture: your site's main message. Upon encountering a site with organizational categories such as fish, dogs, cats, birds, and so on, you might easily guess you were at a pet store. The organization of the site helps to communicate the purpose of the site: "I am a pet store with ... available for your pets." Though this point may seem obvious, there are many Web sites where the message is not clear and may leave you wondering if you are at a boutique or a bakery.

A well-organized site not only "tells" your audience what they can find within, it tells them where they can find it. When we have categories and alphabetical listings to help us, it's much easier to find a CD at the local music store. Imagine trying to locate a Charlie Hunter disk in a store where all the CDs just lie in random piles on the floor. I have actually encountered several LP stores that use this method, and unless you enjoy sifting through piles of dusty vinyl looking for a gem (and you have the time), you are better off at the CD store. Though the LPs are theoretically "organized" (into piles on the floor), you have no way of predicting where a particular record might be. Only after you look through a pile can you say, "I guess it's not in there." The organized store, on the other hand, allows you to find the right information in a predictable manner. Charlie Hunter would be in the jazz section, under H. With organization, knowing where to look is easy. Without organization, even a site with great presentation and interaction will ultimately confuse your audience.

WHEN YOU DON'T WANT ORGANIZATION

At the old vinyl shops, where records sit in massive piles on the floor, it can be a rewarding experience to spend time sifting through the LPs. Occasionally, you will come across something you didn't know existed or would have never thought to look for. The lack of organization, in this case, works to your benefit, allowing you to discover and explore.

For certain Web sites, it might be a good idea to mimic this type of experience. Some e-commerce stores do it in the form of recommendations: putting a list of items related only by your interests on a page customized for you, and allowing you to browse through them. These are far from the "flea market model" of sifting through heaps of items for something that catches your eye. But these days, few people have the time required for flea market shopping, precisely because it can be a very engaging experience.

SORT YOUR INFORMATION

The simplest form of organization is also the most frequently used: the sorting of similar objects into categories or sequences. It is the simplest because, often times, objects "want" to be together. Forks, spoons, and knives, together at dinnertime, invite grouping. They often share the same size, texture, color, and, most importantly, function. As a result, in most homes, these utensils share a drawer in the kitchen. It would be strange to have the forks and knives in one drawer, and the spoons on the third shelf from the bottom of the vanity in the downstairs bathroom. Not only do the objects themselves imply that they are of the same category, but most people expect them to be. Few guests would think to look in the downstairs bathroom for the spoons. More than likely, they will look in the drawer with the forks and knives, perhaps check a few more kitchen drawers, and finally assume that you have no spoons. You can expect the same behavior from your Web visitors. They will look in the categories where they expect to find the information they need. And if they can't find it, they will assume it doesn't exist. When organizing our Web sites, we need to make sure that our categories and what we put in them make sense for our audience and our content. We need to "tell" our audience what they can expect within each category.

Most categorization moves from general to specific. (House wares > Kitchen utensils>Forks>Dessert Fork) This allows us to transfer our knowledge of top-level categories to those below them and thereby increase our understanding. If we know kitchen utensils belong in the kitchen and we know a fork is a kitchen utensil, then we know forks belong in the kitchen.

CATEGORIES: WHAT HAVE THEY DONE FOR YOU LATELY?

Make finding information easier and faster.

Divide information into smaller, easier to "digest" portions.

Emphasize the similarities between information.

Point out the differences between information.

Provide "paths" to information.

Though this example is deliberately simple, the same basic model remains intact for more complex information and is especially helpful when you encounter items with which you are not familiar. (Ahhh, I see, GoLive is a Web design software product. I know this because I followed the path Products>Software>Web design>GoLive.) Higher level categories can provide valuable clues about objects and their function, and they can also give users a sense of where they are in an organized structure and, more importantly, why.

Organizing information from general to specific also carries the benefits of progressive disclosure. Information is much easier to absorb when it comes in smaller, related "doses." Progressive disclosure is especially important online where our screens are limited in size and reading large amounts of text is not favored by most people. (Instead, a common solution is to print large portions of text.) Progressive disclosure provides you with the portion of information you want when you're ready for it. For

NOW I WANT...

Dividing information into meaningful portions allows you to get the answers you need without having to analyze large quantities of extraneous material. Once you understand the basics about Acrobat (it is a program for creating PDF files), you can follow the links to the right to learn more about the product. Are you interested in reviews, customer stories, training, or news? The division of Adobe's information about Acrobat not only lets you make the right choice, it also provides you with an understanding of what is available.

example, when reading about a software product online, you first want the overview. Once you understand the intent of the software, you can get to the specifics of how to use it to get your work done (see sidebar on previous page). Therefore, it makes sense that the technical specifications reside in a subcategory of the software product. By reinforcing the relationships between information, we can provide clear routes that our audience can follow to get the information they need without forcing them to sift through irrelevant material. But, in order for our audience to be able to follow these paths, they must be logical and well labeled.

EVERYBODY'S DOING IT

When you spend some time on the Web, you will find that the most self-explanatory labels for content are the ones pretty much every site uses. Labels such as "Jobs," "Products," "Support," "Store," and "About Us" show up on almost every business site. Though this labeling is good for consistency, you may begin to ask yourself, "How can I keep my company unique and still have clear labels?" The answer lies in visual presentation and Chapter 5.

ACCOMMODATE YOUR AUDIENCE

When deciding on category labels, keep your audience's expectations in mind. Are they familiar with the terms you're using as labels? Do they associate the terms you use with the content under each category? Try to avoid labels that cause your audience to ponder what they might find within each subsection of your site unless you actually want your labels to be a bit mysterious to encourage the exploration of content your audience otherwise might never see. Your audience and their goals should determine the method of categorization you use.

It is also valuable to note the manner in which your audience is most likely to seek out information. Most often, your Web visitors will switch from searching for specific content to casual browsing of your site. They might come in looking for an exact make and model of bicycle and

Labels can be based on topics, user tasks, a sitewide metaphor, specific audiences, or a linear sequence[2]. Take a look at differences in these labels from three different job-search sites.

The labels in this portion of Monster.com are based on user tasks emphasized by the use of verbs: post, start, and search.

New Users Start Here

POST YOUR
RESUME

Job Seeker Login

E-mail Address:

Password:

Login

··> Forget Password?

Employers & Recruiters

··> Employer Login
··> Post Your Job
··> Become a Member
··> HotJobs Products

The HotJobs.com site labels these portions of their organization for specific audiences: new users, job seekers, and employers.

Features

Resource Center

Newsletter

Career Fairs

Advertising Info

This portion of the Headhunter.net site is organized by topics: resources, news, events, and so on.

[2]Peter Morville and Louis Rosenfeld outline these types of organization in their book: *Information Architecture for the World Wide Web.*

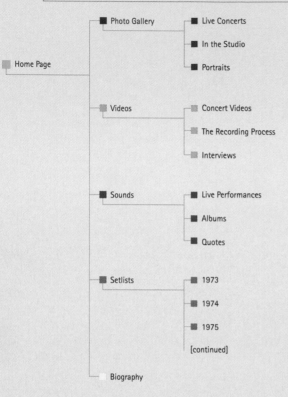

Often times, the way we organize our sites can make them unique or inviting. In the Bob Marley fan site outlined below, the basic content consisted of photographs, sound clips, videos, concert setlists, and biographical information.

A simple and easily understandable organization structure might have been Photos, Videos, Sounds, Setlists, and Biography. Such an organization (on the left) makes it very clear what a visitor might expect to find in the site. However, the site exists for entertainment purposes and focuses on the life of Bob Marley, not on different types of media (photos, videos, sounds). Therefore, the organization system below might be more appropriate.

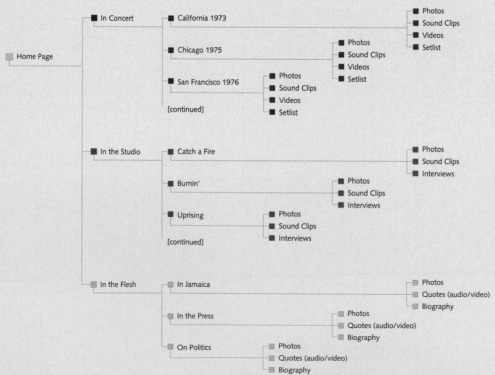

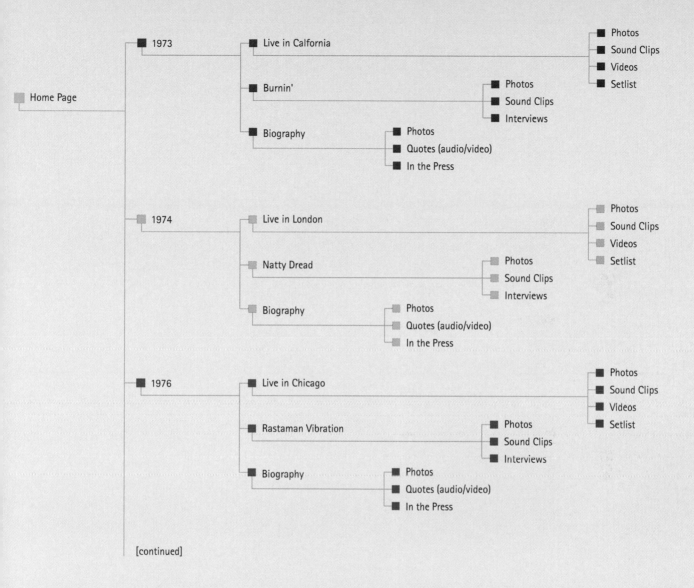

```
Home Page
├── 1973
│   ├── Live in Calfornia
│   │   ├── Photos
│   │   ├── Sound Clips
│   │   ├── Videos
│   │   └── Setlist
│   ├── Burnin'
│   │   ├── Photos
│   │   ├── Sound Clips
│   │   └── Interviews
│   └── Biography
│       ├── Photos
│       ├── Quotes (audio/video)
│       └── In the Press
├── 1974
│   ├── Live in London
│   │   ├── Photos
│   │   ├── Sound Clips
│   │   ├── Videos
│   │   └── Setlist
│   ├── Natty Dread
│   │   ├── Photos
│   │   ├── Sound Clips
│   │   └── Interviews
│   └── Biography
│       ├── Photos
│       ├── Quotes (audio/video)
│       └── In the Press
└── 1976
    ├── Live in Chicago
    │   ├── Photos
    │   ├── Sound Clips
    │   ├── Videos
    │   └── Setlist
    ├── Rastaman Vibration
    │   ├── Photos
    │   ├── Sound Clips
    │   └── Interviews
    └── Biography
        ├── Photos
        ├── Quotes (audio/video)
        └── In the Press
[continued]
```

The site is divided into three categories: In Concert, In the Studio, and In the Flesh. Each section contains a mixture of photos, sounds, and videos from one of these aspects of Bob Marley's life. As you explore the site, you catch glimpses of how Bob spent his time, and where. The experience is much more immersive and might be enhanced even further by introducing linear narratives within each subsection (though this might be detrimental to specific searching). Another alternative is using a chronological organization system, which mirrors the course of Bob's life more accurately.

eventually end up reading user reviews of tires. Or conversely, they might come to browse through your product reviews and end up looking for a specific bike mentioned in an article. Your organization system needs to support both types of activity. At this point in time, the user profiles and scenarios we discussed in the last chapter can really come in handy. When you have an initial organization system put together, try waking through it as one of your "fictional" users. Does it make sense from this

WALKTHROUGHS

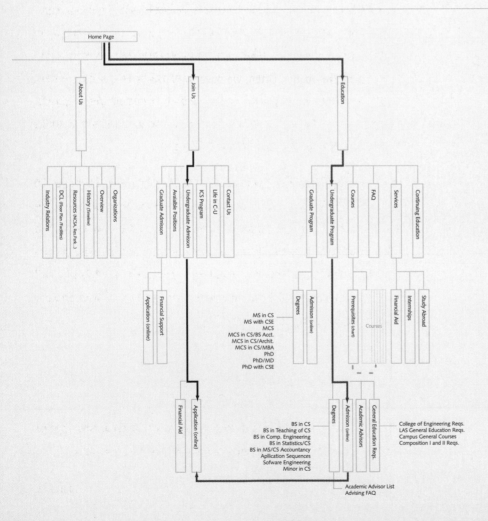

When you have an initial organization for your site in mind, try it out on one of your user scenarios (Chapter 1). Remember to account for different users and goals, as well as the occasional mistake. Not everyone will understand your organization immediately.

In this subsection of a site organization, two possible paths for accessing the online student application form are laid out.

particular user's viewpoint? Can they find what they need? Is it easy for them to switch from casual browsing to specific searches?

Another possibility you need to consider is that visitors to your site might not know exactly what they are looking for, which is where progressive disclosure and logical categories fit in. By starting in a general area, uncertain users can gradually dig deeper into your content until they find something to their liking.

When you understand your audience and their goals, you will have a good idea of how they expect information to be organized. To this end, you might even consider letting them organize it for you. Getting a member of your target audience or simply an outsider (a friend, a neighbor) to comment on how you have decided to organize your content is frequently an eye-opener. Often, we become so well versed in the content of our sites that we begin to see connections that most people do not instinctively make. Or worse still, we miss the obvious relationships because we are too focused on the little details.

A simple way to get input from others is to ask them to do a card sort of your content. Ask your test subject to group a set of index cards (one for each part of your content) into categories that make sense to them. Then ask them to prioritize the groups by importance. You might just be surprised by the results. Testing several people (see sidebar) in this way will give you invaluable insight on how your audience expects your content to be organized. After all, we are doing all this for them.

VISUALIZE IT: SCHEMATICS

When you walk away from the organization process, remember to take home a reminder of the decisions you made. Preparing a visual

THIS IS A TEST...

There is no substitute for input from a target audience member or an outsider. Whether you're developing the organization, labels, or visual presentation of your Web site, do some user testing to make sure that you are on the right track. There is often no need for elaborate or expensive testing schedules; simply getting opinions from potential users or "outsiders" is often enough to catch usability problems. Testing often and early will save you time and trouble in the long run. This book does not cover usability testing in depth; however, Steve Krug and Jacob Nielsen have published great material on "quick and easy" user testing that I recommend reading if you want more information.

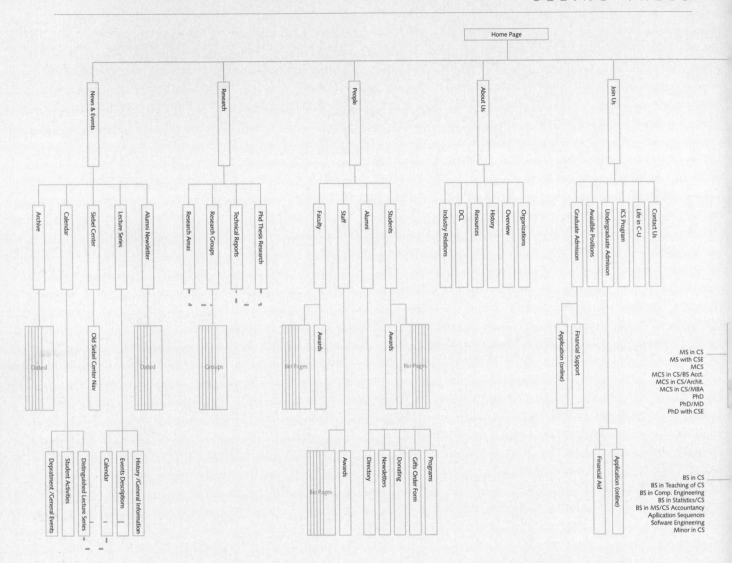

This sample tree diagram outlines the basic structure for the Department of Computer Science at the University of Illinois at Urbana-Champaign (UIUC) Web site. Cross-linking is indicated through dashed lines only when the link is crucial to the organization. Otherwise, the majority of hypertext cross-links and external links are not shown. Limiting the number of cross-links keeps the focus on the main organizational issues. Also note that the lines of the diagram are deliberately light in color. The emphasis in tree diagrams should be on the categories and their labels, not on the boxes around them.

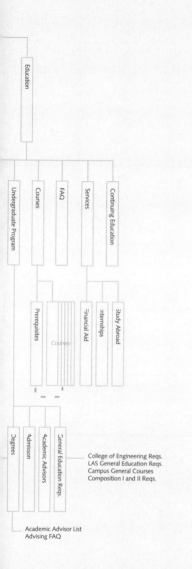

Education

Undergraduate Program

Courses

FAQ

Services

Continuing Education

Prerequisites

Financial Aid

Internships

Study Abroad

Courses

Degrees

Admission

Academic Advisors

General Education Reqs.

College of Engineering Reqs.
LAS General Education Reqs.
Campus General Courses
Composition I and II Reqs.

Academic Advisor List
Advising FAQ

representation of at least the most important portions of your organization will let you see the "big picture" and help you explain your plan to others. Frequently, this visual representation takes the form of a tree diagram. In a tree diagram, each successive level of categorization follows below its "parent" and most often corresponds to a mouse-click. (It would usually take three mouse clicks to get to the fourth row of the tree diagram). By looking at a tree diagram, you can usually tell whether a site's organization is balanced: not too shallow or deep. According to Patrick Lynch and Sarah Horton, authors of the *Web Style Guide: Basic Design Principles for Creating Web Sites* (1999, Yale University Press), sites with a shallow organization system consist of long menu listings and can often confuse users with too many unrelated options. Sites that are too deep obscure content below multiple levels of short menu listings. Neither is a good depth to be swimming in. Most experts suggest presenting no more than seven options at any given menu level. Less is better, but there may be a few times when more is appropriate.

NAVIGATING YOUR CONTENT
[S E C T I O N   T I T L E]

Having a great organization won't help much if you're the only one who knows about it. You need to "tell" your audience how your site is structured so that they can easily get to the things that interest them: You need to supply them with navigation. The navigation elements of a Web site provide your audience with an understanding of your organization and give them a sense of where they are within the site structure. Navigation elements include, but are not limited to search boxes, horizontal and vertical menus, indexes, tables of contents, site maps, directories, charts, hypertext links, and anchor links. These elements can be *global* (pertaining to the whole site) or *local* (pertaining to a subsection or individual page of the site). Most sites do not just pick one navigation element and go with it. Rather, they use a combination of several elements in order to accommodate different user preferences. You can search this book, for example, through the table of contents, page numbers, the index, and more. Regardless of which navigation elements you choose to use on your site, they all serve the same purpose: orientating your audience.

When users feel "lost" on the Web, it's because the navigation isn't doing its job. Navigation should let your audience know where they are, how they got there, and where they can go next. Any useful system for finding your way around, whether in a Web site or a city, should allow you to backtrack, plot your next move, and understand your position. Well-made maps, written directions, and signage systems all make this possible. Through visual and verbal clues, these navigation tools provide us with clear messages that guide and direct us to our destinations. The best way to avoid having users that "can't find what they're looking for" is to have an approachable navigation system that "tells" your audience how to get around your site. We'll spend some time looking at how visual communication principles can assist in making this possible in Chapter 6. But for now, we'll just look at some of the key attributes of navigation systems and the planning we can do to ensure that we're on the right track.

GETTING AROUND THE SITE

Usually, the main navigation system is your site's organization progressively revealed in visual form. I say progressively, because each level of information in our schematics most often translates to one set of navigation menu options. And while the first level of navigation should show up on every page in our site, putting the entire organization on each page is likely to add lots of clutter and just confuse our audience. As a result, we frequently reveal each level of organization only when a user selects its "parent" category.

The first level is included on all the pages within our site in order to provide our audience with a sense of place and security. Your audience will be confident that they can get through your site if they know they can count on a set of consistent links to be there when they need them. In the real world, you're probably more likely to venture into unknown terrain if you have a good map with you. You worry less about getting lost and trust your choice of paths more. A consistent and well-designed navigation system can provide your audience with the same confidence and trust when they venture onto your Web site. Retaining consistency within a navigation system means keeping the location, order, amount, and relative visual characteristics the same throughout the site. A continually moving navigation system with disappearing options is a surefire way to diminish user confidence. Imagine a map where roads disappear only to show up in a new location. How much would you trust such a map to get you home?

Through consistency, we "tell" our audience that they are within one site. We also provide them with a dependable means for getting to any of our top-level categories. This organization allows them to backtrack easily and try another path. Other navigation items that should consistently remain on each page of the site are a link to the home page, a site identifier (often putting in double time as a link to the home page),

Usually, each level of your organization translates to one set of navigation menu options on your Web site.

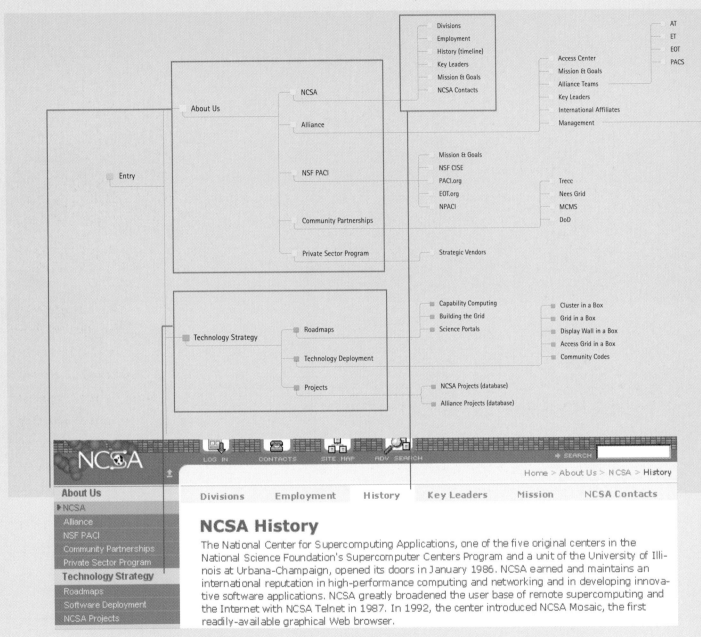

Here, we see the first three levels of organization as navigation menu options on the NCSA site.

global navigation tools (a search box or a link to the site map), global utilities (e-commerce or intranet tools), and contact information.

CONSISTENT NAVIGATION

Navigation elements that should be present on "all" your site's pages are

Home page link

Site identification

Top-level navigation links

Sitewide navigation tools

Sitewide utilities

Contact information

SITE TO SITE

Keep in mind that you not only need to keep your site consistent with itself, you also need to consider the rest of the Web. Users transfer their knowledge of the Web from one site to the other. If every site on the Web puts their search box in the upper right hand corner and you put yours in the lower left, the majority of your audience will be looking in the upper right. For an interesting study on where Web users "expect" to find site elements, read *Developing Schemas for the Location of Common Web Objects* by Michael Bernard (2001)[3].

Remember that the Web lacks any real "physical space." The consistent navigation elements we provide are often the only "you are here" indicators that users get. Therefore, we can't forget to include them on all our pages. This inclusion becomes especially important when someone follows a hypertext link to your site. They bypass the home page and come straight into a random portion of your site structure. How do they know what site they are in? Where in the site are they? What does this new site have to offer them? The consistent navigation elements on your page should put their minds at ease.

Whereas top-level navigation elements orient our audience on a sitewide level, the lower level navigation menus provide direction and awareness within the subcategories of our site. (A good analogy is using a map of the United States to get you to Chicago and then using a map

[3]Bernard Michael L. (2001). *Developing Schemas for the Location of Common Web Objects.* Proceedings of the 45th Annual Meeting of the Human Factors and Ergonomics Society (pp. 1161-1165). Santa Monica, CA: HFES.

of the city to get around town.) Within each subsection of our sites, the subnavigation elements need to follow the same rules of consistency as our top-level navigation. It might help to think of subcategories as being "framed" by the larger site. (See sidebar.) This is all well and good, but once we enter the third, fourth, or even fifth level of our organization, this "framing" can add up to a lot of navigation elements and create confusion rather than alleviate it.

TOO MUCH VERSUS TOO LITTLE

Like maps, signage, and directions, most Web navigation systems consist of words, images, and colors (though motion and sound are also used to provide clues for moving around a site). Through combinations of these basic ingredients, we provide our audience with an understanding of the scope and structure of our sites. Because the content of our site is made of the same elements (text, images, color), we always need to remember that the navigation elements of the site are simply there to help. They should not overwhelm the page, nor should they distract from the content. If we have relevant and clear navigation (quality), we don't need lots of it (quantity). Yet, it is quite common to encounter large Web sites that get overrun by navigation. Menu systems, search boxes, related links, and advertising links can add up quickly and seemingly "take over" a page. Too many navigation elements not only take away valuable space, but also add clutter and noise.

FRAMING YOUR NAVIGATION

NAVIGATION

top level

second level

third level

top level

Top-level navigation elements include the site identifier, your first-level organizational categories, contact information, and any global utilities (such as search). These elements pertain to the entire site and should be repeated on every page to provide consistency and security. Within a top-level category, the second-level of navigation elements should appear on all pages in a consistent and reliable manner.

Once a user enters a third-level category, the top-, second-, and third-level navigation elements and so on are presented on each page. This "framing" provides users with an understanding of the structure of your site, and where they are within that structure. However, it can begin to add up to lots of navigation and little room for content.

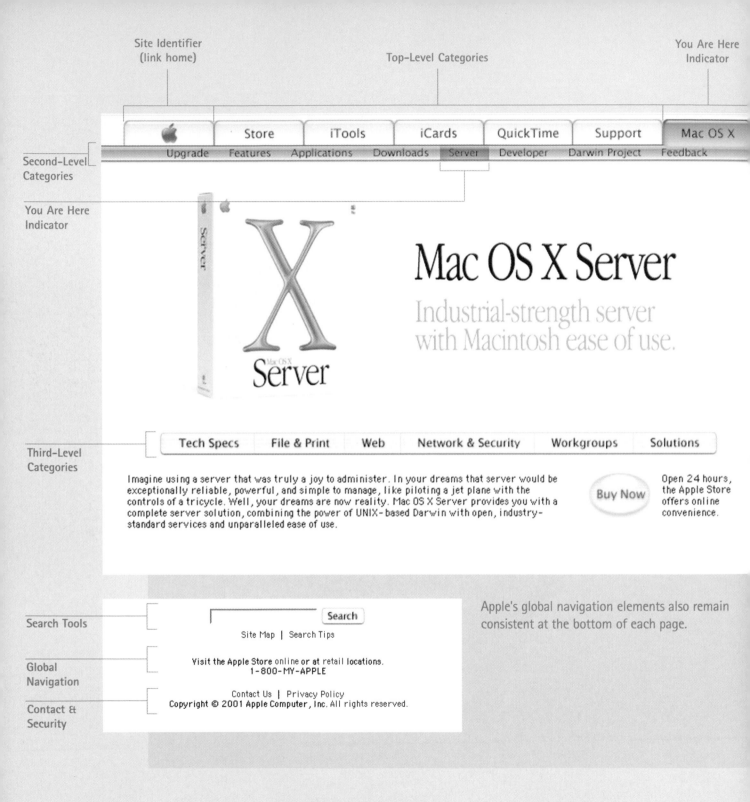

Site Identifier
(link home)

Top-Level Categories

You Are Here
Indicator

| | Store | iTools | iCards | QuickTime | Support | Mac OS X |

Second-Level
Categories

Upgrade   Features   Applications   Downloads   Server   Developer   Darwin Project   Feedback

You Are Here
Indicator

Mac OS X Server

Industrial-strength server
with Macintosh ease of use.

Third-Level
Categories

| Tech Specs | File & Print | Web | Network & Security | Workgroups | Solutions |

Imagine using a server that was truly a joy to administer. In your dreams that server would be
exceptionally reliable, powerful, and simple to manage, like piloting a jet plane with the
controls of a tricycle. Well, your dreams are now reality. Mac OS X Server provides you with a
complete server solution, combining the power of UNIX-based Darwin with open, industry-
standard services and unparalleled ease of use.

Buy Now

Open 24 hours,
the Apple Store
offers online
convenience.

Search Tools

Search

Site Map | Search Tips

Apple's global navigation elements also remain
consistent at the bottom of each page.

Global
Navigation

Visit the Apple Store online or at retail locations.
1-800-MY-APPLE

Contact &
Security

Contact Us | Privacy Policy
Copyright © 2001 Apple Computer, Inc. All rights reserved.

An example of an efficient navigation system that provides awareness without overwhelming the content can be found on Apple's site (left). Note the use of the "you are here" indicators in both the top- and second-level navigation menus.

Site Identifier (link home)

Contact Info

Global Navigation Tools

You Are Here Indicator

Second-Level Categories

Top-Level Categories

CHICAGO SYMPHONY ORCHESTRA

contact us • search & site map • your account • view order

DISCOVER CLASSICAL MUSIC
MEET THE PERFORMERS
CONDUCTORS
COMPOSERS
CSO ROSTER
CSO ON TOUR
CIVIC ORCHESTRA
CSO CHORUS
VISITING ARTISTS
ASK AN EXPERT
BOOK AN ENSEMBLE
AUDITIONS
SEASON AND TICKETS
SHOP SYMPHONY STORE
PLAN YOUR EXPERIENCE
HOW TO GET INVOLVED
ABOUT THE CSO

meet the performers

Dennis Michel
Dennis Michel joined the Chicago Symphony Orchestra in 1998 as second bassoon, after serving as principal bassoon of both the San... read more

110 musicians at the peak of their profession. There's no greater ensemble of classical talent on this continent when the CSO musicians perform. Learn about each of their unique journeys to this incredible musical destination as well as those of the many guest artists that will visit Symphony Center to perform this season.

CONDUCTORS
The illustrious conductors of the Chicago Symphony Orchestra provide artistic vision and leadership to the entire CSO organization. read more

Ask an Expert
We know that many of you have music-related questions about the concert you will attend or have just experienced. We invite you to ask us your questions. read more

Book an Ensemble
Let a CSO Ensemble provide music for your next event For more information about ensemble services, please call 312-294-3267 or use our on-line form to book an ensemble.

The Chicago Symphony Orchestra's site uses a vertical navigation system, but the consistent navigation elements remain the same: site identification, contact information, global navigation tools (including e-commerce tools), and top-level navigation links.

Your audience did not come to your site for the navigation. They came for the content. But they can't find the content without navigation! True, but here is a way out of this catch-22: balance. We need to find the appropriate balance between too much and too little. Too much navigation, and our audience is overwhelmed; too little, and they are lost. Finding the right balance involves thinking twice about the role of each navigation element and its importance to our audience. It also means finding the appropriate visual balance between usable navigation systems and navigation that detracts from your content.

One obvious solution is to simply make navigation look like navigation. Well, what does navigation look like? It seems different on every site. As the Web has matured, certain "standards" have emerged. One of the most common is that navigation usually sits at the top, bottom, or left side of a page. Therefore, even the placement of elements on our pages can clue users in to their function as navigation. Another way is to use background colors to simulate "buttons." But I'm getting ahead of myself. Chapter 6 will cover the visual aspects of navigation design in more depth.

Another popular solution is to use "space-saving" navigation elements to strike an adequate navigation/content balance. Cascading menus, dynamic user-controlled menus, drop-down menus, and breadcrumbs are just a few "space-saving" elements common today. (See sidebar to right.) Each of these solutions has its share of benefits and drawbacks, which you need to be aware of before committing your site to one. Probably the biggest disadvantage to most drop-down, dynamic, or cascading menus is that they require user action to "tell" you what they have to offer. A user must roll over the appropriate menu item in a cascading menu or click to activate a drop-down menu. This extra step can be a particular disadvantage when you're trying to provide your audience with an understanding of your site's contents or when you're trying to

Navigation menus that require user action before they reveal their contents are a common method of saving space and reducing navigational clutter. The site above uses cascading menus that disclose the next level of navigation links when a user mouses over them.

Breadcrumbs are an increasingly common method of providing situational awareness. They show the path from the home page to your current location.

draw them into certain areas. Breadcrumbs, on the other hand, while providing an account of the path a user followed, do little to provide an awareness of the rest of the site (See sidebar to the right). If you do decide to use one or more of these "space-savers," do some quick user testing to make sure that they're an appropriate solution for your particular audience.

PEOPLE ARE DIFFERENT

People find their way around in various ways. Some prefer written directions in the form of step-by-step instructions; some use particular landmarks to guide them, and others prefer the use of maps. Studies have been done to determine which of these methods has the best effectiveness to effort ratio. For example, having a "mental map" in mind when traversing a city provides you with knowledge of all the streets and their positions. Though finding your way might be quite easy, a lot of mental effort is required. Remembering all the streets and their relative position to each other is quite a chore. On the other hand, memorizing a set of directions is relatively easy. But if you get lost, those directions are not nearly as useful as having a map. The truth is that different ways of getting around are most effective at different times. This is why books have a table of contents, an index, and page numbers[4]. You can even flip through the book to look for a particular image or paragraph you need to find. People are also different. Some prefer to use the index, while others can scan the table of contents to determine where they need to go.

A friend that has been to your house several times does not need the detailed directions that an out-of-town cousin might. Your friend might

---

[4]Colleen Bushell has published a paper titled *Design Requirements for Hypermedia* (ZED.2, Virginia Commonwealth University, Summer 1995) in which the navigation concepts and uses of traditional information structures (books, maps) are examined to derive guidelines for designing informative hypermedia. One such guideline details the benefits of "showing several different representations of the information space."

DROP DOWN THE BREADCRUMBS

Home > Folio > Web Sites > | Silver Wrapper Productions | ⬍ |

Though breadcrumbs are useful for showing you your position within a Web space, they provide little understanding of the scope of the entire site and offer no navigation choices beyond backtracking and returning home. Steve Krug, author of *Don't Make Me Think: A Common Sense Approach to Web Usability* (2000, New Riders), compares breadcrumbs to written directions: "The directions can be useful, but you can learn more from [a] map." In the example above, breadcrumbs are combined with drop-down menus to not only provide users with an understanding of their current position, but also an awareness of all the possible paths they didn't take. In the current site implementation, only the portfolio samples use the drop-down method. (If users are interested in one Web design example, it is likely they might want to see more. This navigation features allows them to see the other available samples.) However, the technique could easily be expanded to the entire breadcrumb path (below) to provide a sense of context and scale (where am I, within how much?).

When opened, the drop-down menu provides you with a sense of context: where you are and where you can go.

just need to be reminded of your street name, whereas your cousin might not even know how to get into town. The same types of situations are likely to occur on your Web site. Repeat visitors, first-time visitors, visitors that have a solid understanding of your organization, visitors that vaguely remember how they got to a particular part of your site before, and more all come to your site. To accommodate these differences in

LOOK HONEY, A WEBMARK

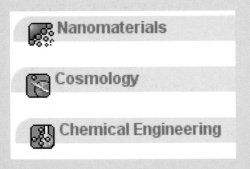

Studies of cab drivers in Paris have shown that few have a "maplike" understanding of the city. Instead, they rely on navigating to and from prominent landmarks (or basic points)[5]. Because the Web lacks any physical space, simulating this type of behavior is difficult. However, we can use unique images (positioned consistently) and color-coding to give sections of our Web sites their own unique "webmarks." Though webmarks probably won't help you navigate a site the way a landmark might help you navigate a city, they can serve as visual cues to jog your memory and let you know you're on the right track when you try to find content you have located before (a common and frequently frustrating activity). In the example to the left, icons adorn each of the second-level sections (~70,000 page) of NCSA's Web site and provide a visual cue to let users know what section they are in.

[5] One of the most effective urban navigation studies was conducted by the French psychologist, Pailhous. He found that Paris cab drivers found their way by a very limited number of routes, related to basic points. (*Plan Your Route* Victor Selwyn, 1987, David & Charles)

users and their objectives, we need to have navigation systems that allow for flexibility and that present information in several ways: breadcrumbs to show the path a visitor has taken through the site, search boxes for specific content retrieval, site maps for the big picture, and more. We can even set up landmarks (or "webmarks") that might help our audience recall where the content they wish to revisit was. Unique images positioned in a consistent manner on pages or the color-coding of various sections of the site can serve as webmarks that can jog our audience's memory and let them know they're in the right place or getting close to it.

Though multiple navigation elements can add the flexibility needed to accommodate the different searching and browsing patterns of your audience, always be aware of the delicate balance between too much and too little navigation. Testing a few navigation mockups is good way to make sure that you're on the right track.

VISUALIZE IT: NAVIGATION MOCKUPS

As with any part of the planning process, it's desirable to create a few visual documents to evaluate possible navigation systems for your site. These navigation mockups are usually black-and-white sketches of where the navigation elements might be positioned, how they might be labeled,

and how they might behave. It's much easier to make functional decisions when the color, typefaces, and design of navigation elements do not get in the way. Using simple black-and-white block diagrams solicits functional feedback rather than personal opinions on design.

It is a good idea to create a mockup of an interior page of your site and test it on a member of your target audience (or any outsider you can get

SAMPLE   NAVIGATION   MOCKUPS

NCSA

Log In   Staff Directory   Site Map   Advanced Search   Search

Divisons   Employment   History   Key Leaders   **Mission**   NCSA Contacts

About Us
    Alliance
    Community Partnerships
    ▶ NCSA
    NSF PACI
    Private Sector Program

Technology Strategy

Science

User Information

News

Archive

NCSA's Mission

The National Center for Supercomputing Applications (NCSA) at the University of Illinois at Urbana Champaign was launched in 1986 with the mission of providing high-performance computing resources to the academic research community and developing new technologies to enable scientific discovery and help to maintain American industry's competitive edge in the global marketplace. In addition the center's education and outreach efforts work to bring the technology revolution to an even wider community, including schools, government agencies, and underserved populations.

a hold of). Show your test subject the page and ask questions like "Where do you think you are in this site?" and "How might you have gotten there?" You might even inquire what sort of information the user would like next, and how they anticipate being able to find it. Often, navigation mockups are only presented to the client for approval. But getting some outside input early on in the design process will save you some costly redesigns later on.

FINDING YOUR PERSONALITY
[S E C T I O N   T I T L E]

So far the majority of planning we have done has been for the organization and interaction of our site. But it can also help to plan some basic aspects of our presentation as well. In particular, we want to get some initial ideas for the personality of our site. The personality of your site determines how it speaks to your audience. Is it screaming, "Get excited about football!" or does it calmly say, "Don't worry, I know getting a home loan is difficult, so I'm going to make it as easy as possible for you." Each of these sites has a different "voice." The voice is reflective of the main message of your site and is "spoken" in a manner appropriate to your audience.

Though the personality of your site is most quickly communicated through the visual presentation (I will discuss this in depth in Chapter 5), it is also evident in the organization, the content, and even the manner in which your text is written. Every aspect of your site, from navigation to color choices, contributes to the site's personality. When all the elements of your site work together to reinforce a common personality, we

DIAMONDS ANYONE?

Though both these sites sell diamonds, they do it in two distinct ways. The personality of each site is evident in not only its visual presentation, but also in the organization and interaction. Read the category labels and notice the different manners in which you pick out a diamond ring on each site.

The **MAGIC** *Eight!*

Take the mystery out of y[...]
diamond jewelry shopping
these eight can't-mis[...]

blue nile™
Education. Guidance. Diamonds and Fine Jewelry.

My Favorites ◆
Financing & Insurance ◆
Order Status ◆
Shopping Basket ◆

| Loose Diamonds | Engagement | Wedding | Holiday Gift Ideas | Product Education |

Home > **Loose Diamonds**

search ►
[ ] ◆ go

shop by product ►
shop by material ►
shop by occasion ►
diamonds: ▼
◆ Diamond Search
◆ Signature Collection
◆ Recommended Diamonds
◆ My Favorites
◆ Recently Purchased Diamonds

related links: ▼
◆ Build Your Own Ring
◆ Build Your Own Earrings
◆ Engagement Settings
◆ Engagement Guide
◆ Learn About Diamonds
◆ Diamond Jewelry

Loose Diamonds

Find the Perfect Diamond ►

 Build Your Own Ring ►

Use our ring builder to match the perfect diamond to your favorite setting.
◆ more

No Payments or Interest for 90 Days ►
Apply for up to $25,000 financing with no interest and no payments for 90 days

Diamond Search ►
To find the perfect diamond, specify the four "C"s with our diamond search.

Blue Nile Signature Diamonds ►

View our most brilliant round and princess-cut diamonds in the Blue Nile Signature Collection.
◆ more

Recently Purchased Diamonds ►
Over 15,000 couples have purchased diamonds at Blue Nile. See a list of the most recently purchased diamonds.

Learn the Four Cs ►

Learn the fundamentals of cut, color, clarity, and carat weight to select the best diamond at the best value.
◆ more

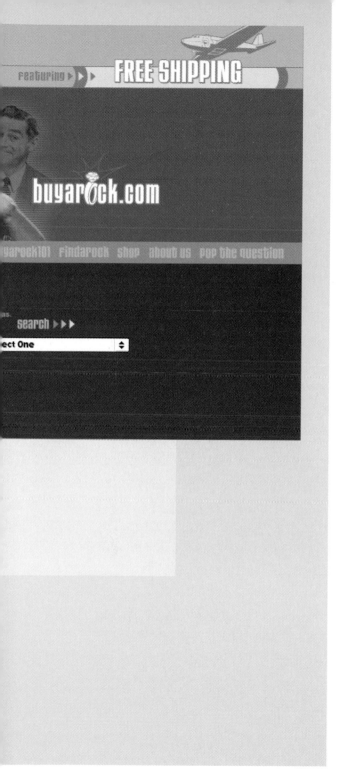

refer to that as a *unified Web experience*. A unified Web experience connects the interaction, organization, and presentation of your site into a cohesive whole. This experience emphasizes the sense of being in "one place" and establishes a dialog with your audience. "We're going to make shopping for diamonds fun." "We have the technical expertise to solve even your toughest problems." But the most important role of your site's personality is to communicate the big picture of your site. Who are you, and what do can you do for me? How are you different (better) than the competition? Given all the things today's Web sites need to do (offer services, provide information, e-commerce, and so on), it is very easy to get wrapped up in the details and lose sight of the big picture.

DESCRIBE YOURSELF

Make sure that the personality you choose for your site is self-descriptive —that is, it tells your audience who you are and what makes you unique. Thinking in terms of real-world examples can help a lot. Rooms, buildings, cities, cars, people, clothes, furniture, and so on all have distinct traits that make them special. Pay attention to your surroundings and take note of the things that bring your site to mind or that seem to "reflect" or could "speak for" your site. More often than not, there is no one item that perfectly embodies your site's message in a manner appropriate to your audience, but a combination of several items might just do the trick. For example, if your site's specialty is Italian cooking, try to visualize the elements that give an Italian restaurant tucked away in a comfortable nook of Little Italy its charisma. Is it the old-world sepia photographs, the poor lighting, the sturdy tables of heavy oak, or the exuberant staff (with accents and all)? Or perhaps an upscale place with tuxedoed staff and a world-class wine cellar is more appropriate, or a family atmosphere with lively music and lots of "flair"? Though all three of these establishments may offer fine cooking, they all have different personalities. Which one is right for you depends on your audience and the message of your client.

As the Web becomes more and more crowded, the importance of personality increases. With millions of sites to choose from, standing out in this "cyber-crowd" is not an easy task. Many sites have gone to extreme measures to be different. Sites use unique and catchy names like Yahoo! and Monster and air Super Bowl commercials with memorable images or outrageous situations. But spending millions of dollars on strange TV spots and using wacky nomenclature are not guaranteed to provide a devoted audience. Having a different voice from the competition lets your site be noticed and remembered, but doesn't help to build relationships with your audience. Rather, a unified Web experience with a consistent and appropriate personality does. Try thinking of your favorite sites. What makes them stand out? Why do you keep coming back to them? How do they "speak" to you?

VISUALIZE IT: SAMPLE COMBINATIONS

When planning your site, keep a record of the images, text, or objects that reflect several possible appropriate personalities and tones for your site. This process can be formalized by creating sample combinations. Sample combinations are created by taking photographs, cutting snippets out of magazines, or grabbing screen images and combining what you find into a single document. These documents allow you to communicate your ideas to others (including your client) and get reactions from your intended audience. Is this an appropriate tone for the information we are presenting? What do these images bring to mind? Excitement? Calm? Sample combinations are an effective means for visualizing some

SAMPLING YOUR SITE'S FLAVOR

Sample combinations, like the one to the left, can help articulate some initial ideas for your Web site's personality. Though this example uses images from magazines, pretty much anything is fair game: photos, sounds, a writing style, and more. The medium or the subjects (in this example, mostly physical objects) of your sample combinations are not relevant. Instead, the style (in this case, a retro/streamline look) that they personify is.

initial ideas for the personality of your site and can jumpstart the visual design process by presenting an appropriate "flavor" for the site.

REMEMBERING YOUR LIMITATIONS
[S E C T I O N   T I T L E]

The Web is intended to be accessible to the entire world. Achieving such an extraordinary goal ultimately requires a lot of compromise on the part of Web consumers and providers. In order to reach a worldwide audience, the Web has many restrictions and constraints. These restrictions often arise from the assortment of different technologies that make the Web run, but they also come from the various cultures accessing the Web from around the world.

THINK TECHNICALLY

Thousands of technical variations on the side of Web consumers can lead to striking differences in our Web site's presentation and interaction. Not all Web access is the same, and as a result, you cannot count on your site looking and working in the same way it does on your machine at home. Different versions of Web browsers, operating systems, Internet connections, hardware, and more contribute to an enormous amount of variables. It is impossible to design for every specific hardware and software combination your audience might be using. Instead, designers need to come up with designs that are flexible and support "graceful degradation."[6] When users visit a site with the most up-to-date technology, they get a design that takes advantage of the latest features in presentation

---

[6]I am not sure who coined the term "graceful degradation," but Jeffery Veen presents the theory behind it quite well in his book *The Art and Science of Web Design* (2000, New Riders).

Microsoft Internet Explorer 5.0 on the Macintosh

Netscape Navigator 6.0 on the Macintosh

Microsoft Internet Explorer 5.0 on Windows

Netscape Navigator 4.07 on Windows

Netscape Navigator 4.7 on the Macintosh

Not all Web browsers display the same code in the same ways. Most notably, older browsers do not support many style features. The example above shows how a navigation system appears on several different browsers (with different style sheet support) and platforms. Note that despite differences in font size and drop-down menu presentation, the navigation retains its functionality across multiple browsers and platforms. Though the presentation is far from ideal in the bottom-most setup (the drop-down becomes visually dominant and navigation should be unobtrusive), users can still get to the content they need.

and interaction. However, when users visit the site with older technology that cannot support advanced features, the site still works, minus a few bells and whistles. In other words, the site loses some niceties (of presentation and interaction), but remains usable: It degrades gracefully. To use our language analogy, some words are lost from our vocabulary, but enough basic ones remain to get our message across. While it may be true that a certain word was the optimal way to express ourselves, we still have a few others that are "good enough." When we decide just how our sites will vary (and degrade), we need to keep several factors in mind: monitors, computers, browsers, plug-ins, and Internet connections.

Monitors can vary in many different ways. There are variations in the overall display area of monitors: fifteen inches or a twenty-two-inch wide screen format? On each one of those monitors, we have resolution differences: 640 by 480 pixels or 1,024 by 768? 256 colors or millions? Also, each monitor has its own settings for brightness and contrast, likely to be set to each individual user's preferences. And that's not to mention the gamma differences between operating systems that make Windows machines seem substantially darker than the display on a Macintosh. One thing these differences tell us is that very subtle variations in color might not get noticed by everyone in our audience. Therefore, important visual cues should not rely on minute color distinctions. Similarly, the differences in screen resolution tell us that we cannot count on everyone in our audience having 800 pixels of vertical space available for our Web site. Instead, we need to create layouts that communicate clearly with a variable amount of pixel height and width.

Differences in operating systems can alter more than just the screen gamma. Typefaces, interface elements, and text sizes are all subject to change as well. We need to be aware of how the fonts we have chosen for our layouts appear on different machines. Comparable differences result from different Web browsers. Text-sizes and interface elements appear differently in even the two most popular browsers: Microsoft Internet Explorer and Netscape Navigator. Each of these browsers has multiple versions, some of which support most presentation and interaction features and others that do not. (As an extreme example, Netscape 2.0 does not even support frames.) In addition, users can adjust settings within each browser such as background color, image display, test sizes, and more.

Scared yet? Don't be. It isn't too difficult to account for the many factors of the Web. The first step is admitting that they exist. Many designers fool themselves into believing everyone on the Web sees their sites the same way that they do. Once you accept the fact that things will change from user to user, you can begin designing in a manner that supports graceful degradation. (More on this in Part 3.) But we're still not out of the woods yet. Designing for everybody does not just mean designing for different computers; it means designing for different people. And when the world is your audience, trust me, there are differences.

THINK GLOBALLY

Because the Web is World Wide, it provides the opportunity to communicate with people of all nations and cultures. While a global audience can be an asset, it is also a responsibility.

Edward Hall, in his book *The Silent Language* (Doubleday, 1977), said, "Culture is communication." What he meant is that many factors beyond speech need to be considered when communicating cross-culturally. Space, time, intonation, and more mean different things to different people, and one must always be aware of the implications. When we communicate online, we need to especially be aware of how our colors, and symbols are perceived and interpreted. For example, in the United States, an owl is often associated with wisdom, whereas in Central American and Celtic cultures, it is a symbol of misfortune. (Apple Computer, 1992) In Eastern Asia, white is the funerary color of choice, while in the United States, we wear black. These types of distinctions also apply to everyday objects, mannerisms, behaviors, and more. If you're planning on reaching a global market or want to focus on a particular country or region, it is a good idea to understand the cultural implications of your designs. Make sure that you understand what your site is "saying," especially when it speaks to a foreign audience.

LIST IT: PRODUCT REQUIREMENTS

Yes, it's time to add another document to our growing Web project folder. When deciding on the global and technical limitations your site needs to accommodate, it is a good idea to list the criteria you need to meet in a product requirements document. A product requirements document is nothing more than a listing of the constraints your audience is likely to bring to your site. Do some of them still use 256-color monitors? Are most of them accessing the Web through low-speed modems?

A product requirements document continually reminds you of the limitations of your audience and outlines technical platforms on which your site should be tested. Some Web sites cater to visitors with high-speed "broadband" connections and offer services that users with slow modem dial-ups cannot easily use. These sites can make use of page elements that take longer to download, such as extensive video or sound files. Other sites target a Web-savvy audience that prides itself on having the latest Web technology. These sites tend to use features that older browsers cannot display. In both these situations, the audience has determined what level of constraints the site must adhere to. When you design your sites, make sure that you are meeting the constraints of your audience, not your personal computer.

SCHEDULING YOUR PROGRESS
[SECTION TITLE]

Even though it is now common to think of projects with tight deadlines as happening in "Internet time," a Web project could very well move sluggishly if you do not plan ahead. Just about every Web site project I have been involved with has slowed down at the same stage: content delivery. Even site redesigns, where the majority of content already exists, slow down when content needs to be updated or created anew. This can quickly turn Internet time into waiting time.

But just like the wait at your doctor's office, this wait is for your own good. Perhaps you have heard the expression, "On the Web, content is king." Most visitors to your Web site are coming for just that: content. (Currently, there is a big trend toward offering services online, but that is what Chapter 8 is about.) They need specific information, or they want to get a basic sense of what is happening or new. Therefore, it is extremely important to meet your audience's expectations and deliver fresh and informative content. You need that content, no matter how long the wait. We have all encountered Web sites that seem more like "ghost sites." Someone put them up and then seemingly walked away. (If you look closely, you might even see cobwebs forming on the pages.) These abandoned sites are a testament to the challenges involved with gathering and maintaining quality content.

Content originates from various sources. In a corporation, each department might be responsible for a different portion. Getting all these departments to coordinate their efforts in a timely manner is a challenge. Also, each department is likely to be busy with its day-to-day chores, so delivering the content for a Web update often gets put on the back burner. That being said, the importance of good Web content is currently recognized by most organizations. These organizations have taken steps to ensure that content on their Web site is timely and up to date. Some have introduced a full-time employee that works with each department to get their information into a Web-ready format, a position that requires someone skilled at writing in the nonlinear style of the Web. While this person is a great asset, it is often not enough.

Not only do the sources of content vary, the content itself varies. Product photos, employee bios, technical white papers, and more make up the content of an average business site. Generating these diverse items involves different timelines and production schedules. Photo shoots and interviews might be necessary, not to mention copy-editing and technical illustrations. Regardless of the type of site you're building, you need to consider the fact that content is going to come in different shapes and sizes and at different times.

At this point, you might be saying, "My client already has all the content they want to put online ready." While it might be true that a good amount of content may already exist in one form or another, it can still be a time-consuming task to get this information into a "Web-ready" format: one that is reflective of the site organization you have set up. Length, wording, and relevance are just some of the factors you need to consider. Also, there is Web-specific content, which often needs to be created from scratch. Given all the challenges of content delivery, you would be well advised to think through the process ahead of time.

VISUALIZE IT: CONTENT DELIVERY SCHEDULE
[SECTION TITLE]

To avoid delays and keep everyone involved with a Web project informed, you need to develop a *content delivery schedule.* A content delivery schedule is usually a listing of the site organization with entries for who is responsible for each portion of the content's completion and when. Remember to include concrete and realistic deadlines. (Nothing gets things moving like the presence of an imminent deadline.) A clear understanding (between content generators and the Web production team) of when things are due will ensure that no one is playing the role of "bottleneck" and holding up your launch date.

CONTENT DELIVERY

NAME	URL	DELIVERY	PROVIDER	RECEIVED
Research	/research/research.html	08.02.00	Renee Holowitz renee@cs.uiuc.edu	X
Research Teams	/research/research_teams.html	08.09.00	John Davis john@cs.uiuc.edu	X
Research Areas	/research/research_areas.html	08.09.00	Sara Mueller sara@cs.uiuc.edu	

This very simple content delivery schedule lists each Web page (for the Computer
Science Department Web site we saw earlier), the person responsible for creating
that particular page's content, and a due date.

LukeW.com 3.0 structure

- index.html

bio
- about_lukew.html
  about_lukew
  - development_services.html
  - design_services.html
  - technical_specs.html
- construction.html
- contact_info.html
- luke_wroblewski.html
- project_history.html
- resume.html
- join_list.html
- clients_list.html
  img

folio
- data_visualizations.html
  img
- game_design.html
  game_design
  - tony_sambino.html
    tony_sambino
    - ch
    img
- illustrations.html
  illustrations
  - justice_brennan.html
  - madre_jeronima.html
  - mine_eyes.html
  - water_seller.html
  - octopus_renderings.html
  - retro_bowlers.html
    img
- interface_design.html
  interface_design
  - bibe_identifier.html
  - fx_trades.html
  - gslis_finder.html
  - kelloggs_intranet.html
  - ncsa_opie.html
  - 3d_data.html
- multimedia_solutions.html
  multimedia_solutions
  - access_interactive.html
  - access_interactive2.html
  - kam_cdrom.html
  - transistors.html
  - thesis_racer.html
    img
- navigation_systems.html
  navigation_systems
  - ilir_dhtml.html
  - octopus_system.html
  - sitemap_system.html
  - lukew2_nav.html
  - jazzfest_nav.html
    img
- presentations.html
  presentations
  - web_applications.html

This partial content diagram for the LukeW site serves as an organization schematic and a progress diagram. The green, yellow, and red dots indicate the status of content, and the red triangles contain notes related to how the content will be generated. The cells with blue background colors indicate folders, the yellow background colors detail future content, and a gray background indicates content that is no longer a part of the site. Though this spreadsheet is a specific solution to a particular site, the kinds of data presented are more than likely the same type of information you will need in your content delivery diagrams.

_creation.html

PART TWO

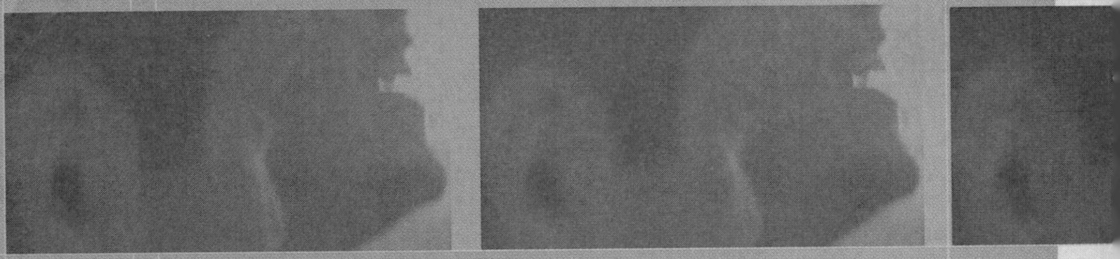

HOW TO COMMUNICATE:
THE THREE "LEXICONS" OF WEB USABILITY

Perhaps the most rewarding aspect of learning a new language is the ability to understand and be understood by other people. Armed with the ability to communicate in this new tongue, you can engage in interesting conversations, build meaningful relationships, and acquire information. The more you use this new language, the easier it becomes to articulate your knowledge and confidently explain your intentions. We want the same level of comfort and assurance when we speak "Web." Effectively communicating with our Web audience results in Web interactions that are meaningful, enjoyable, and efficient.

In the last section, we determined what we want to say to our audience. Now we take a look at how to say it by learning the three *lexicons* (the vocabulary of a particular subject) of Web usability: technical considerations, visual organization principles, and look and feel. Though these lexicons are distinct, we always use them in conjunction with each other when we speak "Web."

You might be asking, why the three lexicons of Web usability? Why not steps? Steps imply a sequence. The three lexicons do not happen in any particular order, they are continually thought of as the Web design process occurs.

TECHNICALLY, IT'S A LEXICON: TECHNICAL CONSIDERATIONS

chapter three

Imagine the difficulty of operating an automobile haphazardly constructed with little regard for how it will be used. All the necessary parts might be there, but if the brake is a button near the sunroof, many of us would have difficulty stopping the car. Or perhaps this car associates obscure meanings with familiar symbols. (In most cars, "R" means reverse and not "Rotate tires.") Driving such a car would be quite a chore, and after a while, most people would give up in frustration (or worse). Although encountering such automobiles is rare, it's rather common to come across Web sites that are just as baffling. These sites are often constructed without adequate consideration of the "technical" aspects that make them (and the entire Web) work. Properly composing our Web pages, clarifying the purpose of our links, using standard Web interactions, and providing meaningful feedback are all ways we can improve the construction of our sites and make communication possible.

GETTING TECHNICAL
[S E C T I O N   T I T L E]

From large four-wheel drive sports utility vehicles to sleek and speedy racers, lots of different cars saturate our roadways. And although these cars look and feel differently, they all work in very similar ways. While you may have driven a pickup all your life, you could easily hop into a small sedan and commute like a pro. Your ability to transfer your driving skills from one car to the next is due in large part to the technical considerations used to design all cars. When you turn the steering wheel to the right, you go right. When you depress the right pedal, you accelerate. In addition to ensuring that your car works properly (it needs to turn, stop, and go), these mechanical details prevent you from having to relearn each automobile you enter. Instead, they allow you to concentrate on where you are going. And, face it: Often, you are not driving because you want to drive, but because you need to get somewhere. The less you need to worry about the car, the more you can focus on your destination. This is also the case online. Web sites are designed to help you achieve your goals: getting information, completing a transaction, and so on. You shouldn't have to relearn how to use the Web every time you visit a new Web site.

That said, there certainly are cars that you want to take out for no other reason than the emotion provided by the automobile. These cars are full of personality and make traveling fun, exciting, or soothing. Chances are, your favorite cars meant a lot more to you than getting back and forth from work. They had a style or attitude you enjoyed. These are traits that go beyond mere technical details of pedals and seatbelts. Personality and attitude come from the look, feel, and contents of the car and can form lasting attachments and relationships. (I will discuss this in depth in Chapter 5.) But you would never enjoy these traits if you couldn't get the car up and down the road. For this reason, the technical details of how people expect cars to work play a prominent role in automobile design.

We need to consider distinct technical details when designing Web sites. These details ensure that Web sites work properly and meet the expectations and needs of Web audiences. Technical considerations for Web usability include responding promptly, unifying the Web, following links, assembling the page, and being accessible. While many of these considerations are intended to increase accessibility or accommodate the shortcomings of current Web technologies, most are designed to make communication easy and informative. These techniques and production details are particular to the Web and help to keep Web traffic moving as smoothly as automobile traffic (excluding rush hour, of course).

RESPONDING PROMPTLY
[SECTION TITLE]

We don't call the Web the information superhighway for nothing. Often perceived as a quick means to access information, the Web can certainly be faster than skimming through books in the library or waiting for tomorrow's newspaper to roll out. When your audience looks for answers online, they expect you to respond in a timely manner. This expectation becomes obvious when you realize that the top two complaints of Web sites users are "I can't find what I am looking for" and "It takes too long." As Jeffery Veen, author of *The Art and Science of Web Design (2000, New Riders)*, says, "You'll lose more traffic to the principle of speed than any other." If you have ever surfed the Web with a low speed modem, you know the feeling. The waiting game can quickly turn the excitement of Web surfing into an experience reminiscent of the airport line. Long download times are frustrating and become especially unnerving when you encounter them in the course of making an e-commerce purchase or trading stocks online. As more services appear within Web sites, these concerns will only become more frequent. Did I just buy an airline ticket, or did my computer crash? The longer you wait to find out, the more your anxiety and displeasure grows.

Although you might be able to count on your audience having high-speed connections sometimes, most of the time you can't. High-speed Web users currently remain, and will remain for some time, the vast minority. Lots of modem users are out there, and the limitations of their hardware and phone lines give them the perception that they are crawling through the sea of Web pages, not surfing. Anytime you can do something to ease this plight, you should. Everything from the download time of a page to the time required to interpret a complex navigation system counts. By optimizing your pages for a quick download, decreasing the "perceived" waiting time, and providing timely and meaningful feedback, you can respond to the needs of your audience in a quick and efficient manner.

GETTING SMALL

Here are a few ways to minimize the file size of your Web pages:

Optimize your code to include just the necessary components.

Reuse images. Once an image downloads, it remains in the browser's cache.

Use external style sheets. Style sheets can mimic complex HTML formatting in just a few short lines, and if linked to from your pages, only need to download once.

Use external script files. Again, one download, and they sit in your browser's cache.

Optimize your images. Use JPEG compression for photos and GIF compression for line art, images with large color areas, and so on.

Reduce the physical size of your images. Cropping images can reduce file size significantly.

PAYING ATTENTION

The attention span of a Web audience is short. They are not interested in spending hours studying your Web pages or waiting for them to load. (Web-based services are another story that I'm saving for Chapter 8.) Until they locate the specific information they need, they are just looking for the next click that will get them there. So how do you design for an audience with attention-deficit disorder (ADD)? You provide them with Web pages that allow them to make quick and informed decisions. You optimize download times, create scannable pages, and minimize complex interactions.

Optimize download times. You are probably aware of at least some of the factors that contribute to download time: page size, large images, multimedia files, and so on. The total file size of your Web page (code, images, and all) influences how long it will take for your page to load on your audience's machine. You can reduce the loading time substantially by reusing components in multiple Web pages (such as images, style sheets, and scripts). After these files download once, they stay in the browser's cache and can be quickly called upon to act again. Also, take the time to optimize (best quality versus smallest file size) the individual components that make up your Web page. Use the minimum amount of HTML code you can to get the presentation effect you need. (Every byte adds up to a longer download.) Or consider using style sheets to replicate the presentation effect. Often times, style sheets can replace long HTML code with just a few short lines. When optimizing your images, don't just rely on JPEG and GIF image compression. Consider also cropping your images to reduce their physical file size.

Create scannable pages: We can also cater to our audience's short attention span by designing scannable pages. A page is scannable if you can quickly glance at it and make sense of the content. Divide your information into smaller, more manageable portions and use visual hierarchy (discussed in the next chapter) to explain those divisions to your audience. This will increase the speed with which your audience interprets the page and allow them to quickly determine which portions are of interest to them. A consistent presentation of your information will also reduce the time it takes to make sense of a page.

Minimize complex interactions: You can also cut down the learning time required of your Web pages by minimizing the use of complex interactions. The primary means of Web navigation is the "click and go" method. Requiring dragging and dropping items into a shopping cart area is unexpected. Most of us expect the Add to Shopping Cart button that requires only one click. Anytime your audience has to pause to figure out how to operate a navigation system or form, you test their patience. And most people with short attention spans are quite testy.

PROVIDING FEEDBACK

We have all been in taxing predicaments where the minutes turned to hours. And we've likewise encountered engaging situations where the

hours seemed like minutes. Perhaps we were distracted by good conversation and the time flew by, or we painstakingly watched the clock tick as we sat in the airport terminal after another delay. Though the actual amount of time might have been roughly the same, our perception made all the difference. When we are aware of our wait, it seems to take the longest. We can counter this perceived delay time by providing the right feedback at the right time.

During the download process, we can rely on simple indications that things are moving smoothly or incorporate small distractions that take our audience's mind off of the wait (see sidebar on next page). We can even influence the loading order of our page elements to present to the most pertinent content first. Jeffery Veen (New Riders, 2000) has detailed a method for using the positioning properties of Cascading Style Sheets to force a "loading order" on a Web page. Using this method, you can give your audience the content that they are most likely to want first and then fill in the gaps while they are engaged. Another means to providing some indication of what will appear on a page is through the use of three attributes of the IMG tag. By specifying the ALT, HEIGHT, and WIDTH attributes of your images, you can give your audience a sense of what the page will contain and how it will be laid out (see the "Being Accessible" section of this chapter). By taking your audience's mind off the wait, you create the perception that things are faster than they really are.

Feedback is also required during interactions that might lag because of server delays or complex data manipulations. If a search is likely to take a while, use a small animation and explanatory text to tell your audience that things are progressing. You should consider using such feedback loops during long downloads and during extended periods of inactivity

A FEW CURES FOR ADD

Location: 🐌	http://www.lukew.com/			
Logo	LukeW.com home page	Open Bio Menu	Open Folio Menu	Open Coolio Menu

Loading LukeW.com

Please be patient,
LukeW.com will be loaded
in seconds.

When downloading, the LukeW.com home page uses three methods of accommodating the short attention span of Web users. Specifying the ALT, HEIGHT, and WIDTH attributes of the IMG tags that make up the top row of navigation gives users an understanding of the layout and contents of the page and also lets them select an option without having to wait for the image to download. The "loading message" is positioned using Cascading Style Sheets and is rendered before the rest of the page. The LukeW.com mascot stomps his feet and checks his watch as the clock behind him ticks on. He also becomes irate if the download takes too long. This entire "distracting" animation is about 2 KB and disappears when the page is loaded. It is also worth noting that the loading animation has a built-in delay and causes it not to appear to most high-speed users. (They don't need to be distracted; the page is already loaded.)

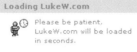

that often accompany user requests. Providing feedback is also important to give your audience a sense of where they are within your site (see navigation design in Chapters 2 and 6) and indicate why their request for action may have failed. For example, if a search query comes up empty, include some feedback that explains why the search might have failed and what might be done to get a more successful result (see sidebar). Feedback is an important part of communication, and I will revisit it throughout this book.

SORRY, TRY AGAIN

After an unsuccessful search, Google provides just the right amount of feedback on why you might have come up dry.

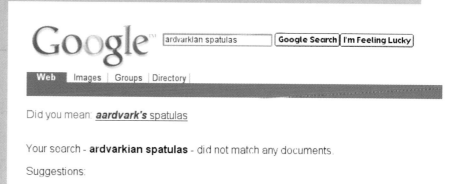

Did you mean: **_aardvark's_** spatulas

Your search - **ardvarkian spatulas** - did not match any documents.

Suggestions:

- Make sure all words are spelled correctly.
- Try different keywords.
- Try more general keywords.
- Try fewer keywords.

UNIFYING THE WEB
[SECTION TITLE]

Most of our languages consist of sounds, which form words that we logically group into sentences. This general model allows us to make sense of the letters we see on this page. We can discern sentences by noting the location of punctuation marks, and words by the spaces surrounding

DIFFERENT IS BETTER?

Getting an innovation to stick is often difficult. Larry Constantine and Lucy Lockwood have outlined the following reasons you might be better off sticking to the standards:

The nonstandard might not be better.

Dramatic improvement is needed to justify the introduction of a nonstandard.

Radical departures might not be accepted.

Consistency is important, especially online.

Nonstandards add to the mental load of your audience.

Nonstandards may slow learning.

It is easy to be different, but it is hard to do it better.

Paraphrased from the *Inventing Interfaces*, lecture presented at User Interface 2000 by Lucy Lockwood and Larry Constantine.

them. Even when we are presented with an unfamiliar language, we can rely on our understanding of these fundamental rules to find sentences, words, and eventually meaning. *Por ejemplo, aquí hay palabras en Español.* We can rely on our understanding of "how language works" as long as the new languages we encounter follow the same basic model we already know. Similarly, we can comfortably navigate a road we have never encountered because we have a clear understanding of the "driving model." Certain signs tell us to stop, while others tell us to merge or watch out. We count on these signs to work the same way from road to road and state to state. Streets that broke the *unified model* of driving by altering the purpose of common signs would be accident prone, to say the least.

The Web also has a unified model of behavior, and though breaking it won't cause interstate pileups, it will confuse and frustrate your audience. Staying within the established framework of the Web will not only save your audience grief, it can save you time and trouble as well. It is often much easier to take advantage of what people already know about and expect from the Web than it is to devise unique rules for your own site. Unless your solution is vastly superior to the standard, your audience probably will view it as an inconvenience (see left sidebar). Most people are not willing to take the time to learn something new and would rather just use the methods they already know[1]. Instead, make use of the work already done by thousands of other Web designers. During the Web's evolution, new standards have slowly emerged (the shopping cart icon on e-commerce sites, for example), and you can take advantage of the knowledge your audience has gained from repeatedly encountering these elements. It is especially important to adopt the fundamental principles that work to unite the entire Web.

[1]Steve Krug emphasizes that "We don't figure out how things work. We muddle through." (*Don't Make Me Think: A Common Sense Approach to Web Usability*, 2001, New Riders)

The unified model of the Web is based on a browsing metaphor (hence the reason Microsoft Internet Explorer and Netscape Navigator are called *Web browsers*). Whether you are following a hypertext link or making use of your Web browser's Back button, your primary means of interaction is navigation. Links, menus, search boxes, and your browser's tools (see sidebar below) are all designed to support your ability to wander the information superhighway. The way we use these navigation tools is common to all Web sites, and Web users count on them like drivers count on traffic signs.

YOUR BROWSER'S TOOL SHED

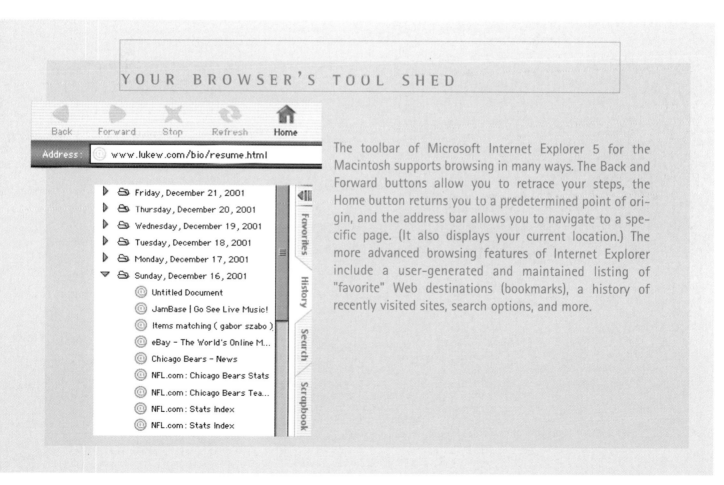

The toolbar of Microsoft Internet Explorer 5 for the Macintosh supports browsing in many ways. The Back and Forward buttons allow you to retrace your steps, the Home button returns you to a predetermined point of origin, and the address bar allows you to navigate to a specific page. (It also displays your current location.) The more advanced browsing features of Internet Explorer include a user-generated and maintained listing of "favorite" Web destinations (bookmarks), a history of recently visited sites, search options, and more.

It is worth noting that sometimes browsing is not the best form of interaction for your audience's goals, and navigation tools may not be necessary or even appropriate. More and more services are appearing online that go beyond simple searching and browsing of content. These services require unique forms of interaction not readily supported by the browsing model dominant in today's Web technology (see Chapter 8). For now, just realize certain situations may exist where searching and browsing are not the most important criteria. (Sometimes you might park your car and just listen to music. No traffic signs are needed.) For the bulk of the Web, however, they are.

BREAKING UP IS EASY TO DO

A few of the most common ways in which Web sites break the unified Web model are

Disabling Web browser navigation tools

Introducing nonstandard Web interactions

Overriding link cues

Incorrectly using Web conventions

BREAKING THE MODEL

Disabling the navigation tools of Web browsers, introducing nonstandard Web interactions, overriding link cues, and incorrectly using conventions are some of the common ways in which Web sites break the unified model holding the Web together. Often, these "breaks" are the result of a poor use of technology or presentation. Sacrificing the integrity of the Web for a sharper presentation or snazzy use of technology is like leaving the engine out of a car to make room for a 50-CD changer or giant fuzzy dice. For the show car that never leaves the automobile dealership, this might not be bad. It could even be recommended. But for the car that gets us to and from work, the engine is essential.

KEEP 'EM BROWSING

The network of roads that connects our countries and cities is specifically designed with our cars in mind. Because cars are the predominant form of transportation, everything from the size of road lanes and parking spots (though there are some bigger ones for trucks and smaller ones for motorcycles) to the height of street signs is carefully constructed to accommodate our automobiles and their abilities. The World Wide Web and its vehicle of choice, the Web browser, have a similar relationship. Travel on information superhighways is designed for the Web browser and its capabilities. In fact, each Web site needs to do its part to make sure that browsing is consistent throughout the Web. Imagine entering a city that disabled your car's ability to park. You would be hard pressed to get out and do some shopping. Of course, no city in its right mind would knowingly strip its visitors of the ability to spend their money, but some Web sites are not as gracious. In fact, there are many ways in which Web sites disable Web browsers and deny their visitors the ability to go about their business.

The Back button, bookmarks, the history menu, and the location bar are frequently used navigation features of Web browsers. The sense of security provided by the Back button allows us to follow new and perhaps risky paths through Web sites, confident that we can retrace our steps and try again. Bookmarking allows us to save sites in our browser's memory so that they can be easily located in the future. A record of the Web sites we visit is kept in our browser's history menu. The presence of the location (address) bar gives us a sense of where we are on the Web, allows us to "jump" to any location to which we know the URL, and can be copied and shared. Despite the effectiveness of these browser tools, many Web sites disable them in a variety of ways: creating new "browserless" presentation windows, building a site with frames, or using a browser plug-in (which does not support the browser tools) to present content.

Because of the Web's inherent display size variables (see Chapter 2), Web site designers often resort to a forced presentation size for their site. A common method for this is using the Javascript scripting language to open a Web site within a new Web browser window of fixed pixel height

"BROWSERLESS" WINDOWS

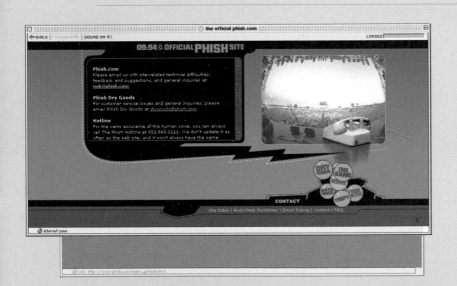

This figure is an example of opening a new browser window without the browser tools. The new window allows the Web designers to choose the amount of space available for presentation. Because the exact size of the window is known, all four sides can be used to present navigation. (In this case, the navigation appears on the bottom.) Notice that although the browser tools are removed, the designers have supplied Back and Forward buttons for the site.

and width. (See sidebar on left.) Because the size of this new window is known, designers can create layouts optimized for the window's dimensions. Quite often, this new browser window is specifically opened without the standard navigation tools of the browser. There are a variety of reasons for removing the browser tools: to remove "navigational clutter" (some browsers have an excessive amount of toolbars), to focus attention on the site's content, to force visitors to use the interaction model of the site not the browser (see Chapter 8), or to maximize the display area available to the site. In some cases, these reasons might justify removing the browser tools, but most often, they do not (see sidebar on next page). You should especially rethink removing the browser tools when presenting a Web site with links to other sites. Though the absence of browser navigation might work fine for your particular site (provided you have accommodated for the loss of the browser tools with your navigation), once a visitor leaves your site, they have no way of returning without the Back button. By removing the Back button, and the rest of browser tools, you have separated your site from the rest of the Web. Without visible browser tools, visitors can't easily bookmark your pages, print your content, or copy your URL (to send to a friend or link to your site).

Though removing the browser navigation tools can disorient your audience, an even more confusing situation is when the tools are present but not working. Web browser *plug-ins* (add-ons that enhance the presentation and interaction features of standard browsers) and *frames* (Web pages divided in multiple rows and columns of additional pages) are often the culprits in this usability crime.

Frames are often used to maintain stable navigation throughout a site. While the changing content remains in one frame, another consistently displays the navigation menus. This provides a stable manner for traversing the site and may decrease download time (the navigation frame only has to be loaded once). But these advantages are quickly outweighed by the disadvantage of disabling browser navigation tools com-

NO NEED TO BROWSE HERE

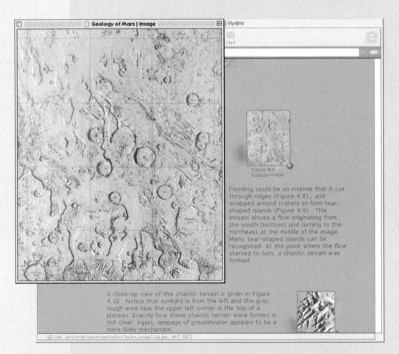

An appropriate use for new browser windows is illustrated in the Geology of Mars site. Images of the surface of Mars are presented as thumbnails within the descriptive text of the site. This helps the page download quickly (by using small thumbnail images), while keeping the images adjacent to the text describing them (for reference). When someone chooses to examine the images in more detail, the larger image is presented within a new "browserless" window. There is no need to retain the browser tools in this new window because there is nothing to browse: just the image. When they are done viewing the larger image, the audience may close the new window or return to the original page and the new window will close automatically.

mon to the whole Web. Frames, like many plug-ins, do not work within the unified model of the Web. When multiple portions of content are presented through plug-ins or frames, the absence of specific URLs disables bookmarking, and renders the Back button and location bar of the Web browser nonfunctional. Macromedia's Flash (perhaps the most common plug-in in use today) can be used to illustrate the problem. The URL for a site contained within a Macromedia Flash file only references the Flash file itself and not the distinct content within that file. As you browse content within the Flash file, the URL in your browser's location bar remains unchanged. As a result, bookmarking and the Back button do not work as you might expect. Although new versions of Flash have an effective runaround for this issue, many other plug-ins still don't. And runarounds that can give framesets unique URLs, are often cumbersome and problematic.

Another concern with plug-ins is accessibility: Your Web audience might not have the latest plug-in needed to view your content. For this reason, many sites have developed two versions: the plug-in enhanced version and the readily accessible HTML version. But creating and maintaining two Web sites is a lot of extra work (unless you take the time to build automated solutions) and consequently not a good solution. If plug-in use is a clear benefit for your audience (the increased presentation and interaction provided by the plug-in helps you meet your goals), you should make use of plug-in detection technologies. If your visitor has the proper plug-in, you can present them with the "enhanced" content. If

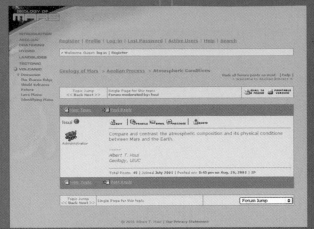

GETTING FRAMED

The use of frames in the Geology of Mars site illustrates the problem common to many plug-ins and frames. Though the content within each of the Web pages is very different. the URL is the same. The URL is continually pointing to the frameset HTML page and therefore does not change. This breaks the unified model of the Web and causes problems with bookmarking. the History menu. and so on.

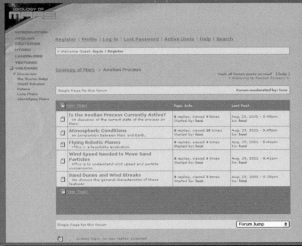

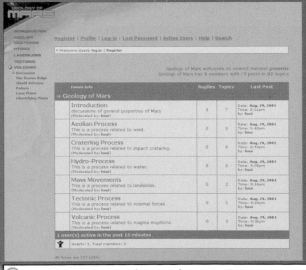

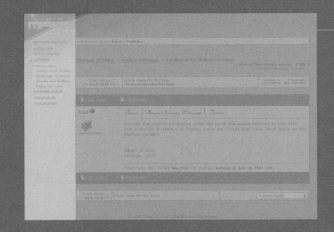

It is common to see sites that rely on browser plug-ins to present their content offer their audience a choice of the "enhanced" or standard version of the site. (An alternate solution is to use browser plug-in detection technology to see whether the plug-in is installed and then automatically bring up the appropriate site.) This guarantees that audience members who don't have (and don't want to install) the plug-in can still view the site's content. Even those with the plug-in might sometimes opt for the standard version in hopes of a quicker download.

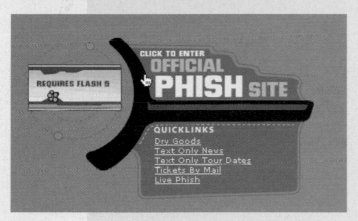

Building and maintaining two distinct versions of your Web site involves a lot of extra work. Instead, it is possible to offer only the most common or frequently changing content in an alternate format. In the intro-duction page for the Phish.com site, you may choose the enhanced version or jump to text-only versions of the news and tour dates.

not, you can provide them with a concise explanation of why they should download the plug-in and how they can do so. Telling them that acquiring the latest version of a plug-in will only take a minute of their time and provide a useful and efficient way to view your content is a good way to encourage them to add the plug-in functionality to their browser. If your audience believes the plug-in will help them achieve their goals, they are more likely to go through the added effort.

NONSTANDARD INTERACTIONS

Once your audience puts in the extra effort to get the right plug-ins for your site, reward them by presenting the content within the plug-ins in an appropriate manner. Many plug-ins make it very easy to design unique and innovative interface elements. This can be advantageous when presenting content that requires a particular form of interaction not easy to create with standard HTML. However, it can become troublesome when nonstandard interactions are required for common tasks. We are used to steering our cars with a wheel, not a track ball. In fact, if you were asked about the expected function of a track ball, odds are you would not answer "drive around town." When asked about a steering wheel, however, the odds are in driving's favor. Though it may be easy to create pull-down menus of any shape or size within Macromedia Flash, odds are your audience will not recognize them as pull-downs unless they bear some similarities to the standard pull-down menus common to most Web pages. The same is true for other interface elements such as input fields, buttons, and navigation links. Simply because unique forms of interaction are possible with the use of plug-ins does not mean that they should be used in favor of understood Web standards (unless they are appropriate for your audience, as may be in the case with entertainment and art sites). When developing within HTML and CSS, there are certain things you can and can't do. These restraints are often for your own good. A limit on the spectrum of possible interactions keeps Web pages consistent with each other. This allows users to transfer their knowledge from site to site. When developers create unique interface elements with plug-ins, Web audiences need to learn how to make use of those elements. If every site did it differently, this could quickly become a tiring process.

INCORRECT USE OF CONVENTIONS

While browsing the Web, you have probably come across many similarities between Web sites. You might have noticed that navigation menus most frequently show up at the top or left of a page and that underlined text indicates the presence of a link. These similarities have slowly become conventions through persistent use. Though there are few conventions on the Web compared to other media— books, for example, have familiar tables of contents, indexes, page number, chapters, and so on— it is still important to properly use the ones that exist: the positioning and presentation of site identifiers, navigation menus, and links.

The most common location for a site identifier (in English-speaking Web pages) is in the upper left corner. The majority of Web sites online adopt this convention, and users have come to expect it. Using this part of the page for the section title might confuse members of your audience that rely on it to identify your site. Similarly, when your audience encounters colored or underlined text within a paragraph on your site, Web conventions tell them that they have located a link. Underlined text that is not navigable is likely to be interpreted as a mistake. The next two sections go into more depth about some of the Web-wide conventions you should adopt for the placement and presentation of your links and page layouts.

[FOLLOWING LINKS]
[SECTION TITLE]

When traveling from place to place, we rely on our interstates and roads to get us to our destinations. When traversing the World Wide Web, it is the links that get us to where we need to go. But unlike our highways, we rarely know where Web page links will take us. While highways have an established system of signs to guide drivers, many Web links are poorly labeled and misleading. Adding to the confusion is the variety of links we are likely to encounter within a single site or Web page. Different kinds of links get us to different types of content and in different ways. When designing links, you need to not only be aware of the types of links you are using, but of your audience's needs as well. This means "telling" your audience where a link will take them and why they might want to go there.

DIFFERENT DESTINATIONS

Our network of streets includes narrow roads, fast roads, dirt roads, and more. Whereas the highway is likely to get you close to your goal quickly, a few smaller roads are often required to get to your exact destination. Though each road has its own particular characteristics, they all serve the same purpose: to get you where you want to go. Similarly, several different types of links get us to the content we seek online. *External* (links leading to different Web sites), *internal* (links to pages within the same site), *download* (links that lead to, often large, non-Web files), *inline* (links to content within the same page), and *action* (links that correspond to events outside of browsing) links are all likely to show up within the same Web site or page. Each of these links has its own purpose, but they all work together to get you where you want to go.

External links: External links provide paths from your site to specific sites you have determined to be informative or relevant to your audience's goals. Though it may initially seem counterintuitive to recommend that your audience leave your site, it can actually be beneficial[2]. If you provide external links to content your audience finds useful, the referral will be appreciated and reflect well on your site. External links can also serve to supplement the content you are providing with additional or supportive information. Linking to external product reviews, background information, a "second opinion," and so on allows you to make use of content created and maintained by others to support your goals. Remember to be selective in the links you choose. When your audience encounters poor

[2] Jakob Nielsen has discussed the merits of "outbound links" as content for your site in his book *Designing Web Usability: The Practice of Simplicity*. (1999, New Riders).

content "recommended" by your external links, they will be less likely to trust your site for quality information a second time. Being particular about your external links also reduces the number of options your audience has to contend with. Unless your site is a *portal* (with content consisting mostly of external links), include only a few well-selected external links to complement your content. Not only will this serve your audience better, it will reduce your workload as well.

Internal links: Internal links are probably the most common links around. And the most prevalent internal links are sitewide navigation systems and embedded links. Links within your navigation systems are unique because their positioning and presentation is responsible for orientating your audience and more (see Chapter 2). *Embedded* (usually within blocks of text or images) internal links, however, direct your audience to relevant or supplementary information elsewhere within your site. They are much closer in function and appearance to external links than to navi-

LINK LISTS

In this portion of an NCSA third-level page, the links within the text are important navigation elements. The Advisory Committees listed are followed by explanatory text, necessary because most people are unlikely to know the responsibilities of each committee. Though these links are "within" the text, they are separate enough to be distinguished as distinct navigation choices.

Home > About Us > Alliance > **Advisory Committees**

Advisory Committees   Affiliates   Key Leaders   Mission   Partners   Teams

Advisory Committees

Executive Committee
　The Alliance Executive Committee is an advisory body representing all Alliance scientific and technical focus areas. Face-to-face meetings are held quarterly to review the Alliance's progress toward its technical goals.

External Advisory Council
　The External Advisory Council is comprised of leader in the fields of public policy, telecommunications, and computer science and advises the Alliance on issues in government, academia, science, academia, industry, and education.

Steering Committee
　The Alliance Steering Committee includes the Alliance's top managers and represents all Alliance programmatic areas and activities. The committee meets biweekly via a conference call.

User Advisory Council
　The User Advisory Council consists of Alliance customers—users of its high-performance computing resources. The council advises Alliance management on its directions and provides valuable input about operations and user services. Membership is periodically rotated to reflect changes in the user base.

gation menus. That said, you should not count on embedded links as the sole means of getting your audience through your site[3]. Web users expect embedded links to supply additional or related information relevant to the specific portion of text they happen to be reading or skimming. Web conventions, developed over time, have reinforced these expectations. The exception is when links are displayed in list form and followed by descriptive text (see sidebar to the left).

Download links: Not all links lead to content that can be displayed within a Web browser. Just about any kind of document can be linked to from a Web page. AIFFs, WAVs, MOVs, AVIs, BMPs, PDFs, DOCs, and PPTs just barely begin to scratch the surface of the different file types available online. Links that lead to any file that might not display within a Web browser window are referred to as download links. *Download links* are used to provide information in formats more appropriate for particular content and support the need to go beyond what is possible with standard Web pages and images. For example, PDF files are often used to accommodate large documents. Printing 80 HTML pages one by one is an inferior solution to downloading and printing one PDF document. PDF files easily support complex layouts that are better suited for the large documents likely to be printed by your audience. Microsoft Word documents (DOCs), also often linked to from Web pages, are easy to edit and frequently used as templates. These and other download links should be used when your content is better suited for a format other than Web pages or images. Providing higher resolution content, condensing multiple portions of content into a single unit, providing an optimal interaction format for content, and distributing applications are just a few of the reasons to include download links in your site.

[3]Jared Spool, et al (Web Site Usability, 1998, Morgan Kauffman) have found a "strong negative correlation between embedded links and user success in finding information". Therefore, embedded links should provide complementary information and not serve as an important form of navigation.

Inline links: Some links do not "take" your audience to a new location or page. Instead, they guide them through the content of the current page. We call these *inline* or *anchor links*. When selected, inline links jump (scroll) further up or down the page. This technique can be very useful for directing your audience to relevant portions of long Web pages[4]. While it's a good idea to divide your Web pages into separate, more manageable "doses" of content, there are times when longer pages are necessary, and dividing the information is not an appropriate solution. In these cases, inline links can provide a macro (big picture) view of the page's content and simultaneously give your audience the ability to navigate the page (see sidebar right). A common use of inline links is in the form of an Up link. This link, located at the bottom or throughout a long page, provides a quick way for your audience to jump to the top of the page. It's often a good idea to include an Up link when the site navigation is located at the top of the page. After reading through the page's content, your audience may want to navigate to a different portion of your site, and the Up link provides a convenient way to get back to the sitewide navigation options. Try to avoid inline links in short Web pages (if a page is too short, the inline link will appear to have no effect) or embedded within text. In both these cases, encountering an inline link might confuse your audience and do more harm than good.

[4]Jared Spool, et al (*Web Site Usability*, 1998, Morgan Kauffman) state "our findings suggest that within-page links did more good than harm in helping users find information."

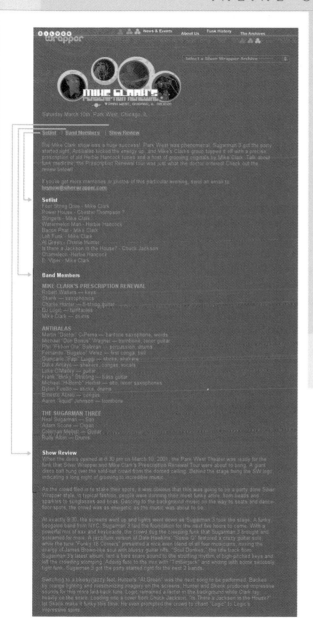

Inline links can provide an overview of the main content areas of a Web page, while simultaneously helping with navigation. In this example, the inline links (setlist, band members, and show review) provide a macro, or big-picture understanding of the content on the page. Though this Web page might be considered long, all the content is specific to the event being presented. Therefore, it makes sense to include it on the event's page and use inline links to provide an overview and means for accessing the sub-sections of the page. The arrows in the image show where each inline link "jumps" to.

Action links: *Action links* trigger events other than browsing. Probably the most common action links appear as Submit or Reset buttons in Web forms and as Go or Search buttons next to input fields. These links sometimes do not "take" your audience anywhere. Instead, they complete a transaction or activate dynamic content. Opening a new Web browser window to present content is a widespread form of action linking. Action links are more common in Web services than in pages designed for searching and browsing.

MARKING THE TRAIL

Because there are many different types of links and link destinations, it can be quite difficult for your audience to anticipate where a link may take them. Will it lead to a long page in a different Web site, or open a new browser window with a descriptive image? Because of these ambiguities, your audience needs to be "told" what they can expect from the links they encounter. *Indication* can help "mystery" links become articulate links that speak to your audience and let them know where they are going. We can provide indication for our links with descriptive wording, adjacent information, pop-ups, and colors.

Descriptive wording: There is no substitute for using *descriptive wording* for links. The more information the actual link can provide, the less your audience has to think about what lies on the other side. For example:

> *Check out our <u>numbers</u>, or*
>
> *Check out our <u>third-quarter financial report</u>.*

The second option provides a clearer indication of what you can expect to find by following the link. While the preceding example clarifies the link by adding words, sometimes removing words is more effective. In general, you should not let your links get too long. Long links are difficult to scan, can contribute to visual clutter, and are more prone to word wrapping between lines of text. Try to choose descriptive words that match the content destination of the link. In the preceding example, if your audience arrived at a page titled "third-quarter financial report," their expectations would have been met. If they were led to a page titled "company profile" that had a two-sentence reference to the success of the third quarter at the bottom of the page, they are more likely to be disappointed. When you make a promise to your audience through a link description, make sure that you deliver.

Adjacent information: Though the change in wording in our preceding example helps to clarify the link, it still leaves a lot of unknowns. How large is the financial report? What kind of information does it contain? Does clicking the link download a Microsoft Excel spreadsheet or open a detailed image in a new window? Trying to answer all these questions with descriptive wording will only lead to a confusing and distracting links. Instead, we can provide some additional information about the link with *information adjacent in space* and pop-ups. If we revisit the preceding example, we can provide a better indication of where our financial report link leads.

Check out our <u>third-quarter financial report</u> (258KB PDF).

DOWNLOAD CLUES

 Macromedia Dreamweaver Support Center
Downloads

Macromedia Dreamweaver 4.01 Updater Download

deutsch

Download the Windows German Dreamweaver 4.01 Updater <u>DW401_Updater_De.exe</u> (2.9MB)
Download the Macintosh German Dreamweaver 4.01 Updater <u>DW401_Updater_De.sea.hqx</u> (7.8MB)

english

Download the Windows English Dreamweaver 4.01 Updater <u>drm401up.exe</u> (2.9MB)
Download the Macintosh English Dreamweaver 4.01 Updater <u>drm401up.sea.hqx</u> (7.8MB)

The download links for Macromedia's Dreamweaver Updater include the descriptive title of the file followed by the full file name (as a link) followed by the approximate file size. Using the full file name of the updater helps Macromedia's audience make sense of the document that will be saved to their desktop. (The file name is truncated to comply with operating system procedures for file names.) Instead of including the file type near the file size, it is part of the link.

Now we have made it clear that the report is a 258KB PDF file. By including the approximate file size, we give the audience a better understanding of how large the file is and how long it might take to download. We also let them know that they will need a program capable of displaying PDF documents in order to view the third-quarter report.

When linking to standard Web pages or images, it is not necessary to detail the file type. But for most download links, you should include some adjacent information detailing the type of file. This prevents unwanted external programs from opening on your audience's computer and lets them know the technology needed to view the link's contents. Indicating file sizes for links is not necessary unless a significant download time is associated with a given file or the file size is substantially larger than your audience might expect. File sizes are often included adjacent to download links (such as video and multimedia links), to forewarn users of a lengthy wait.

Pop-ups: Though adjacent information can provide immediate clarification of links, it can also add a lot of visual noise and clutter to a page. Consequently, we want to keep the adjacent information we include with

Sometimes it might be beneficial to use graphics as adjacent link clarifiers. A small image next to a link can emphasize the importance or category of a link. This is especially useful for inline links. A small arrowhead can quickly communicate the effect of selecting an inline link, as in the example below. Note that the Up link is located at the end of the page to the right, exactly where you would finish reading the page.

you have read to the page
nt to return.
▲ UP

Access Int Samples

✳ Interface Only 248 KB

🏛 Rocket Science Story

🏛 Clearing the Air Story

🖾 Interface Screen Shot 116 KB

Open a new window
with this image.

🔘 Download

NOTE: Access Interactive 2.0
requires the Flash 3.0 (or higher)
plug-in from Macromedia. You may
download it by following the link
above.

This example uses a small image to distinguish between external, internal, download, and action links. The first link requires the Flash plug-in, the second two are distinct internal Web pages, the fourth link opens a new window with a 116 KB image, and the last link is an external link to Macromedia's site. Though the audience is initially unlikely to know the type of link each icon represents, they will notice the difference between the images. Once they rollover a particular link, a pop-up further clarifies what they can expect. Because this system is used consistently throughout the site, the audience can rely on it for an understanding of different link functions.

our links to a minimum. Often, file type and size take up more than enough space. But files size and types do not answer all the questions we might have about a link. For more information, we can turn to *pop-ups*. Pop-ups appear only after a user has moused over a particular link. Though they present no immediate information (pop-ups require user action, whereas adjacent information does not), pop-ups can supply valuable information about the link and what a user can expect when following it. This can save your audience time that they might have otherwise spent following unhelpful links. Link pop-ups can be implemented very simply with the TITLE attributes of HTML anchor tags (within browsers that support them), or as Dynamic HTML (DHTML) scripts.

<A HREF="page.html" TITLE="Link to a page.">

TITLE attributes offer no visual control or image support within the pop-up. They also appear differently from browser to browser. For most links, these simple text boxes work fine. However, when you need more control over the presentation and content of pop-ups, DHTML is the way to go. DHTML pop-ups offer a large amount of visual control (colors, fonts) and can include just about any type of Web content. However, DHTML pop-ups carry a lot more overhead with them and are much more difficult to build and maintain. Regardless of the method you use to implement pop-ups, use them to present supportive, and not vital, link information.

Unvisited and visited links: So far we have used indication to help clarify what your audience should expect from each of your links. However, we can supply them with even more information by properly using *link colors*. Links can exist in four states: unvisited, visited, active, and poised. The two most important distinctions are between visited and unvisited links. Without being otherwise specified by Web developers, they appear as bright purple and blue, respectively. Or was that blue and purple? Despite the arbitrary color-coding of these links, they let your audience

Access Int Samples

※ Interface Only 248 KB

Rocket Science Story

Clearing the Air Story

Interface Screen Shot 116 KB

Download

NOTE: Access Interactive 2.0 requires the Flash 3.0 (or higher) plug-in from Macromedia. You may download it by following the link above.

A pop-up created using the TITLE attribute of a link.

Commercialization Process 180 KB PPT

Dynamic HTML lets you control the visual presentation of pop-ups, including colors, typefaces, and content. In the example below, pop-ups provide thumbnails for an image gallery. This lets the audience preview each photograph before they commit to a lengthy download.

know which links they have followed and which ones remain unexplored. This provides a valuable form of feedback and helps users track their progress.

Though being able to tell where you have already been in a Web site by link color seems like a good form of indication, it has some flaws. First, Web browsers mark visited links (displayed in the visited color) for a set time interval. This means that when you revisit a site, some of the links you explored previously will be marked as visited. This might become confusing if you are relying on link colors to narrow your choices. Conversely, you might revisit the same site, and the links you explored before will no longer be marked as visited because too much time has passed. The other problem with link colors is that they are rarely kept the default blue and purple colors (though some usability experts suggest they should be). Most Web content providers alter these colors to match their color schemes or designs.

The good news is the choice of blue and purple is basically arbitrary. There is nothing about the color purple that says "visited." So using different colors is not likely to affect link understanding. However, keep in mind four guidelines when selecting visited and unvisited link colors.

Always distinguish between visited and unvisited links. Despite issues associated with revisiting sites and browser time limits on visited links, an understanding of where they have been before can help orientate and educate your audience.

Use a less saturated or grayed-out version of your unvisited link color for your visited link color. When looking at a bright green link next to a faded olive green link, the unsaturated color seems "used" or visited. This convention eliminates the need to remember arbitrary color-coding schemes. (Blue links mean what again?)

Make certain that both your visited and unvisited link colors have ample contrast to the text and background color in which they appear. Providing contrast makes scanning for links easier and clearly distinguishes what is and is not a link. You will learn more about contrast in Chapter 4.

If possible, use colors from your navigation systems for your other links. If your navigation consists of red buttons, using the same red for your unvisited links mimics the functionality of the navigation. Your audience will only have to learn once that red means "link" and can then apply that knowledge throughout the site.

Here we have a unvisited link, distinguished by a saturated contrasting color and helps your audience scan the page. In contrast, a visited link should use a less saturated form of the link color.

A poised link needs to "light up", and could use background colors or underlining to do so.

poised link
unvisited link
visited link

A sample of color combinations for links. Note that the unvisited link color stands out from the body text, and the visited link color is a less saturated version of the unvisited link color.

THE COLOR OF LINKS

A common way to distinguish links from the rest of Web content is through the use of underlines. By Web convention, any text (especially colored text) that is underlined is a link. However, underlining all your links (especially within tight navigation menus) can be distracting. The text is the important thing, not the line below it. For this reason, links often appear without the underline. Thankfully, distinctly colored text within body text is also indicative of a link.

Here we have a unvisited link, distinguished by a saturated contrasting color and helps your audience scan the page. In contrast, a visited link should use a less saturated form of the link color.

A poised link needs to "light up", and could use background colors or underlining to do so.

poised link
unvisited link
visited link

Two common ways of maintaining underlined links and reducing clutter are using underlined links only within text and not navigation systems, and revealing the underline when a user is "poised" over the link.

This sample is of a poised link with background color, or an added underline. Do not dramatically change the text of poised links. Using bold, italic text or changing the size of poised links will shift the entire block of text around the link.

Active and poised links: Besides visited and unvisited links, many browsers support active and poised links as well. *Active links* are links currently being followed, and only shift to an "active color" for the split second they are clicked on or otherwise activated. Because links only remain in the active state for a short time, the active link color only confirms that a link was selected. However, this might come in handy if you meant to click a different link, and you can catch yourself before the incorrect page begins loading. Because of such situations, it's a good idea to use a distinct active link color. However, it's much easier to prevent an incorrect selection beforehand than it is to catch and correct one after the fact.

Poised links provide indication that a link is about to be active and are implemented using the HOVER property of Cascading Style Sheets (which is unfortunately poorly implemented in older versions of Netscape Navigator). When you place your mouse pointer over a link, the link is "poised" to be selected, and the poised link color is displayed. This makes it clear which link will be followed and greatly helps to reduce incorrect selection. Poised link colors should use a more saturated or brighter version of the unvisited link color or introduce a background color. The increased contrast makes the link "light up" and appear ready to go. Unique poised linked colors are especially helpful when many small links are grouped close together, a very common situation in large Web sites.

[ASSEMBLING THE PAGE]
[S E C T I O N   T I T L E]

When building the individual roads that connect our cities and towns, certain specifications need to be met. These "rules" result in roads that are predictable and articulate. Drivers know what to expect and where they can find it. We can count on the yellow line in the center to tell us whether passing is safe, and we know that the large white arrows will guide us to the turning lane. Individual Web pages bear many similarities to these roads: They need to be understood at a glance, they need to be consistent with each other and with the rest of the Web, and they need to be clearly labeled and easy to navigate (and if you're lucky, they get a lot of traffic).

Whereas we could construct a road with some gravel and hard work, Web pages tend to be a bit more demanding. There are certain elements that all Web pages "should" have: a page title, a site identifier, an indication of when the page was last updated, at least some navigation choices, and contact information. When used properly, these elements help to orientate your audience and provide them with the information they need to make sense of your content. Your audience will be better able to understand the significance of these elements if their location is dictated by Web conventions and individual Web site consistency. According to Web

PAGE PARTS

All Web pages *should* contain

A page title (in the TITLE tag and visible on the page)

A site identifier and link home

An indication of when the page was last updated

At least some navigation elements

An indication of who can be contacted about the page

CONTENT!

conventions, the site identifier should remain in the upper left hand corner of the page and serve as a link to the home page. (See sidebar in Chapter 2.) The contact information (though it can also show up elsewhere) should appear in the page footer along with copyright and privacy or security information. When looking for copyright information, your audience is likely to go to the footer first. Though navigation choices can be found just about anywhere on a page, Web users will most frequently expect them to appear at the top and left side of an English-speaking page. These sitewide navigation choices often include tools or utilities common to the entire site. Search tools, e-commerce utilities, or specialized personal services are a few of these elements. An indication of when the page was last updated can clarify whether the content on a page is recent or dated and frequently appears near the page title (although many sites include it in the footer).

Page titles, most commonly found left justified at the start of body text, have three duties. Page titles need to match the "incoming" links' promises. That is, if links elsewhere within your site refer to a page as "Financial Info," the page title needs to be a close match. "Our Financial Information" makes it rather clear that your audience is on the right page. However, "Daily Dollars" might lead them to question their location.

The page title not only needs to match incoming link expectations, it also needs to match returning expectations. The best way to accomplish this is to use the HTML TITLE tag.

<TITLE>AB Bank: Financial Information</TITLE>

Including a TITLE tag that specifies the page is to be remembered as "Financial Information" keeps the browser's history menu and bookmarks (unless modified by users) reflective of the page's content. So when your audience attempts to return, their bookmarks and history will contain a title that accurately describes your page. The TITLE tag differs from the page title in one important manner: It should contain a reference to the site (and possibly descriptive category) in which the page was found. You should not include the entire navigation path within the title tag, because your audience is unlikely to use the page title as navigation (as the title bar is not navigable), and the name will be truncated within a browser history or bookmark menu. (See sidebar to the right.)

KEEP CONTENT DOMINANT

Despite the need to include navigation, utilities, contact information, and more on each page, the emphasis should always be on the page's substance. In some cases, this substance may be navigation (as in destination or navigation pages), or it might be contact information (as in pages with multiple phone numbers or addresses). Regardless of what each page provides for your audience, the rest of the page elements only play a supportive role. Navigation is designed to get you to the content you need and then effectively "disappear," or at least not prevent you from understanding the page's content. Many sites have pages that are over saturated with elements that compete with or impair your ability to concentrate on the gist of the page.

There are two ways to avoid this scenario. One way involves evaluating the elements on your pages (through user testing and discussion) and eliminating as many extraneous or ineffective elements as possible. The second way is to use the principles of visual organization to create a page

TITLE TAGS AS EVIDENCE

▷ 🗁 Thursday, December 27, 2001
▽ 🗁 Tuesday, December 25, 2001
    @ LukeW | Geology of Mars
    @ LukeW | Resume
    @ LukeW Interface Designs
    @ NFL.com: Stats
    @ NFL.com: Stats
    @ NFL.com: Stats
    @ NFL.com: Chicago Bears Team..
    @ Untitled Document
    @ Untitled Document
    @ http://www.somesite.com/som...
    @ http://www.somesite.com/som...
    @ http://www.somesite.com/som...

In the screen shot from Microsoft Internet Explorer above, the pages without predefined titles appear as either untitled documents or URLs. The URLs are not useful for understanding what we can expect to find on each page; neither are pages with the same name (nfl.com above).

A descriptive page title can serve as a reliable record for your audience. When Web browsers catalog a user's actions online, they use the page title to distinguish pages. Likewise, when saving a page using bookmarks, if a user does not enter a descriptive name, the page title is used as the default value. Using clear page titles within the TITLE tag of your Web documents helps your audience relocate your site with ease.

There are two guidelines for the TITLE tags: Include the site name before each page description and do not use the page title as a complete "navigation trial." Including the site title lets users know where the page came from, whereas including the full path from the home to the current page is unlikely to get fully displayed in the history or title bar of a browser. Instead, include only short phrases that clarify the content of the page (as in the "LukeW | Geology of Mars" title in the example.) The full path, Home>Folio>Web Site Designs>Geology of Mars Site, is less effective.

layout that puts the focus on the content and not the supportive elements of a page. In the next chapter, we will discover the visual principles that can make this happen.

Above the fold: From a technical standpoint, however, we can do some things to give content the type of attention it deserves. One is to consider the implications of designing *above the fold*. Above the fold refers to the portion of a Web page most likely to be seen by your audience. The term has its roots in newspaper printing. When a newspaper is distrib-

THE FOLD

Keep the most important content "above the fold" created by Web browser window screen sizes.

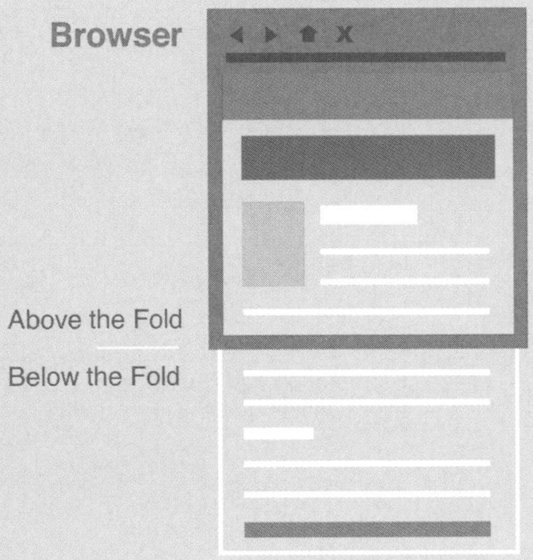

Browser

Above the Fold

Below the Fold

uted, it's folded in half for easier transportation and display. As a result, only half the front page's content can be seen when the folded paper lies on the shelf. Newspaper editors make sure that the day's most important stories are placed "above the fold" where they will be seen. A similar situation occurs with Web pages. Although there is no literal fold, Web pages face being cut off by the bottom of the Web browser. While it's impossible to know where that fold line will occur (your audience's screen resolution, browser tools, operating system, and browser window size all influence the cut-off point), you can still design your pages to account for its presence. Because the lowest screen resolution to account for is 640 x 480 pixels, you can count on about 300 pixels (after taking browser tools and menus into account) to remain above the fold. The limited amount of space you have to explain the your page is another important reason that content should be the dominant element on each of your Web pages.

Scannable: You can also maximize the communication abilities of your content by presenting it in a *scannable* manner. Because most of your audience is unlikely to read through all the text on your Web page (unless they think they have found the content they need), a scannable page can provide a quick understanding of what is available. Descriptive page titles, section headers, and embedded hyperlinks can all supply a glimpse of the page's intentions. By making these elements visible and recognizable, you can focus your audience's attention on the content of the page. Dividing your content into shorter, easier to manage portions can also enhance scannability.

BEING ACCESSIBLE
[S E C T I O N   T I T L E]

Not only do we need the roads we build to be understandable (so that we know how to navigate them), but they also need to be accessible. Too narrow a road, and most cars won't be able to fit. Not clearly marked, and odds are most of us won't find it. But roads only need to worry about a particular nation's cars, trucks, buses, and bikes. Unlike the World Wide Web, roads don't have to accommodate the entire world and a multitude of unique devices. The Web has to contend with traffic from cell phones, computers, pagers, personal digital assistants, and information appliances of all shapes and sizes. There are blind people, young people (many without driver's licenses), technology-savvy people, disabled people, foreign (at least to you) people, and more out there cruising the Web pages you put up. The sites you build need to be accessible to the many different types of visitors you are likely to receive. There are several ways to remain accessible to the general audience that comes to your site. Considering technological variations, properly using images, and retaining established URLs are some of the more important ones.

When planning your site, it's important to determine what level of Web browsing technology you will support (see Chapter 2). Newer browsers have better support for advanced presentation and interaction features, but are not yet used by everyone surfing the Web. Usability guru Jakob Neilsen recommends supporting all browsers less than two years old. This means 4.0 (and later) versions of Microsoft Internet Explorer and Netscape Navigator (both released around 1998) are fair game. As such, cascading style sheets and many Dynamic HTML enhancements are possible without excluding a large portion of your audience.

However, older browsers are still out there, and your site should at least gracefully degrade (see Chapter 2) to be usable on these older browsers. If possible, try not to have important portions of your site require new browser features. Or at least consider making a version accessible to less advanced browsers. This is especially important, because members of your audience may be using a text only browser (such as Lynx), a specially adapted browser for the visually or otherwise impaired, or a cell phone's, PDA's, or other device's built-in browser. If your site makes extensive use of new browser features, provide these users with an alternate route to access your content. You might also want to do this if you are heavily relying on plug-in technologies to make your site run. Not everyone in your audience will have the latest version of the plug-in you are using, and in some cases the plug-in may not be available for the device they are using to access your site. Many sites that extensively use plug-ins to present their content offer an alternative version of the site, or portions of the site, to remain accessible to their audience. That said, you should only use plug-in and new browser technologies when they complement your content or enhance your audience's understanding of your site. Instead of using technology for technology's sake, use technology for your audience's sake. They will appreciate it a lot more than the technology will.

PROVIDE ALT-ERNATIVES

Like plug-ins and new browser features, improper image use can cause accessibility problems for members of your audience. Using a text-only browser, or a standard browser with images disabled (some users select this option to speed up downloads) are just two of the many ways images can be left out of the Web layouts you so carefully constructed. If the images are necessary to understand the page's significance, your audience might be in trouble. As a result, you should not rely too heavily on images to present your content. Sites that rely entirely on images for their presentation are slow to load and can be troublesome for image-free browsing. This certainly does not mean you should not use images, but when you do, you need to present ALT-ternatives for the images included in your site. For each image on your site, include the ALT attribute of the IMG tag to identify the image for those who can't view it.

<IMG SRC="horse.gif" ALT="Brown horse grazing in a meadow.">

When someone cannot see the images, they will see the ALT text instead[5]. If you have provided a descriptive ALT attribute, your audience will still have a sense of the content on your page. When your image consists of words, such as "enter our store," the ALT attribute should contain the same text. In other cases, the ALT attribute needs to describe the image as best it can without becoming overly long. For a photograph,"Bruce Banner, CEO of Hulk Enterprises" is more effective at communicating the importance of the image than "scrawny guy with glasses, brown hair, and a nervous smile." Not only does the ALT attribute help members of your audience that cannot see your images, it also comes in handy when waiting for a page to load. If you have supplied ALT attributes for each of your images, members of your audience have a "sneak peek" at the images coming down the pipe to their screen. Most browsers will display the ALT attributes of your images prior to downloading them. If you have also included WIDTH and HEIGHT attributes in your image tags, they will also display the size and positioning of the images with outlines, giving your

[5]This is why use of the ALT tag is critical to meet section 508, handicap accessibility requirements for Web sites.

audience a sense of the page's layout (see sidebar in the "Paying Attention" section). Once they see an ALT attribute that coincides with their goals, many users will not wait for the full page to download. Instead, they will select the outline with the ALT attribute that meets their needs and be on their way.

LEAVE A FORWARDING ADDRESS

The first step to accessibility is having something to access. There is a good chance members of your audience might be using your "address" to come to your site. Your Web address (or URL) might have appeared on a TV commercial, on a recently distributed flyer, or been sent by a friend. Referrals to your URLs not only come from your advertising efforts, they appear all over the Web in the form of links. Many other sites may link to your content if they believe the information you offer is beneficial to their audience. Similarly, many search engines store your URLs and present them as navigation options to their users. You need to make sure not to "break" these established URLs. Abruptly renaming pages or changing directory structures severs the ties that your page had to the rest of the Web. Many of these ties can take a long time to establish, so cutting them off can be costly. If you do need to alter the URL of your pages, make certain that you leave a forwarding address. A simple page that tells your audience the page has moved or an automatic forward to the new URL are better than leaving your audience out to dry with a "file not found" error.

chapter four

When you look to a map for information, you probably spend very little time actually reading text. Instead, you get most of your information from the map's visual presentation. Blue areas indicate bodies of water, while green areas represent parks. If two towns appear in the same size font, they probably have a comparable amount of residents. Maps, like other visual means of communication, tell you an awful lot with very few words. Because it is the primary means for getting around your site, your visual presentation should work similarly. By properly using visual communication principles, you can explain the content and function of your Web site to your audience and get them to where they want to go.

SPEAKING VISUALLY
[S E C T I O N   T I T L E]

Can you recall the number of times someone has pointed out to you that a picture is worth a thousand words? Most of the time, you probably just shrugged in agreement and didn't give it much more thought. But think about how many words it would really take to accurately describe even a simple photograph. You could talk about the size of objects in the photo and how one object compares to the others. That might lead you to discuss the relationships between the objects: one is in front of the other, two look very similar, the third is made up of smaller parts. You could even get into the colors, spelling out the hues present in each item. What about the subject matter: How did it get there, and why? What about the location? The time? As you can see, you'll be closing in on a thousand words in no time.

Pictures, like all visual experiences, quickly communicate an awful lot. If you have ever tried describing someone to a friend, you know the value of having a photograph on hand. One glance at the photo is all it takes. With only words at your disposal, you might never do the person justice.

But visual communication is not limited to photographs. Basically, anything you can make sense of with your eyes can "speak" to you visually: maps, books, Web pages, and so on. Just looking at any of these objects quickly provides you with a wealth of information. It would be foolhardy not to take advantage of this golden opportunity when you design Web pages. After all, the Web is a visual medium. But designing effective Web presentations means a lot more than just making pretty pictures. Though a picture may very well be worth a thousand words, the words I come up with might be quite different from the ones you produce. Remember that Web pages have specific messages. They tell your audience what kind of information they can find, how to get to that information, and more. Therefore, you want to paint an informative (yet engaging) picture for your audience. By using visual organization principles, you can compose Web pages that not only say the right thing but also say it clearly and coherently.

More than likely, you're already using visual organization principles without being aware of it. When taking notes, you might distinguish main topics with larger text or small images, such as bullets. Or you might have your desk organized into meaningful piles of papers, of which a quick glance tells you whether any unpaid bills are left. In both these cases, the placement or visual treatment of information provides you with valuable clues about how to interpret what you see. Not only do you know each large or bulleted word indicates a topic in your notes, you also know the text underneath it is on that topic. When looking at your desk, not only do you know whether there are any unpaid bills, you know how many there are. In both cases, the visual organization charges what you see with meaning.

The relative position, color, scale, and style of your information should not be an arbitrary choice. They need to be well thought out so that they can educate your audience on how to interpret and make use of your Web site. By manipulating the treatment and placement of elements on your Web pages, you can create meaningful distinctions and similarities between information. Those distinctions then help to establish a graphic language that your audience can rely on to make sense of your site. For example, you can present all your unvisited links as underlined lime green, or all your navigation links on the left-hand side of a page with a light blue background. If you apply this graphic language consistently, your audience will know what sort of behavior and information to expect from your Web site elements quickly and easily. *Left-hand side and light blue background? Okay, that's navigation, I don't need that right now...* Without having to spend time reading, your audience can make sense of the information.

Your audience can also apply what they have learned to different situations. *This text has the same light blue background as the navigation. I bet it is a link.* And that is good news for the short attention spans you're likely to encounter online. (See Chapter 3.) Establishing a graphic language with visual organization principles, not only allows your audience to better scan your pages, it also lets them confidently navigate them. Orientating your audience and guiding them through your navigation systems is much easier when you have visual organization tools on your side.

A consistent graphic language can communicate the where, what, and how of Web pages. (The why and who are in Chapter 5.) Where can I find the navigation system? Where have I already been in the site? What is on this page? What will I find if I follow this link? How can I finish this transaction? How much information exists on this topic? These questions and more can be answered visually, saving you and your audience the need to wade through piles of text and instructions. The next section will introduce you to the basic principles that we use to visually organize information. Understanding the basics will help you make better decisions when it comes time to "speak" to your audience.

SEEING INFORMATION
[S E C T I O N   T I T L E]

In order to understand how to visually organize information, we need to be aware of how we make sense of what we see. When looking at an unfamiliar presentation of information, we begin by recognizing similarities and differences between things. This observation allows us to group information into meaningful categories. For example, all the odd-shaped blue areas on a map are visually similar. Once we learn that one such area is a lake, we can attribute that property to all the other objects that are similarly depicted. Thereby, we save the time needed to locate the name of each blue area to determine whether or not it is a lake. Not only do we know that every odd-shaped blue area is a lake, we know that odd-shaped green areas are not lakes. As a result, we can quickly glance at a map and determine the amount of possible fishing spots near us.

The process works because the map uses a consistent graphic language. If lakes were depicted in green, blue, or pink and so were parks, we would have our work cut out for us when we wanted to fish. Similarly, suppose that we determine that, in our map, all city names appear in a black sans-serif font on an orange background. We can then begin to draw conclusions based on the relative size of that text. The larger the text appears, the larger the town. This relationship allows us to quickly compare our possible fishing destinations and pick one that is far from the lights of a big city. Although these examples are deliberately simple, they showcase how visual relationships (similarities and differences) between things can help us to interpret what we see.

The way these individual elements and groups relate to the whole is even more important. Once we recognize the relationships between things, we look to make sense of the whole picture through a unified "story." When looking at our map from before, we can say, "Here is a large city with two parks next to lake." We are able to piece together this story by observing the similarities and differences between the elements on the map and then applying our understanding of those relationships to the big picture. This grouping of related elements to establish an informative structure (a story) is the essence of visual organization.

UNDERSTANDING PERCEPTION

Several principles tell us how the members of our audience will piece together their story: proximity, similarity, continuance, closure, and assimilation. *Proximity* tells us that elements placed closely together, when compared to elements far away, will be perceived as a new element: a group. The closer the elements are to each other, the more likely they are to be seen as a unique visual group. *Similarity* can reinforce this perception. Similarities of size, shape, color, direction, and texture work to group distinct elements together visually. So elements with a lot of common visual characteristics are likely to be grouped together, whereas distinct elements are not. (We will take a look at how to create some of these relationships in the next section.) *Continuance*, on the other hand, tells us that several different elements are likely to be grouped together if their differences are the result of a basic pattern: for example, a series of identical circles progressively deceasing in size. *Closure* says that we also have a tendency to group elements by filling in the space between them to create larger, more simple forms. In other words, we tend to fill in the gaps.

So far, the principles we have looked at all tell us why we tend to group visual information. Though this information is important for understanding how we make sense of a visual presentation, there is more to the psychology of perception than that.

Assimilation says that our visual perception is often influenced by our past experiences and knowledge. That's why we concentrate on designing for our specific audience and their experiences —especially their experiences with the Web (see Chapter 3). Assimilation is responsible for a characteristic that psychologists call *isomorphic correspondence.*

Proximity, similarity, continuance, and closure all determine how viewers group information in a visual presentation.

| Proximity | Similarity | Continuance | Closure |

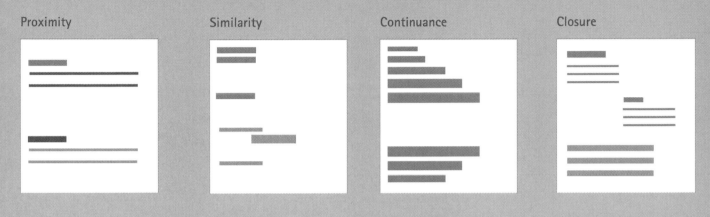

Though it seems like quite a mouthful, isomorphic correspondence is the relationship between the appearance of a visual form and a comparable human behavior. For example, we associate the red coils on a stove top as potentially harmful. When looking at an image of such coils, we can almost feel the hurt if we were to touch them. You have seen isomorphic correspondence used on the Web many times. When a link is visually represented as a three-dimension button, we associate it with pushing.

Though it is important to know how we make sense of visual information, it is not enough. We want to visually communicate a specific message to our audience. That means that we need a large amount of control over the relationships and stories that our audience will observe within our presentations. We need to create elements that carry the

meaning we intend for our audience to interpret. Remember, communication is only effective when the author's intended meaning is a close match to the audience's interpreted meaning. This is especially true with visual communication. Sending the right message means being aware of how the visual organization of a site is communicating.

Knowing how people group visual elements is a good start. It helps organize information into meaningful groups: This group is navigation, and this one is content. The preceding principles tell us the psychological manner in which we group visual information. When we want to communicate a certain idea or functionality for a certain set of elements, we can rely on these principles. Though the way each individual interprets visual information is likely to be unique, the majority of people can perceive these basic relationships. It is exactly these relationships that we make use of when we visually organize information to give it meaning.

INTENTIONALLY

DIFFERENT

We can create visual similarities and differences (relationships) between objects through the use of color, texture, shape, direction, and size.

COLOR

DIRECTION

Visual relationships are the fundamental basis for all systems of visual organization. Remember that when presented with a layout of information, the first things we notice are the relationships between the various elements in the layout. Creating visual relationships requires an understanding of what makes things different. Is one element bigger than the other? Is one red and the other blue? Does one have rounded corners, while the other is straight? Though lots of variations are possible, we can group distinct visual characteristics into one of five main categories: color, texture, shape, direction, and size. Introducing variations in one or all of these categories creates *visual contrast* (see sidebar below).

The amount of visual contrast between two objects is related to the amount of variation in their visual characteristics. The more two objects contrast, the more likely it is that they will be perceived as distinct (unrelated) objects. You can maximize the amount of contrast between two

TEXTURE

SHAPE

SIZE

objects by introducing variations in all of their visual characteristics. This will imply that the two objects are very different. Conversely, introducing variations in only one visual characteristic will result in two objects that seem more related. It is important to note that we only understand contrast because we are familiar with *harmony* (balance). We perceive things to be in harmony if they are similar in most ways or in all ways. Harmony is very pleasing, comfortable, and satisfying. As a result, we look for it in visual presentations. It is our desire for harmony that makes contrast stick out and grab our attention.

Visual relationships are also created through the placement of elements. By being aware of how you are positioning elements within your layouts, you can suggest relationships, create emphasis, and imply importance. Placement needs to be considered in relation to the entire layout, as well as in relation to the other elements within. When two elements are close together, they appear to be related or at least more closely associated than elements that are farther apart (proximity). By manipulating the space around objects, we can also emphasize certain elements over others. When a good deal of white space (an empty area within a layout) surrounds any given element, the element sticks out much more than if it were surrounded by additional elements. This strategy can work to focus your audience's attention on a particular area of your layout or separate unrelated elements. This ordering of elements can hold significance as well. An element positioned above another element is frequently perceived first, as are elements to the left (in Western cultures).

Now that we have an understanding of the basic ways to distinguish objects (grouping, contrast, and placement), let's look at the big picture: using those relationships to tell a coherent "story." A story not only explains what you see, it does so in a meaningful order. As with any other narrative, we need to start at the beginning and end at a logical conclusion. We accomplish this visually by organizing the elements within our layouts into a visual hierarchy. Elements within a visual hierarchy have an easily identifiable order of importance or emphasis. In other words, something gets noticed first, second, and so on. This ordering helps to guide you through the information you see in a logical progression: one that helps you to make sense of the information. It also helps to unify all the elements into a cohesive "whole," in which the meaning of each element is understood.

As an example, let's look at a poster advertising the circus's arrival in your town. When you first glance at the poster, the heaviest (highest in the visual hierarchy) visual elements are probably circus images (such as

VISUAL HIERARCHY

A visual hierarchy:

Creates a center of interest that attracts the viewer's attention

Creates a sense of order and balance

Establishes a pattern of movement to guide a viewer through a composition

VISUAL MANIFESTO

A clear visual hierarchy guides you through the information in this poster. The heaviest visual elements are the images of musicians and the title: Soul Manifesto. Of next importance and visual weight are the dates and location. The ticket information carries the least visual weight of all the elements in the poster.

elaborate elephants or amazing acrobats) or even the word "circus." By placing these elements at the top of the visual hierarchy, we make certain this is what gets noticed first. This is important for our "big picture" understanding: The circus is in town. Before we get into the details, we need to have an overall sense of what we are dealing with. If we look at the opposite end (the bottom of our visual hierarchy), we are likely to find "less vital" information, such as the ticket price. Could you imagine the reverse: a poster that emphasized the ticket price over the rest of the content? Odds are, few people would know the circus was in town. Instead, they would shrug as they passed by giant "$7.50" posters, not bothering to read the fine print that says "Oh, by the way, circus."

When interpreting the poster, we depend on the visual hierarchy to make sense of the information. Starting at the top and gradually moving down, we build our narrative as we go. Okay, circus, Barnum & Bailey, June 3 –5, at the Rosemont Horizon, tickets are $7.50, got it. Not only do we understand the big picture, we make sense of the individual elements as well. When presented with the text "$7.50," we understand it to be the cost to enter the circus. Without the big picture information, we would be hard pressed to know what the $7.50 was for.

So how do we build effective page hierarchies? We use visual relationships to add more or less *visual weight* to our elements. Visual weight can be loosely defined as the degree to which an element demands our attention and keeps our interest. For example, very large red type would have more visual weight than a small gray dot next to it. However, a very elaborate image with lots of detail would hold your attention longer than the red type. In both of these examples, the difference in visual weight is created by the contrast between the two objects. The detailed image has more texture than the type. And the type is larger in scale, in a brighter color, and has a more complex shape than the small gray dot.

The distribution of visual weight within a layout is the key to creating an informative visual hierarchy. The visually dominant elements on a page (the ones with the largest amount of visual weight) get noticed the most. These elements determine where our story begins: They form the center of interest or focal point. The rest of the hierarchy then helps to establish a pattern of movement that guides a viewer's eyes through the rest of the composition. We move from the first focal point to the second, the third, and so on, picking up pieces of the narrative as we go. The relative position of each element in the hierarchy provides us with valuable clues about its importance and "place in the big picture." Not only does a balanced layout provide a clear path for recognizing and understanding information, it also establishes a sense of order that helps to create a cohesive "whole" instead of a collection of unrelated parts.

KEEPING IT BALANCED

A common problem with nearly all hierarchies is that everyone wants to be at the top. But in corporate structures, as well as visual organizations, we simply can't have it. If every element on your page is fighting to be the focus of your audience's attention, nobody wins. Instead, your audience is left darting from one "desperate for attention" element to the next, and they lose sight of the big picture quickly. Effective visual hierarchies rely on balance to maintain a coherent system of relationships. You can think of this balance as a seesaw effect. When one element becomes more dominant, the others become less dominant. Achieving a unified, harmonious layout that guides viewers in the manner you intend is a matter of balancing this seesaw. Only some elements should be dominant; the rest need to fall in line. Where each element falls in the visual hierarchy depends on the message you are trying to communicate.

DISTINCTIONS & HIERARCHY

NO VISUAL HIERARCHY

PAGE HIERARCHY

A visual hierarchy presents the information on a page in an understandable and logical manner. The distinct visual weight of each element guides you through the page in an informative and appropriate manner and provides valuable insights on the role of each element relative to the whole.

VISUAL WEIGHT

Type

Though the red type catches your eye first (bright color and unique shape), the texture and details present in the image hold your attention much longer. The gray dot carries the least visual weight of the three elements because of its simple shape and lack of contrast with the background (light gray and white are only slightly contrasting).

[SECTION TITLE] EDUCATING YOUR AUDIENCE

Be it a map, a city, or a book, we have a much better chance of finding what we need when we know how something is organized. Yet we often lack the time and patience (especially online) that it takes to read through a set of instructions or a manual to learn how something works. Instead, we pick up on whatever visual clues we can find and use those (and our experiences) to paint ourselves a picture of how things work. For example, in the city block, you see numbers on buildings that appear to be ascending. You quickly determine which direction your destination is and off you go. You can expect a similar behavior from your Web audience. They will scan your page, pick up on a few visual clues, develop a mental model of how the site works, and be on their way. As a result, it is important that the visual clues you provide for your audience are informative and consistent. If the building numbers in our city block example suddenly shifted to descending order or existed solely for decoration, you would have to start over.

Through well thought out applications of visual hierarchy, contrast, relationships, and placement, you can communicate a lot to your audience. In addition to telling them where they are within your site structure, you can explain the various elements they will encounter from page to page and provide a sense of how they can accomplish their goals. In other words, you can explain the where, what, and how of your Web pages. The next few sections present a number of ways in which visual organization can educate your audience and help them build correct mental models of your site. If any of these considerations seem obvious to you, then we're on the right track. The goal of visual organization is to make things as clear as possible for your audience so that they do not have to think too much about how to use your site.

EXPLAINING WHERE

Although the Web lacks any real physical space (remember Chapter 2), there are many reasons why a sense of "where" you are within a site is crucial. Not only does knowing where you are provide a sense of comfort and confidence, it also supplies valuable information about other places you can go and how you can get there. In other words, it allows you to understand the structure of a site. To return to our map analogy, when you can pinpoint your position on a map, you can clearly see the roads and destinations available to you. Though most road maps are not able to indicate your present location (maps of the future will), Web sites do. In fact, your Web site can use visual organization in several ways to orientate your audience. Through consistency, contrast, and hierarchy, Web pages can make it clear where in the Web, within a particular site, or even within a page users are.

When Web users come to your pages, they do so in a variety of ways: through search engines, URLS in magazines, links from other sites, and so on. Because you have no way of knowing how in the Web they got to your site, you need to let them know where in the Web they are. It is here that Web conventions pay off, and the site id you have included (see Chapter 3) quickly tells them they are now in your site.

But the consistent (with Web conventions) placement of site elements is not the only clue you have. A consistent graphic language can distinguish your site from the rest of the Web as well. Using a cohesive set of styles throughout your site and each page in it establishes a sense of place that is readily distinguishable by Web users. Reusing colors and design motifs (especially those that echo portions of your site identifier) within the different elements on each page can make this distinction even more pronounced. For example, you can use a shade of green from

about us

THE TEAM
WHO WE ARE
WHY WE'RE HERE
EXPERIENCE
GUARANTEE
RETURNS POLICY
SHIPPING
SECURITY

shop   buyarock 101   pop the question   buyarock.com

free shipping

Your order from buyarock.com will be shipped to you free within 7-10 days, via insured overnight Federal Express or UPS. You will be notified via email of your shipping confirmation. Many orders may be able to ship more quickly, but each piece of jewelry is created by hand to your specifications after you place your order.

Your diamond jewelry from buyarock.com will arrive in an attractive black velvety jewelry box. The buyarock.com name will not appear on that box.

 MORE

CONTACT US:
customerservice@buyarock.com
1-800 574-7099

---

buyarock.com   shop   buyarock 101   about us   pop the question

DIAMOND Anniversary Bands

Click on any item to see its many diamond size and quality options. Shop with confidence as every diamond we sell larger than 3/8 carat is accompanied by a Diamond Grading Analysis and a Gemprint® Registration Certificate, which records your diamond's unique "fingerprint."

The products shown here may also be available in different mountings (i.e. platinum, white gold, or yellow gold). The options can be seen by clicking on the Take A Closer Look buttons for each product.

Take a CLOSER LOOK

Take a CLOSER LOOK

Take a CLOSER LOOK

Take a CLOSER LOOK

---

pop the question   shop   buyarock 101   about us   buyarock.com

Show & tell

Show off your ring!
OR GET A SECOND OPINION

However you choose to use it, the exclusive buyarock.com Show & Tell feature allows you to choose a piece of diamond jewelry and save it in your own file here on our site. Then you can direct your friends, family, and anyone else to come and check it out. It will remain in your special file for one week after you post it there. All you need to do is browse our extensive selection of diamond jewelry and when you see a piece you like, click on it to see an enlarged view. In that view you'll see directions on how to enact the Show & Tell feature and share your selection with anyone you wish. That's a great way to announce your engagement and show off your ring or any new diamond jewelry from buyarock.com.

 START
Shopping

A DISTINCT LANGUAGE

A unified graphic language helps to create a sense of "place" for a Web site. In the buyarock.com Web site, common type treatments, color accents, and graphic elements (such as shapes, line drawings, and photographs) help to create a cohesive site. Whether you are looking at the shipping policies of the company or shopping for anniversary bands, the consistent graphic language of the site reassures you that you are in the same site and helps you to make sense of each page's content.

your company logo as background for your navigation buttons or repeat a graphic element in different contexts on a page. A page with a graphically unified set of elements not only works better as a distinct whole, it also makes it easier to create contrast between individual elements. It is much easier to locate a different element amongst many similar elements. Its uniqueness stands out.

The benefits of a consistent graphic language are even more evident when your audience moves around within your site. Not only does retaining an established graphic language between pages reassure your audience that they are within the same site, it also can provide valuable clues to where within that site they are. Color-coding each subsection of your site is a common way to communicate position (using similarity). Color-coding is most effective when the sections of your site have distinct differences. These distinctions could be based on user tasks, specific audience members, or content. The various colors of the sections provide an indication that your audience has made a distinct change in goals (see sidebar on the next page).

However, you can give your audience a sense of their position in more subtle ways. Through the use of visual contrast, hierarchy, and small multiples within navigation systems, you can communicate a sense of scale, structure, and location. For example, visual contrast within a navigation system is an effective way to communicate the current "level" of the site. The more prominent (often larger or bolder) elements in a navigation system are understood to be at a higher or "parent" level than less prominent elements. This visual relationship provides a better understanding of the site structure. The elements higher up in the visual hierarchy are perceived as "bigger" (and because they are more general categories, they often do in fact describe large parts of sites). The elements lower in the visual hierarchy are smaller, more specific categories. The graphic language matches the actual structure of the site.

COLOR BY CONTENT

Amazon.com uses a color-coding system to distinguish its distinct stores. Color-coding assures you that you are shopping for the appropriate merchandise (in this example, books or DVDs). Also note how the color scheme is repeated throughout the page. The interface elements (Go button) and section titles (Welcome to Books) all reiterate the section's color scheme. This helps establish a firm sense of a distinct "place."

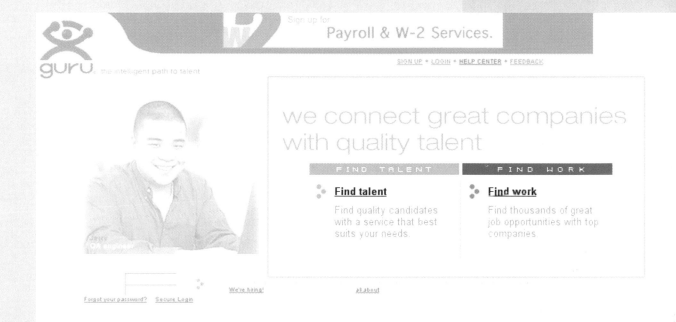

The Guru.com Web site uses color-coding to distinguish its content for two distinct audiences. Visitors to Guru's site are presented with an initial choice (are you looking to do work, or are you looking for someone to do work for you?) distinguished by colors. The colors are then carried throughout each specific audience's content.

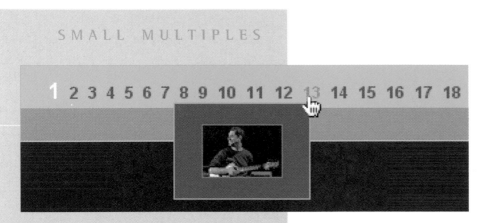

SMALL MULTIPLES

Small multiples can provide a sense of relative scale. In the example above, each number indicates an additional photograph. A quick glance at the list tells you how many photos are available without taking up lots of space with thumbnails or lengthy descriptions.

The image above shows graphical small multiples at work within a linear sequence. Because you are meant to view this content linearly, the small multiples do a nice job of showing you where you are and how much you have left to go.

This use of visual hierarchy also provides a sense of relative scale. A sense of scale (how much content is behind each link) is rather difficult to communicate on the Web. However, the contrast between navigation elements (size, style) can indicate the amount of content in each category relative to the whole. This visual relationship is by no means an accurate representation of the amount of content, but it does provide some basic understanding. Scale can also be communicated more explicitly with small multiples. *Small multiples*[1] work best when content is presented in a linear sequence (often a series of steps) because the content descriptions can be reduced to small images or numbers (see left sidebar).

We can also use contrast to provide a more obvious indication of your location within a Web site. By visually contrasting a user's current location from the rest of the navigation elements, you can create a definitive signal that says "you are here." This effect is most commonly achieved with contrasting background images or type, an adjacent image, or all three (see sidebar on next page). Remember that when we make

Edward Tufte describes small multiples in depth in his book *Envisioning Information* (Graphics Press, 1990).

STRUCTURAL CLUES

The relative scale of the navigation choices in the Apple menu provides an indication of the structure of the site. The larger items are broader categories with more content, while the smaller choices are narrower, more specific choices.

sense of what we see, the similarities and differences between things readily stick out. You can exploit this perceived difference between navigation elements to indicate location. You have seen this tactic many times before: on maps in the subway, in the mall, and so on. On such maps, you usually see an arrow or dot displayed in a color that strongly contrasts with the background next to a message that says you are here. Although the indicator needs to stand out, you don't need to go overboard on the contrast. Remember that the smallest effective difference will do. Because of Web conventions, your audience may very well expect to see a "you are here" indicator in the navigation and be confused if they don't find one.

The benefits of a consistent graphic language do not end at the sitewide level. They're applicable down to the actual elements that make up each page of your site. The relative scale, position, and style of each page element (in other words, the page's visual organization) can tell your audience an awful lot about its intended use and importance. It can also provide your audience with a sense of where they are within a page. Such orientation is especially important within long pages and pages requiring sequential interaction (such as forms).

Preserve Your Sanity.

Take advantage of these resources to help you with your new Mac OS X Server.

| Store | iTools | iCards | QuickTime | Suppo |

Upgrade Features Applications Downloads Server Developer Darwin Proje

Tech Specs   File & Print   Web   Network & Security   Workgroups

YOU ARE HERE

Using contrast within a navigation system can help indicate your audience's current position within your site. In this example, the top, second, and third-level navigation menus have "you are here" indicators. Notice that within the second and third-level menus, the amount of contrast is reduced to the *smallest effective difference*. The "solutions" indicator is just dark enough to stand out, but not enough to be distracting.

EXPLAINING WHAT

Organizing all the elements that make up each of your Web pages can be a daunting task. On any given page, you might have a site identifier, navigation systems (perhaps several levels deep), navigation bread-crumbs, contact information, sitewide utilities (search boxes, shopping carts), privacy information, external links, internal links, download links, inline links, page titles, and so on — not to mention the text and images that make up the actual content on the page.

Imagine how difficult it would be for you, and especially your audience, to make sense of all these varied elements if they were just dropped on a page in one big pile. To make it even more interesting, imagine if everything in this pile was displayed in the exact same 12-point black Helvetica text. How would you know what was a link? How could you even know what you were looking at? Though this example is rather extreme, it quickly points out the vital role of visual organization. By applying a consistent graphic language of positioning, style, and scale to our jumbled mess of black Helvetica, we can begin to make distinctions between the various elements on the page (see sidebar on next page). Through these distinctions, we can answer the question, "What am I looking at?" The visual organization of each page can communicate valuable information about the similarities and differences between ele-ments and their relative importance. In other words, it can saturate the page's elements with meaning. And once your audience understands the significance of your page elements, they can use that knowledge to make sense of pages throughout your entire site.

When every element on your page is given the same visual treatment, making sense of what you see is difficult. Remember that meaning is created by noticing the similarities and differences (relationships) between things. When those relationships are applied consistently and intentionally throughout a site, your audience can rely on the visual qualities of elements for understanding. Whereas a consistent graphic language can tell your audience what each page element is, the visual hierarchy of the page can explain the relative importance of each element. For example, in the last image on the right, the navigation elements are less dominant than the content. A good way to see this relationship is to squint your eyes when looking at the images. The more important portions of the page stand out, while the less important (thereby lower in the visual hierarchy) recede.

All Page Elements Equal

Distinctions and Hierarchy

Navigation

Page Title

Subsection Title

Footer

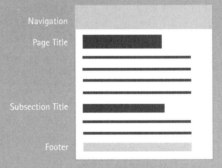

Further Distinctions

Site Identifier

Secon- Level Navigation

Sitewide Utilities

Embedded Links

Just like we organize the content of a Web site into a meaningful structure that tells our audience what they can expect to find within (see Chapter 2), we do the same thing for our individual Web pages. Your pages likewise need to be divided into meaningful "chunks" —this portion is navigation, this one is footer information, and so on. By making visual distinctions between the different page elements, you make it easier for your audience to interpret the information on your pages (through visual perception principles). Not only do page element distinctions increase the scannability of pages, but they also ease the interpretation of these pages. When you can quickly recognize page elements and their function, you are able to find what you need on a page.

The visual representation of page elements should be reflective of the element's function, consistent throughout the entire site, and properly placed within the page's visual hierarchy. Following these guidelines allows your audience to understand the role of each element. For example, the page's content should be higher in the visual hierarchy than

VISUAL SCANNING

A quick visual scan of this content page from the Chicago Symphony Orchestra's site shows the three types of page elements available. Through the use of white space and graphic elements (the thin black line and top image), the three sections are visually separated, making it easier to understand to interpret the page.

meet the performers

William Eddins
RESIDENT CONDUCTOR

William Eddins is the Resident Conductor of the Chicago Symphony Orchestra (the first in its 111-year history) and a frequent guest conductor of major orchestras throughout the world. In September of 2002 he will become the Principal Guest Conductor of the National Symphony Orchestra of Ireland.

In March of 2000 Mr. Eddins received the Seaver/NEA Conducting Award, a triennial grant of $50,000 awarded to exceptionally gifted young American conductors.

Recent engagements include the New York Philharmonic and the symphony orchestras of San Francisco, Cincinnati, Atlanta, Detroit, Dallas, Baltimore, Indianapolis, Milwaukee, Houston, San Antonio, Kansas City, Grant Park, Omaha, Columbus, Austin, and Colorado, as well as the Louisiana, Dayton, Los Angeles, Jacksonville, Tulsa, and Buffalo Philharmonics, and the Los Angeles Chamber Orchestra.

He has upcoming performances with the St. Louis Symphony, Philadelphia Orchestra, Minnesota Orchestra, Nashville Symphony, New Jersey Symphony, Saint Paul Chamber Orchestra, Colorado Symphony, San Antonio Symphony, and the Lexington Philharmonic. Internationally, Mr. Eddins has conducted the Adelaide Symphony Orchestra (Australia), the Barcelona Symphony Orchestra (Spain), the Lisbon Metropolitan Orchestra (Portugal), the Natal Philharmonic (South Africa), and the Berlin Staatskapelle.

Page 1 2

Eddins with the CSO
March 28, 2002
Rossini: Overture to *William Tell*
Lutoslawski: Cello Concerto
Rimsky-Korsakov: *Sheherazade*, Op. 35
For more info and tickets

Upcoming performances
Thu 03/28 CSO
Fri   03/29 CSO
Sat 03/30 CSO
Tue 04/02 CSO
Wed 04/17 CSO
Thu 04/18 CSO
Fri   04/19 CSO
Sat 04/20 CSO
Sun 04/21 CSO
Sat 05/11

Section title
Page title
Body text
Navigation
Supportive Info

A similar effect occurs within the content area. Here, we see visual hierarchy being used to distinguish the various elements on the page. For example, the page title is given a higher place in the visual hierarchy because of its positioning (near the top of the page), the amount of spacing around it (the title is offset from the rest of the page), and its unique visual treatment. Because it is set in a distinct font style (italic, gray, larger size), it contrasts with the rest of the page, causing it to be noticed. Also take a look at how the contrasting color of the embedded links allows for a quick and easy scan of the page's content for additional information.

GENERAL HIERARCHY

Generic Page Hierarchy

Top-level Navigation

Site Identifier

Second-level Navigation

Sitewide Utilities

Page Title

Embedded Links

Subsection Title

Footer

A typical page hierarchy (highest to lowest): Content, navigation, and supportive information. Each of these sections has its own internal hierarchy generalized below (highest to lowest)

Generally, the hierarchy of each page is based on distinctions between the content, navigation, and supportive information of each page. A typical page's hierarchy is content, navigation, and supportive information (from highest to lowest). The only standout is the site identifier (a supportive element). It is often placed at an equal hierarchy to the navigation. This outlines the basic page's hierarchy from highest to lowest. Though very generalized, this hierarchy can provide you with an understanding of the relative importance of each page element's role. However, in many situations, it's advisable to deviate from this formula, such as when you're highlighting specific content or advertising. Your content, audience, and their goals should determine the exact hierarchy for your site.

Content

Page title

Subsection title

Embedded links

Supplementary information (captions and so on)

Navigation

Location indicator

Top-level menu options

Subnavigation options

Trace route (breadcrumbs)

Supportive

Site identifier

Sitewide utilities (search, site map, and so on)

Footer information (privacy, security, contact, and copyright information)

FOR EACH ELEMENT

The visual representation of each element on a Web page should be

Appropriate for (indicative of) the element's function

Applied consistently throughout the site

Properly positioned (in a manner reflective of its relative importance) in the page's visual hierarchy

the navigation. The navigation plays a secondary role to the content. It gets your audience to where they want to go, but needs to recede into the background so that they can pay attention to what is really important: the content. After all, they didn't come to your site for the navigation.

Similarly, embedded links need to be distinguishable from the text surrounding them, so their function is clear. Yet these links should not be at the same level of the page's hierarchy as the page title. The page title describes the content of the entire page, whereas the links provide additional supportive information. Because the title is more important to your audience's understanding of the page's content than the embedded links, the title should be higher in the page's visual hierarchy. Applying this same type of thinking to each of the page elements creates the generic page hierarchy outlined in the left sidebar. A well thought out visual hierarchy should supply considerable information that allows your audience to make sense of what is on each page and why.

It is also to your benefit to reuse the graphic language you establish for your site as much as possible. For example, if your navigation system features blue text on a light gray background, you can reuse that vocabulary within the embedded links of your site by coloring your links the same blue and introducing the light gray background color when the

IMPROVING READABILITY

Because a well-designed page hierarchy rightfully emphasizes a page's content over the navigation and supportive information, it also helps to ease readability. When noncontent elements are lower in the page hierarchy, they are less distracting to readers. You can also bring more attention to the content through the proper use of white space. When your content has room to breathe, it not only stands out more, but is easier to follow and scan as well. We will look at this topic in more depth in the "body text" section of Chapter 6.

links are poised. Once your audience understands that particular blue indicates navigation, they can quickly grasp the function of different elements they encounter within your site. Though this technique is probably most valuable when moving from page to page, it can also prove useful within pages (see sidebar below). The vocabulary you establish should always be used consistently. As soon as you break the pattern, your audience is no longer certain whether their expectations will be met. Is this a link or simply colored text? Make certain that the similarities and differences between your page elements are meaningful and not arbitrary. Otherwise, your audience will not be able to make sense of what they are looking at.

KNOWLEDGE TRANSFER

In the example from apple.com, the graphical treatment of the top-level navigation is echoed in the second and third-level navigation choices. It is also repeated in the Buy Now button. Apple's audience only has to learn that the three-dimensional elements are navigation once, because the visual treatment is repeated throughout. Note that the three-dimensional rendering of the navigation choices is reflective of their function. They look like clickable buttons.

When you know what you're looking at on a map (this line is a highway, that area is a lake, and so on), and where you are in relation to those objects, you can confidently determine how to get to your destination. The large red and blue highway might very well be faster, but the narrow winding country road could include beautiful scenery as it passes through a state park. Your grasp of the map's visual organization allows you to make informed choices and you can focus your attention on what is really important: getting somewhere (not the colors of roads and lakes). At that point, the map really becomes useful. The visual language of the map recedes into your subconscious, and you are able to make knowledgeable decisions without concentrating on what each element on the map means. Likewise, the visual organization of your Web site should not be the focus. Instead, it should become transparent, quietly helping to make your Web site useful and usable. Remember, the goal of visual organization is make things as obvious as possible so that your audience does not have to think too hard about how to use your site.

Once you have a firm grasp of the visual organization of your Web site, you can use the consistent graphic language you have established to speak to your audience in a variety of meaningful ways. You can guide them through your content and through complex interactions. Armed with an understanding of a page's visual hierarchy, you can emphasize certain portions of content when they are important or subdue elements when they are supportive. Using the similarities and differences (visual contrast) between content, you can suggest distinct choices and separate content (see sidebar below). More importantly, you can apply portions of your graphic language to new page elements and interactions to explain their role to your audience.

FORKS IN THE ROAD

Using visual contrast (created by distinct colors), the Guru site presents its audience within an obvious choice: find talent or find work. The visual distinction emphasizes the uniqueness of the two options.

FIND TALENT	FIND WORK
Find talent	**Find work**
Find quality candidates with a service that best suits your needs.	Find thousands of great job opportunities with top companies.

These applications of visual organization answer a lot of the "how" questions your audience may have for your site. "How can I find more of this type of information?" You can answer this question visually by representing similar information in the same manner —perhaps by using the same font color and size or adjacent image. Another visual clue would be the relative position of the information. If it's grouped closely, it's more likely to be related than not. The visual similarities of the

Adobe
everywhere
you look™

Store | ▸ Products   Support   Corporate   Adobe Studio | Search | Contact us

Web   Print   Digital Video   Digital Imaging   ePaper

Downloads   Tryouts   Registration

Adobe Acrobat 5

buy/upgrade

downloads

product info

solutions

customer stories

reviews & news

support

training & events

related products

System requirements

Language versions

Licensing programs

The best way to share documents online

What good is a document you can't open? Whether you create business plans, spreadsheets, graphically rich brochures, or Web sites, Adobe® Acrobat® 5.0 software lets you convert any document to an Adobe Portable Document Format (PDF) file. Anyone can

The visual similarities between groups of links on the Adobe site indicate their relationships. In the example above, the gray links (separated by dotted lines) all lead to additional information on Acrobat 5. Their distinct, yet consistent, representation and proximity make it clear that they are related.

amazon.COM.

WELCOME   ADDRESS   ITEMS   WRAP   SHIP   PAY   PLACE ORDER

Ordering from Amazon.com is quick and easy.

Enter your e-mail | johndoe@doe.com
address:

○ **I am a new customer.**
(You'll create a password later.)

◉ **I am a returning customer,
and my password is:**

▶ Sign in using our secure server

Forgot your password? Click here

Has your e-mail address changed since your last order?

The secure server will encrypt your information. If you received an error message when you tried to use our secure server, sign in using our standard server.

**Amazon.com Safe
Shopping Guarantee**

We guarantee that every transaction you make at Amazon.com will be safe. This means you pay nothing if unauthorized charges are made to your credit card as a result of shopping at Amazon.com.

▶ **Learn More**

The only way to place an order at Amazon.com is via our Web site. (Sorry--no phone orders. However, if you prefer, you may phone in your credit card number, **after** filling out the order form online.)

HEY YOU, LOOK OVER HERE

The most prominent visual element on this page (the yellow and blue sign-in button) makes it clear what the next step is. The button is very high in the page's visual hierarchy: Squint your eyes and see for yourself. Though the amazon.com logo is larger, the fact that it uses the same colors as the rest of the page decreases its visual contrast and places it lower in the visual hierarchy. Also take note of the fact that the button is rendered in a manner reflective of its function. It looks like a three-dimensional button. How do you sign in to Amazon? Enter your e-mail, password, and sign in. The white space around the input fields and visual hierarchy make it clear.

information tell you that it's related. This technique is used in most navigation systems. When choices in the navigation are displayed in a similar manner and in close proximity, it's obvious that they are related. This visual relationship tells your audience how to get around your site. Just pick one of these navigation options and off you go.

You can likewise rely on the visual differences between information to communicate with your audience. In a typical e-commerce interaction, your audience is likely to ask, "How do I go to the next step?" Visual contrast can field this one when you use it to emphasize the next step in the check out procedure. By placing the "Next" indicator higher in the page's visual hierarchy, you can rest assured it will not be overlooked by your customers.

We only touched on a few simple ways to use visual organization to your and your audience's advantage. Once you have an understanding of what it means to visually organize information and the benefits of doing so, you can make informed decisions when designing your Web sites. Remember that your content, audience, and their goals should form the basis for your designs.

WHO ARE YOU? GET A PERSONALITY
chapter five

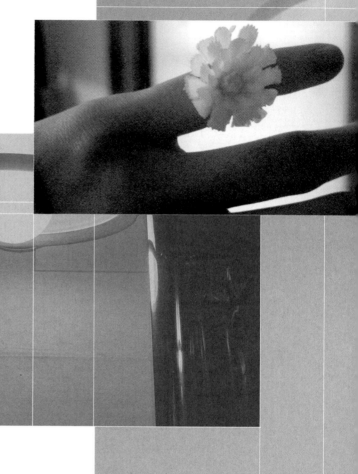

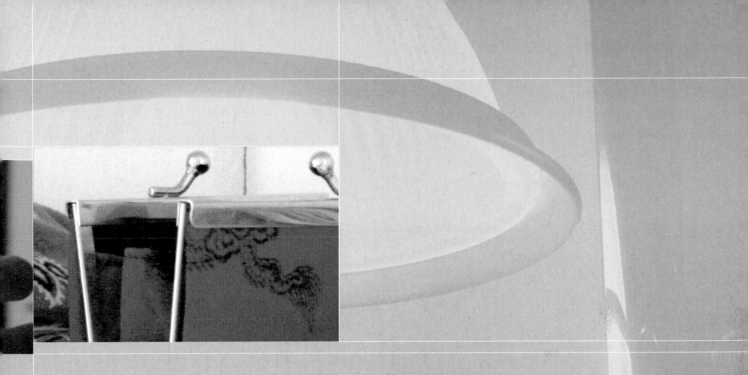

Our most memorable experiences are those we can not only see and hear, but also feel. Building such experiences on the Web requires an understanding of how the design of your Web site creates a personality that interacts with and speaks to your audience. A Web site needs to be both effective and affective: not only usable but likable as well. Therefore, designing an appropriate and engaging personality for your site is not the icing on the cake (as visual design is sometimes called): It is the recipe that determines your final result and whether or not it will appeal to your audience.

WHAT IS PERSONALITY?
[S E C T I O N   T I T L E]

All communication between people is filtered through their personalities. Your personality determines how you react and how others react to you. It is the part of you that makes you a unique individual and sets you apart from others[1]. As a result, it is also how people remember and define you.

This practice comes so naturally that personalities are not just reserved for people, but instead attributed to many different things, natural or manmade. Associating a personality with an object makes it unique and therefore memorable. *That movie is funny and intelligent.* The unique traits we identify with certain objects not only help us to better identify them, but also strengthen our relationships with them. We know we can count on certain objects to be helpful, reliable, fun, informative, and more. Reeves and Nass have argued that people especially attribute human characteristics to new media[2] (such as the Web). Perhaps the ability of such media to communicate with images, sounds, and motion closely mirrors our own skills. Or maybe the complexity possible in new media keeps us as interested and engaged as another person might. Whatever the reason, new media applications are quite often perceived as distinct entities with particular characteristics.

As with all new media, the combination of organization, interaction, and presentation creates and supports the personality of a Web site. And while we can use nouns to describe the individual components that make up Web pages, (photos, data, buttons, and so on), we turn to adjectives (funny, elegant, soothing, and so on) when describing their collective end product: the Web site's personality. A site's personality is directly responsible for its emotional impact: how it "feels." Is it enjoyable? Is it relaxing?

ONE'S PERSONALITY

"The effectiveness with which one can achieve positive reactions."

"Designates those things about the individual that are distinctive and set him apart from other persons."

"What is most typical and deeply characteristic of a person."

"The reaction of other individuals to a person is what defines his personality."

-Paraphrased from *Theories of Personality* (Wiley & Sons, 1970).

---

[1] Hall and Lindzey outline several different definitions of "personality" in their book: *Theories of Personality* (Wiley & Sons, 1970).
[2] Their book, *The Media Equation: How people treat computers, television, and new media like real people and places* (Cambridge University Press, 1996), presents the results of numerous psychological studies in an effort to support this assertion.

What kind of experience does the site provide for its audience as they surf through? Everything from the tone in which the content is written to the labels on the navigation menus contributes to the personality of a site. That is why, more so than any other design consideration, the personality of a Web site is responsible for a unified Web experience. Making sure that you have a consistent and clear point of view throughout your site allows you to build cohesive experiences for your audience instead of just a set of interconnected Web pages. It is these kinds of experiences that your audience attaches to and wants to repeat.

While everything within your site contributes to its personality, it is most quickly communicated and reinforced through your visual presentation. Your site's personality is directly reflected in the type, colors, and visual elements that make up each one of your pages. This is why the look and feel of your site should not be thought of as the last step in the Web design process. Instead, it should be the continual unification of every aspect of your site under a consistent narrative —one that perpetually communicates and reinforces what makes your site unique and worthwhile for your audience while establishing lasting emotional ties. In other words, you want to tell your audience a story, an informative and memorable one at that.

PERSONALITY A.K.A.

Though I use the word *personality*, many terms also refer to the same idea:

> Look and feel
> Tone and manner
> Attitude
> Narrative voice
> Emotional impact
> Particular flavor
> Unique identity

LOOK AND FEEL

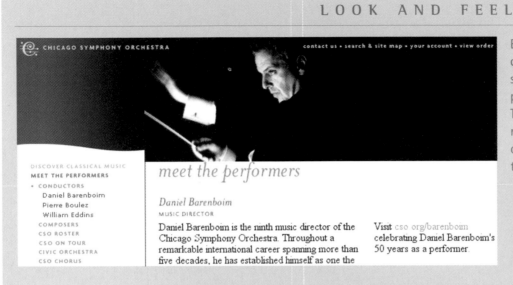

Everything on the cso.org site contributes to the feeling of sophistication and elegance present throughout the site. The colors, the type treatment, the photos, and so on all work together to tell a consistent story.

Creating a look and feel for your site is a natural part of the design process. You probably already have images or ideas that you associate with your site's content and message. They may come from previous experiences or from your understanding of what makes your site unique. To clarify, think of the associations you make with your content. What kind of imagery do you think of?

Each of the concepts of your site brings distinct colors, typefaces, imagery, and ideas to mind: a unique look and feel (see sidebar above). The combination of these visual elements (the look) elicits an emotional response from the viewer (the feel). Your site's look and feel gives it a particular flavor (or personality) that helps to get your message across: Who are you, and why should I care?

The personality of a site comes through almost instantly. Therefore, you need to be certain it is saying what you intend. Think of the words "wedding" and "rugby." What kind of imagery do you associate with each word? Is it soft, velvety, flowing text with a cool pastel color scheme or a strong, dirty, and dynamic typeface with dark solid tones? Clearly, one of these says "wedding" quickly and confidently, while the other does not

Both the rugby and wedding sites seen here feature a delicate touch that seems more appropriate to marriage than rugby. The Rugby Source site manages to give the sport some elegance with its look and feel, but it certainly didn't match my expectations.

It is worth noting that the image does add some strength to the layout, but it is quickly offset by the delicate type treatments in the navigation system and background.

WHY HAVE A PERSONALITY?

Truth be told, this is actually a trick question. When it comes down to it, you really don't have a choice in whether or not you have a personality. Even if you were to restrain every part of your behavior that might betray your true demeanor, you would still end up with a personality: boring and cold. The same is true for Web sites. Even if you deliberately don't think about your site's personality during the design process, you will end up with one anyway. The colors, content, and visual elements (or lack of all

LESS IS MORE

37signals simple for sale

Signals

00 Start Here
01 We See People
02 Manager of External Reporting?
03 <blink>12:00</blink>
04 Not Full Service
05 Size Does Matter
06 $6,000,000,000
07 Are They Experienced?
08 Experience
09 And I Quote
10 Refugees
11 Copy Righting
12 Occam's Razor
13 Eight Seconds
14 Breadcrumbs
15 83%?!
16 Short Story
17 No Awards Please
18 eNormicom.com

19 Suits Who?
20 Sloganeering
21 A not "Q"
22 B2whatever
23 Sightings
24 My Cousin's Buddy...
25 Just Because You Can...
26 Make it Useful
27 Simplicity by Design
28 Tulipomania
29 Linkin' Logs
30 ASAP
31 Reference
32 Highest
33 What's in a Name?
34 Our Team
35 We Come in Peace
36 Signal vs. Noise
37 SETI

Work (new 11/19/01)

Case studies for some of our latest client projects:

• Transportation.com
• Advertise with Dex
• Kicksology
• MissileLock
• Zen Hospice Project
• More...

Other

Internal projects, press clips, appearances, and other goodies:

• Design Not Found
• Signal vs. Noise
• eNormicom.com
• ShirtSignals
• NYT article
• 37Fakebank
• More...

Though you might initially think that plain text on a white background is not much of a personality, the folks at 37 signals are ready to prove you wrong. Though their site has no images and very little color, it has a very distinct and elegant personality —one that reflects the design philosophy of the firm and is appropriate for their audience (designers and potential clients). The stark presentation of the numbered links makes them all the more inviting and interesting.

three) of your Web site all make an impression on your audience, intentional or not. Therefore, it is in your best interests to be aware of the personality you are creating for your site and make certain that is telling the story you want.

When creating Web sites, we rely on the site's personality to provide emotional impact and a consistent point of view for our audience. The personality of your site provides the answers to the "who" and "why" questions of your audience in a clear descriptive voice. Whose site is this? Who is it for? Why should I be interested? Why should I trust it? By answering these types of questions, the personality helps to communicate the big picture of your site. When you realize that the focus and main message of many sites is blurred or lost under the haze of too many Web site elements and competing viewpoints, the value of a focused personality is obvious. An appropriate and evocative personality not only tells the right story to your audience, but it also provides distinction, appeal, and wholeness to your site. If properly applied, these characteristics create meaningful and engaging communication that make visiting your Web site an enjoyable experience.

THE POWER OF PERSONALITY

A well designed personality:

Tells the right story

Provides distinction

Appeals to and engages your audience

Unifies your site

When good information is given a poor presentation, its value may not be appreciated. The before and after shots of an article database show you how look and feel can influence perception of information.

It might be helpful to think of the personality of your Web site as similar to your product or company's branding. A *brand* can be thought of as an idea or impression made on your audience by their experiences with your services or goods and their presentation. The most influential form of branding is "the design, quality, and performance of the product" (Braunstein & Levine, 2000). However, on the Web, your site frequently is your product, and therefore its presentation and interaction are vital to creating a positive impression on your audience. An elegant and professional presentation can provide a convincing reason to trust an unknown site. This is especially true if you offer services that are only available online. I have redesigned the interface to several online information presentations, and though the actual information does not change, the perception of that information often does. For example, users that did not make use of the information resource prior to the redesign will often say, "I did not think the information was valuable, but the presentation of the data (after the redesign) gave it more validity." Though the value of the information really did not change, the perception did. Presentation can significantly alter a user's perception of reality. (Think bottled water.) But remember, a poorly designed presentation can create a negative impression, just as a well-designed one can create a positive one.

BRANDING ONLINE

On the Web, your site often is your product. Therefore your branding, "the design, quality, and performance of your product," is really your site's personality.

Branding has several other advantages that are especially apparent online. Because an effective use of branding creates customer loyalty and even dependence, online branding encourages return visits to your site and helps to create lasting relationships and emotional ties with your product or service. As Marc Braunstein and Edward Levine, the authors of *Deep Branding on the Internet* (Prima Venture, 2000), have said, "People go to a search engine when they don't know; they go to a brand when they do." In the preceding information resource redesign example, users continually return to a data source they perceive to be valuable. Branding also reinforces a particular and relevant idea for your product, helping to communicate the big picture of your site that helps to answer the "who" and "why" questions of your audience. But ultimately, branding your site through its personality creates a unique voice that engages and invites your audience —that is, it tells a story.

SAY THE RIGHT THING

The personality of your site allows you to get the correct message to your audience quickly and efficiently. *Am I here for rugby scores or to plan my wedding?* A quick glance at your site should remove any doubt. But with great power comes great responsibility. You need to be certain the story you are telling your audience is not only right, but right for them. But how do you know what is "right" when the appropriateness of a personality differs from site to site and audience to audience? Thankfully, the planning you did in Part 1 will help you to evaluate the different directions you might choose for your site's look and feel and come out with the best fit.

Having spent significant time defining your target audience and their shared culture, you now have an effective measure against which to gauge the appropriateness of your identity. How will your audience respond to the personality you have decided on? Will they be flattered or insulted? Will they feel empowered or uncertain? Remember that you need to meet your audience's expectations. If you do not consider how your audience requires your content, you will leave them feeling ignored and unimportant. This is especially true of their emotional expectations. If your site "feels" wrong, your audience is likely to be confused, or worse still, upset. To return to the wedding example, the personality of a wedding site needs to be comfortable and elegant. Visitors to the site have very fixed notions of what is appropriate and are unlikely to react favorably to anything out of place. The attitude of a rugby site would definitely not be a welcome sight when it comes time to select a wedding dress.

The right personality makes a connection with your audience that they will appreciate and remember. This is the first step to building a lasting customer relationship: letting your audience know you have thought of them. People want to feel involved. They want to belong. Instead of doing things the way you see fit, look at it from your customer's perspective. How do they expect this information to be displayed? What does this particular image say to them? Your audience will appreciate it, and the makings of a relationship will be underway.

BE UNIQUE

Why be different? Well, if we are to trust the ad campaigns of Dodge trucks, Apple computers, and Arby's sandwiches, different is better. Okay, but why? First of all, being different means being distinguishable. Your personality, just like your Web site's personality, helps to differentiate you from others. And when "others" consists of the millions of sites scattered across cyberspace, being different can really come in handy. If your site stands out, your audience is more likely to give it a chance or at least some thought as they surf by. Similarly, your site may stick out in their minds as they come across a need that you're able to fill for them. When every site looks the same, people have no compelling reason to choose one over the other, unless they are familiar with the firm or perform a comparative analysis (most often of price) to determine their best choice.

Not only does being unique distinguish you from the competition, it, more importantly, helps to explain who you actually are. A recognizable Web site personality can define a business and reinforce familiarity. After all, if something is distinct, you tend to remember or at least recognize it. This is great news for the notoriously short attention spans of Web visitors. The sooner they can figure out who you are and what you have to offer them, the more pleased they will be. But being recognizable among the crowds of Web pages strewn throughout cyberspace is no small feat and is especially difficult when you need to be recognized for the benefits you bring to your customers. It is hard enough to just look different when compared to millions of sites, much less to be known as different. This is why a superior Web experience does not rely on presentation alone. The organization (content) and interaction (service) of your site both reflect strongly on your personality.

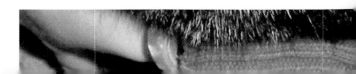

A MONSTER PERSONALITY

Not only does Monster have a distinct and memorable personality, it is recognized as being a great resource to find jobs online.

Having quality content or interaction systems (such as effective online customer support systems) reflects favorably on your site's personality and can help give you the type of distinction presentation alone might lack. In fact, many sites with a poor visual presentation remain popular on the merits of their content alone. Does their audience enjoy bumping through the site's awkward graphics and hard-to-read labels? No, but the personality of the content (it could be high-quality, funny, worthwhile, and more) makes the rest bearable. Would their audience be happier if the personality of the presentation matched the personality of the content? Of course. They like the content, don't they? Such a site would be well served to improve its presentation. Not only would it enrich their current customers' experience, but a presentation that reflects the site's content would tell the site's story to newcomers as well. *Hey, we have quality content, come take a look.*

INVITE AND ENGAGE

FOR YOUR EYES ONLY

Many sites provide "personalization" features that allow you to create a Web experience that is tailormade to your likes and dislikes. Not only can you choose to see only the content that interests you, but you can also select your color scheme and layout. Though most of these interfaces still require a lot of input from you to be appropriate, sites that automatically "adapt" to your personality are just around the corner.

At some point, all of us have selected our dinner destination with just a passing glance. *Hey, that place looks nice. Let's go in there.* The character of a building or its décor may seem inviting or intriguing enough to convince us to give it a try. This scenario isn't restricted to dining out. It occurs everywhere, and especially online. *Hey, this site looks trustworthy. Let's see if they have what I am looking for.* Just like physical structures (restaurants, hotels, homes, and so on) can be inviting or foreboding, so can Web sites. A unique and appropriate Web site can attract us with its visual presentation just as a restaurant can with its facade. And this doesn't just apply to first-time customers. When we return to the same restaurant, we still appreciate the impression its character makes on us. Our familiarity with the visual presentation of the establishment reassures us that the content (the food) will likewise be as we expect. If the façade of the restaurant looked run-down when compared to our last visit, we would, more than likely, question whether the food took a similar dive. For this reason, to say a site is inviting is a measure of how appealing it is to its intended audience, first-time visitor or devotee.

Usually, this appeal is emotional. Something about a site or physical structure elicits a positive reaction from us. It could be the color, the type treatment, or a particular visual element. It could be that it says the right thing to us or that it stands out from the crowd. Whatever the exact reason, we make a positive connection with its personality. The site becomes more tangible: something we can feel and relate to (and ultimately trust). This connection allows us to explore and interact with the site. We feel we know its character and move from search to purchase confidently and comfortably. The personality of the site not only lets us know we are welcome; it keeps us engaged and interested.

Just like the ambiance of a cozy restaurant can persuade us to linger after dinner and slowly finish our drinks, the personality of a Web site can likewise keep us engrossed. Web sites with personality do not simply provide information: They provide an experience. Experiences are memorable and involve a lot more than facts. As Nathan Shedroff has said, "Experiences are the foundation for all life events and form the core of what interactive media have to offer." (New Riders, 2001) Because experiences are immersive, they keep us engaged and interested. A quality Web experience is more akin to talking to a good friend than struggling through a dense math textbook. You actually enjoy yourself, instead of continually checking to see when you will be done.

BRING IT ALL TOGETHER

Whether the company is selling tennis shoes, basketball shorts, or golf socks, Nike manages to retain the characteristics of its personality (brand). That means you can expect the same quality and commitment to innovation from your golfing slacks as you do your Air Jordans. This relationship is beneficial to both parties. You know you can count on having a quality pair of slacks, and Nike can count on customer confidence and loyalty, even in new products. The Nike brand (its unique story) brings divergent services together under the same narrative.

Similarly, a consistent personality for your Web site can unify your various services and content under a common "feel" or attitude. The connection your audience makes with your site can reflect positively on your content, products, and services. A quality experience on an e-commerce site can lead to the perception that the goods available there, likewise, measure up to the same standard. You can also use this perception to introduce new services to your audience. When you apply the same look and feel to your latest service, your story continues, and the associations your audience makes with your brand are expected and invoked.

A consistent personality is also useful for bringing together the various pages and content of your site. If all the sections and subsections of a site "feel" the same way, a sense of place is created, and your audience thinks of your site as a distinct entity. I mentioned this before when discussing a "unified graphic language" (Chapter 4), but now extend the discussion to include the entire user experience: organization, interaction, and presentation. Bonding your site with personality creates a coherent identity and a continuous story for your audience to follow and appreciate.

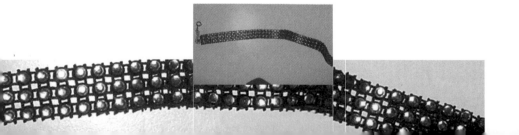

HOW TO GET A PERSONALITY

As you know by now, every site intrinsically has a personality. It comes from the presentation and substance or "design, quality, and performance" of your site. Because the personality is there whether you like it or not, the real question becomes "How do you get the right personality for your site, one that reflects your particular message and is appropriate for your audience?" You want a personality that will attract and engage your visitors and distinguish your site from the rest of the Web with both its attitude and its assets.

Presenting your site in an appropriate tone and manner requires some initial decision-making and an understanding of how the components of your site contribute to its look and feel. In other words, how can color, type, visual elements, and interaction establish an attitude that is prevalent throughout your site? As I mentioned before, the personality of your site is most quickly communicated through its visual presentation. Though every person is likely to react a bit differently to it, certain general tendencies can help you understand what the visual presentation is saying to your audience. Principles in color theory and typography can tell you how the visual characteristics of your site are likely to be interpreted. And a deliberate choice of visual elements and interactions can reiterate your main message. Through these techniques, you can design a consistent personality that breathes life into your site.

INVESTIGATING THE POSSIBILITIES

In Chapter 2, I briefly touched on some planning you could do to get early ideas for your site's personality. These ideas were recorded on sample combinations that help visualize some possible directions. Though sample combinations are a great place to start, when you finally decide on your personality, you will have to consider several factors:

History: What is your client's current branding strategy? Do they have an established graphic language? Do you need to consider carryovers from previous site designs?

Audience: How will they react to the personality? Is it appropriate? What do they expect from your site?

Competition: How can you stand out from your rivals? What story are they telling?

Connotation: What associations come with your product? Do they match your site's personality?

Coming up with the right look and feel for your site involves a lot of research and reiteration. Don't expect to get it right the first time. Instead, explore several directions and reap the benefits of the design process: think, design, test, and repeat.

"Color adds tremendous meaning to communication as it vitalizes the visual message, delivering an instantaneous impression that is, most often, universally understood."

PANTONE guide to communicating with color. (Grafix Press Ltd, 2000)

USING COLOR

Perhaps no other design element has as much influence on how we feel in a space (a Web site, a home, and so on) as color. Colors can instantaneously change our moods and alter our opinions. They can make us comfortable, put us in a state of awe, or get us excited. Our

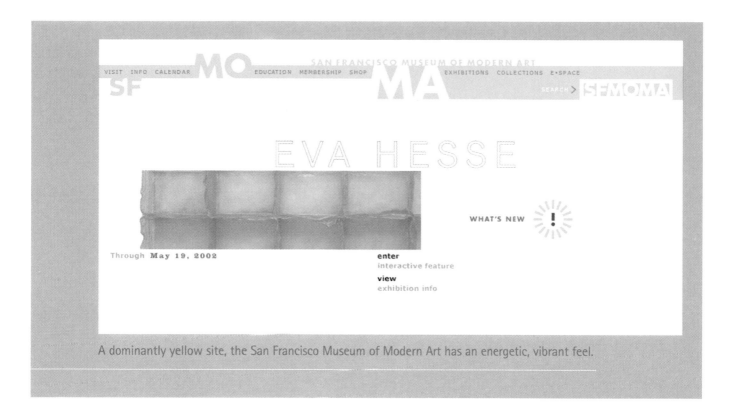

A dominantly yellow site, the San Francisco Museum of Modern Art has an energetic, vibrant feel.

personal experiences, shaped by unique circumstances and societal influence, determine our responses to color. Our reactions can range from smitten to sickened and come charged with emotion. Color psychology outlines how we react to colors and provides us with the knowledge we need to elicit positive responses to the colors that shape our Web site personalities.

For example, we tend to associate the color yellow with energy and life. Ask nearly any child to draw the sun, and they instinctually reach for the yellow crayon. Yellow's connotation with energy and its brightness also means it is sometimes perceived as "speedy." Even the large numbers of cabs seen whizzing through busy city streets may also have some influence on this perception.

COLOR CHARACTER

Red: Vibrant, passionate, love, war. A very strong and attention-grabbing color, red is charged with emotions.

Violet: Regal, sacred, sensual. In deep shades, violet is luxurious. When lightly tinted, it is aromatic and spiritual.

Blue: Cool, dependable, sophisticated, sky, water. Blue is full of depth, constant yet dynamic.

Green: Fresh, relaxing, earth. Green is very balanced and calm, a natural color.

Yellow: Sun, energy, warmth. Yellow is welcoming and full of life, a happy color.

Orange: Strong, vital, hot. Orange is the warmest of colors, a healing and playful hue.

If you're interested in more information on color responses, pick up a book on color theory.

Contrast our associations with yellow to our feelings for the color red. Red is associated with love and war, two of the most emotionally charged words around. As a result, red demands our attention and is effectively used for stop signs and to mark danger. The importance of red is highlighted by the fact that cultures with only three defined words for color always identify black, white, and red before any other color[3]. Designers, familiar with red's ability to take charge of composition, use it knowingly to focus our attention on important information. Specific groups rely on red's strength to interpret meaning in their daily jobs. Investors, for example, know when they see red that their investments are heading south. (As a result, they're probably not willing to decorate their homes with red hues.)

As you can see, the associations and emotions that come with colors are deep rooted. Color instantly gives everything it adorns a unique character. The world around us, our place in it, and our past all influence the moods and ambiances that colors create for us. Though as individuals we are likely to have differences in how we interpret colors, certain associations and reactions that are common to us all. By understanding these, we can successfully make use of the emotional qualities of colors to create appropriate personalities for our Web sites. We can formalize some of these by looking at the basic principles of color theory that tell us why and how colors work.

Edward O. Wilson outlines the growth of color terms in his book *Consilience: The Unity of Knowledge* (Vintage, 1998).

Predominantly red, the Irving Plaza site remains welcoming and warm while creating a sense of excitement.

The Color Wheel: The color wheel is an important reference for understanding the fundamental relationships of colors. The wheel is broken up into three types of colors: primary, secondary, and tertiary. *Primary* colors are fundamental (they cannot be made by mixing other colors) and include red, yellow, and blue. The *secondary* colors (green, orange, and violet) are derived by mixing equal amounts of the primary colors. The *tertiary* colors (yellow-green, blue-green, blue-violet, red-orange, and yellow-orange) are a combination of secondary and primary colors.

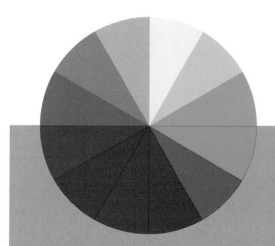

THE COLOR WHEEL

The color wheel presents the visible spectrum in a circular arrangement that illustrates the relationships between colors. When all 12 colors of the color wheel are properly positioned, they create a natural spectrum.

Warm vs Cool: Colors can be described as either warm or cool. The distinction comes naturally to us from our experiences with the world around us. Warm colors (red, orange, and yellow), found at the top of the color wheel, are inviting and cheerful because we associate them with the heat we encounter from the sun and fire. Cool colors (blue, violet, and green), on the other hand, are universally seen as calming and composed because we see them in the sea, sky, and forests. (It's worth noting that violet and green are unique because they can appear warmer or cooler depending on their composition. The more red in a violet, the more hospitable it appears.)

The distinct effects of warm and cool colors are important to consider when designing spaces. Too many cool colors, and a space can seem cold and unfriendly. Too many warm colors, and it can become stuffy and hot. Additionally, warm colors are said to *advance*, which means they make surfaces appear closer to you than they actually are. Cool colors, on the other hand, tend to recede, which is why they make great background hues. They sit back and do not compete with the information you need.

You might notice that predominantly cool-colored sites tend to show up more frequently than warm-colored sites. With screen real estate already at a premium, and lots of information to squeeze into every layout, few sites are willing to increase the congestion by adding lots of advancing warm colors.

COLOR THERMOMETER

Warm colors: Red, yellow, orange

Warmest color: Orange

Cool colors: Blue, violet, green

Coolest color: Blue

Can appear warm or cool depending on proximity to other colors: Green, violet

HOT AND COOL

The predominantly cool color scheme of the Cintara site is composed and intelligent. The warm colors present in the Nitro snowboards site, on the other hand, create an excited and aggressive feel.

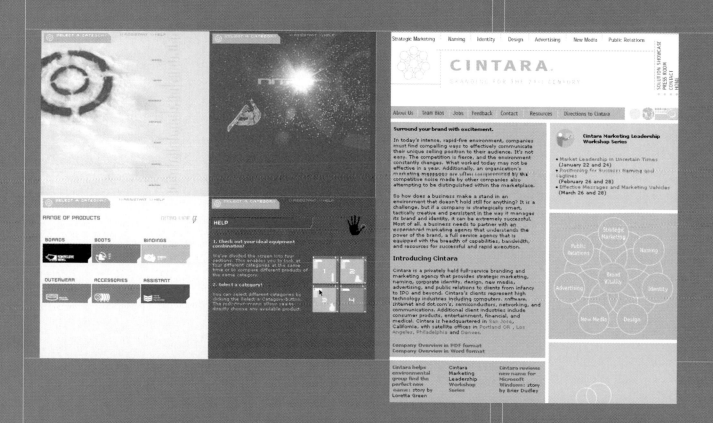

ADVANCE AND RECEDE

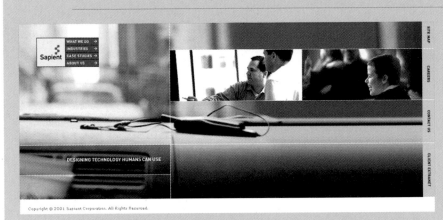

On the Sapient home page, the cool colors of the background image recede, while the warm colors (red and orange) advance. This works to bring the navigation system to your immediate attention. The effect is especially pronounced because orange and blue sit opposite each other on the color wheel. As a result, there is a lot of contrast between them.

Contrasting Colors: Colors that sit opposite each other on the color wheel are referred to as *contrasting colors*. When used with equal brightness, these colors have a tendency to compete with each other for attention and result in color schemes that are active and full of energy. This visual phenomenon is referred to as *simultaneous contrast*. For example, you're likely to encounter simultaneous contrast in a lot of sports team identities, such as the orange and blue of the Chicago Bears or the purple and yellow of the Minnesota Vikings. The further apart two colors sit on the color wheel, the more they contrast with each other. Therefore, if you want to add some tension or excitement to your Web site's personality, consider widening the gap between your colors.

SILMULTANEOUS ENERGY

The visual phenomenon known as simultaneous contrast occurs when two contrasting colors are used with equal brightness. Their pronounced differences are made all the more vivid by their opposite nature. Blue, in this case, appears at its brightest when positioned next to orange (as seen in the Nike Town site). The same blue next to purple appears a lot more relaxed and especially tranquil when paired with another blue. As you can see, how a color "speaks" to you largely depends on the colors next to it.

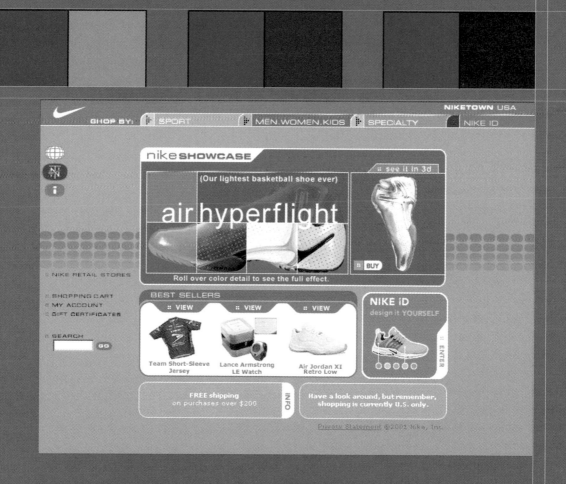

Contrasting colors are also often referred to as *complementary*. The opposing nature of the two colors results in a balance (for example, cool blue and warm orange). Recall from Chapter 4 that we are constantly seeking balance in our surroundings and our lives. Because of this, a combination of two contrasting colors can provide the harmony that we seek and make compositions feel complete and comfortable. This is especially true when one color is dominant, and the other emphasizes the qualities of the dominant color by providing a contrast to it: a complement. Such a use of contrasting colors can create personalities that feel complete or together.

A COMPLEMENTARY BALANCE

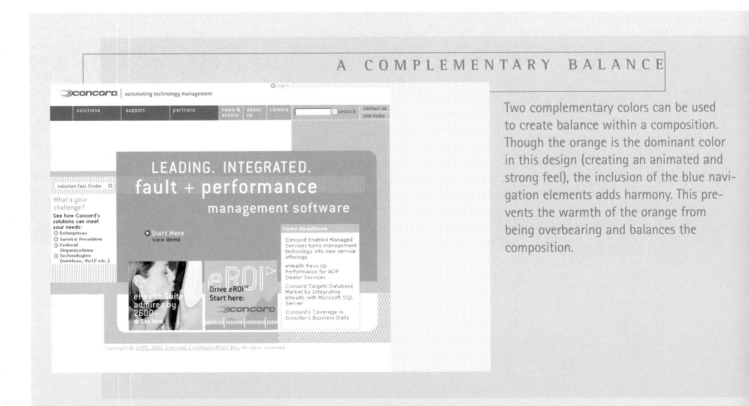

Two complementary colors can be used to create balance within a composition. Though the orange is the dominant color in this design (creating an animated and strong feel), the inclusion of the blue navigation elements adds harmony. This prevents the warmth of the orange from being overbearing and balances the composition.

The contrast naturally present in complementary colors is the perfect way to bring attention to certain portions of a layout. In the Streams.com site, it brings important links to the attention of the audience.

Contrasting colors can also be used effectively to bring attention to important areas of your site. When one color dominates and the other is used sparingly as an accent, you can draw attention to certain elements of your site. This is useful when you emphasize elements that describe your site, such as a logo or tag line.

Analogous Colors: Colors next to each other on the color wheel are referred to as *analogous* or *harmonious* colors. These colors work well together because they are closely related. For example, violet, blue-green, and blue violet all share a common base color: blue. Because these colors blend well together, they create pleasing or tranquil personalities. Analogous color schemes can be expanded to include several neighboring colors, thereby increasing the range of the scheme. This can create personalities that are more complex and diverse.

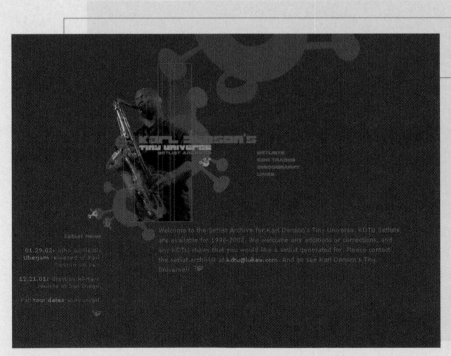

NEXT TO YOU

Colors that neighbor each other on the color wheel create comfortable and visually pleasing presentations. In this example, red-violet, yellow, orange, and pink create a tepid and vibrant personality.

A monochromatic color scheme stands in stark contrast to the majority of Web sites. In the Linkdup.com site, a palette of blues keeps the interface unified and unobtrusive, allowing the color accents (site images), which make up the site's content, to attract and keep the audience's interest.

The Monos: Sometimes the most appropriate color scheme may consist of only one color. Monotones are schemes that use a single neutral color (such as gray or beige) of varying tints and shades. *Tints* are created by adding white to a color, and *shades* appear through the addition of black. Monochromatic color schemes use varying tints and shades of a single color. Both monotone and monochromatic color schemes can express a simple, contemplative personality and create unique sites that stand out from the color-rich palettes of most of the Web. However, they both are difficult to keep interesting as well. The amount of contrast available between the softest pink and the darkest red is often not enough to create visual interest and instead you may have to rely on texture or pattern to keep things moving in your visual hierarchy.

Dominant Personality: When choosing color combinations that embody your site's personality, it is important to maintain a dominant color. The dominant color establishes the mood for your site and keeps your audience's attention focused. If every color is competing for attention, no one wins, and your site's personality comes across as schizophrenic and disorganized. The sense of a coherent narrative is lost, and your site is left trying to tell too many stories at once. Instead, select the story that is the most interesting and appropriate for your audience and let the dominant color tell it.

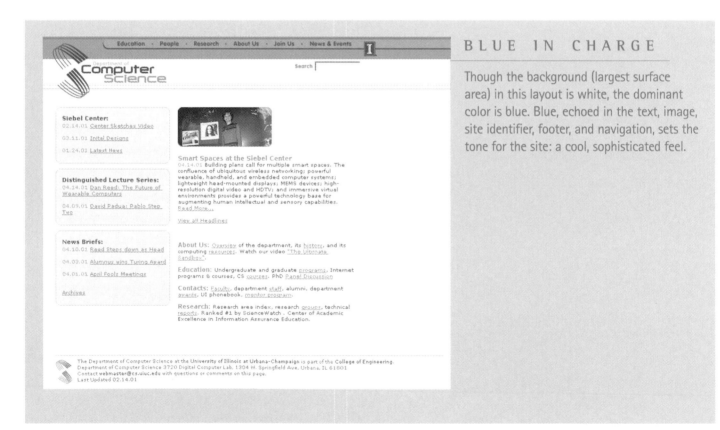

BLUE IN CHARGE

Though the background (largest surface area) in this layout is white, the dominant color is blue. Blue, echoed in the text, image, site identifier, footer, and navigation, sets the tone for the site: a cool, sophisticated feel.

Established Conventions: Another important point to note is that many color schemes have symbolic meanings associated with them. Color combinations can bring political, racial, and even corporate messages to mind. This can be a powerful form of branding, and most companies do have "corporate colors" reflective of their corporate message. For example, it might be difficultto create a site in red, white, and blue that does not bring America to mind. If you're trying to create a patriotic site, this association is to your advantage. If you're not, you may be sending your audience the wrong message. As another example, using a color scheme of yellow, red, and blue (the three primary colors) brings ideas of simplicity and basics to mind.

Perhaps the most established of all color combinations are those found in nature. These color schemes are universally seen as harmonious because they are common to us all[4]. For this reason, colors found in nature are often used in interface design.

[4] Edward Tufte claims that "a good way to avoid charkjunk [disruptive visual elements] is to use colors found in nature, particularly toward the lighter side, such as grays, blues, and yellows of sky and shadow." (*Visual Design of the Interface*, IBM, 1989)

WHAT TYPE ARE YOU?

From grunge fonts (Rustboy.com) to techno type (the Whitney site), your choice of
typeface adds character and emotion to your site.

USING TYPE

Contrary to popular belief, all text does not have to be read to be understood; type can also communicate visually. Just like colors, *typefaces* (designs of type) each have a distinct character and tell a different story. We count on typefaces to explain which movies will scare us and which ones will make us laugh. Typefaces let us know which laundry detergent is gentle and which one is tough on dirt. They influence the magazines we read and the clothes we wear. Your choice of typeface can support the message of words, or in the case of company names, it can provide a message. What does IBM mean? The choice of type lets us know we are dealing with reliable technology systems.

The feelings your audience associates with different typefaces can largely be attributed to their unique visual characteristics: how closed-in or open they are, how tall versus wide they may be, or how angular or smooth they appear. The *gestalt* (set of elements considered as a whole) of each typeface contributes to its unique character (see sidebar below). Certain typefaces (with thick stocky letterforms) appear strong and rugged, while others (with thin curvy letterforms) are delicate and refined. More than likely, the typeface you use on your baby shower invitation is not the same one that adorns your favorite hockey team's uniform.

TYPEFACES

The elements that contribute to the unique character of each typeface are

The height of capital and lowercase letters

The contrast between the thick and thin portions of letters

The height of ascending and descending letters, such as d *and* q

The thickness of the letterforms (bold, thin, and so on)

The spacing between letters

The smoothness, crispness, or roughness of edges

The presence of decorative elements such as serifs, terminals, and hooks

The style of the face (italic, mono type, and so on)

Perhaps the tallest hurdle you will encounter when looking for the perfect typeface is the sheer number of choices available to you. With the advent of the Web and personal computer, typefaces have become easy to make and even easier to distribute. In an effort to narrow your choices, it might be beneficial to look at some general categories of typefaces.

Old Style: Developed out of traditional handwriting, these typefaces have an inviting, elegant, and classic appearance: Garamond, Bembo, Palatino, Times.

This is an example of Garamond.

Modern: Though still graceful, modern typefaces are more stylized and may appear less friendly than old style faces: Bodoni, Didot, Walbaum, Pergamon, Corvinus.

This is an example of Bodoni.

Slab Serif: These typefaces stand out and have thick serifs and a strong appearance: Clarendon, New Century Schoolbook, Courier, Rockwell, Serifa, American Typewriter.

`This is an example of Courier.`

Sans Serif: Without decorative serifs, these frequently geometric typefaces are functional and practical: Futura, Syntax, Formata, Univers, Gill Sans, Helvetica.

This is an example of Gill Sans.

Grunge: These frequently distorted and energetic fonts are about fun and emotional impact: Ammonia, Bedbug, Dead History, Psycho Poetry, Where's Marty.

This is an example of Ammonia.

Techno: Combining a space age feel with high-tech mechanics, these fonts are often the choice for technology corporations: Alien Mushrooms, Bad Excuse, Decipher, Legion, Stuntman.

THIS IS AN EXAMPLE OF STUNTMAN.

Retro: Mimicking the signs of the '50s, '60s, and more, these fonts have a unique style that adds lots of character: Parisian, Moonglow, and all the fonts at FontDiner.com.

This is an example of Sparkly.

Pixel: Mimicking the anti-aliased presentation of screen fonts, these typefaces reflect the pixilated nature of the computer screen: Eight Bits, Five Bits, Genetica, Sevenet, Spekvetica.

THIS IS AN EXAMPLE OF GENETICA

Scripts: These fonts emulate handwriting and include old world black letters, gorgeous calligraphic strokes, and cartoon lettering: Apple Chancery, Aria, Balmoral, Isadora, Edwardian Script, Ex Ponto.

This is an example of Edwardian Script.

In addition to your choice of typeface, the surrounding elements and spacing of your type helps determine what your audience hears. Placing an elegant script typeface in the midst of computer imagery can make a strong statement on the merits of rarity alone. Placing a lot of space in between letters can make a typeface feel more delicate or open. Tightening the letter spacing can make a typeface feel more complete and solid.

USING VISUAL ELEMENTS

Though colors and type play a big role in setting the tone for your site, numerous other visual elements come into play as well. Images (in the form of line art or photographs), abstract shapes, textures, and patterns can strongly influence the look and feel of your site. Though such visual elements can complement or distract from your main message in an infinite number of ways, the principles behind why a certain visual element works and another doesn't are the same for photographs and shapes as they are for colors and type. When deciding on visual elements for your site, consider

Appropriateness: Is this visual element right for your audience? Does it support the story you are trying to tell?

Interest: Does this visual element help to keep your audience engaged? Does it take attention away from important information?

Unity: Does this visual element reinforce your narrative? Is it consistent with the look and feel of your site?

Images: Images are basically static representations of reality. As such, they are a powerful means of communication. Because they are rich in texture and shape, photographs and line art attract and hold your audience's attention (see Chapter 4). As a result, they can break up static text and create areas of visual interest in a layout. Images also communicate concepts quickly and effectively (remember a picture is worth a thousand words). Therefore, you should always select photos and line art that support your site's personality. If your emphasis is on being a "people-centric" company, then by all means include images of people. In fact, consider using closeups that showcase their individual traits and identify them as distinct individuals. If, on the other hand, your emphasis is on

A DRIVEN PERSONALITY

The mostly monochromatic color scheme of the Nissan cars site makes use of similarly tinted images to communicate a message of speed, power, and refinement. The "worm's eye" view and the blurred background elements of the photo help set the tone and mood for the site. But it is the combination of many visual characteristics that really define the personality of this site:

Cool colors: Refined and composed

Blue: Bold, dynamic and full of depth (ocean, sky)

Monochromatic: Contemplative, almost Zen-like qualities

Contrasting colors (the touches of orange): Excitement and visual interest

Abstract shapes (squares): Strong and stable, crisp

Type: Crisp, modern sans serif font

Images: Speed and power, knowledge, and elegance

All these visual characteristics work together to tell Nissan's story and create a coherent look and especially feel.

speed, consider blurred photos of motion or transportation systems to get your point across (see sidebar on previous page).

The style of image you choose can also influence your site's personality. Grainy, out of focus, black-and-white photos can contribute to an old world feel, whereas, a polished modern cartoon style can create a fun and relaxed atmosphere.

GOOGLE DOODLES

Though Google's home page is relatively simple (it is basically a search box and logo), a lot of personality is communicated through variations to the Google logo (as seen in these Winter Olympics features). These small, yet important details have helped make Google one of the most well-liked and used sites on the Web.

Abstract Shapes: Abstract shapes such as boxes, spheres, and so on can communicate a lot of ideas through their visual characteristics. For example, a box with sharp and crisp edges appears correct, strong, and secure. As such, it would be appropriate for a construction company or industrial manufacturer's site. The right angles and defined forms bring to mind math and machinery. In contrast, such shapes would not be reflective of the personality of Barbie.com. Barbie is more at home in flowing, organic shapes with soft edges and delicate forms. This example brings up the most apparent distinction between abstract shapes: *organic* versus *manmade*.

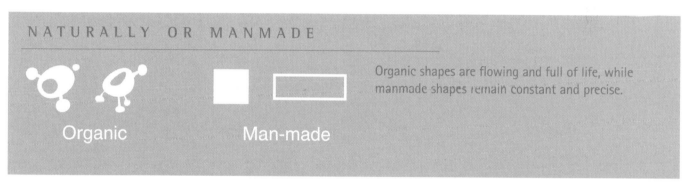

NATURALLY OR MANMADE

Organic   **Man-made**

Organic shapes are flowing and full of life, while manmade shapes remain constant and precise.

SHAPING
OUR PERSONALITY

All shapes have a distinct voice that contributes to our site's personality.

Square: correct, stable, mechanical, deliberate

Circle: complete, vibrant, alive

Triangle: dynamic, smooth, quick

Organic: natural, unique, spontaneous

Organic shapes are imperfect and resemble forms found in nature. They tend to be more round and flowing than manmade shapes, which usually consist of right angles and crisp, well-defined edges. Though many Web sites stick exclusively to one type of abstract shape or the other, there are many instances where a combination of the two best tells your story (see sidebar below).

TEXTURE AND SHAPE

⊕HermanMiller.com   for the Home   ☽ ☾ ♥ ☾ ?

Search

for the home

The Collection

Modern classics to suit your lifestyle.

Home Office Products

Desks and ergonomic chairs that fit right in.

☽ Contact Herman Miller for the Home
☾ Ways to Buy from Herman Miller for the Home

Within the nearly monotone color scheme of the Herman Miller site, organic and manmade shapes work together to tell the right story. The organic shapes (within the round navigation buttons), and the manmade shapes (the squares and rectangles) mirror the design aesthetic of Herman Miller's products: functional yet flowing furniture. Organic shapes reflect the uniqueness and emotional qualities of the products, while the manmade shapes communicate stability, strength, and correctness. Also note the use of patterns in this site. Not only do the grid lines imply rigid design specifications, they echo the textures present in the products.

Textures and Patterns: Textures and patterns provide a tactile sense of your site's personality. Does it feel soft to the touch? Or is it rough and rugged? Like shapes, textures can be organic or manmade. Manmade textures and patterns, such as grid lines (see sidebar) and other geometric patterns, bring to mind precision and detail, whereas organic textures tend to be more casual and earthy. Because textures tend to be very detailed, they can easily take over a personality. Remember, your eyes are drawn to areas of complexity (see Chapter 4). The Herman Miller site (left) is a good example of making sure that patterns play a supportive role. Because they are rendered with very light lines, the patterns do not take over the personality or the visual hierarchy of the site.

USING INTERACTIVITY

Communicating a personality through the types of interactions present in your site is a significant part of creating an engaging and appropriate experience for your audience. Should your site be serious, consisting of data queries for cold hard facts? Or is it better off being playful, with fun, almost game-like interfaces? Perhaps you are best suited creating a more mysterious interface that your audience needs to explore. The personality of your site and your audience's goals should determine which route you take. But when attempting unique forms of interaction for your site, keep in mind the issues surrounding standard Web interactions (Chapter 3). Introducing a new way of interacting with your site might actually result in an inferior user experience when the interactions you employ end up confusing your audience.

PART THREE

START COMMUNICATING:

ONLINE THAT IS!

In all fields of human endeavor, once you learn the basic characteristics and principles of a craft, you're empowered to create original, effective, and impassioned work. The sculptor with a detailed understanding of his medium's strengths and weaknesses is able to use his knowledge to chip stone into art. The bridge builder with an informed grasp of his requirements and constraints can create practical and long-lasting structures. The Web designer is no different.

Now that you have an understanding of the "terms" that make up the three lexicons of Web usability — technical considerations, visual organization principles, and look and feel — you're ready to start communicating to your audience. This section presents many possible applications of the lexicons that ensure the page elements, home page, services, and dynamic content of your site accurately and elegantly say what you want.

chapter six

Just as elementary particles combine to create the very fabric of life, Web site elements work together in a variety of ways to weave the very Web itself. All Web sites, in one way or another, make use of basic Web page elements, such as navigation systems, forms, images, links, and so on. How they combine and present these elements gives each site a distinct personality and determines the experience the site's audience will have. When creating Web page layouts, it is important to understand the role of each element, its place in the page's hierarchy, and how its visual organization and presentation can communicate these qualities to your audience.

WORKING THE ELEMENTS
[S E C T I O N   T I T L E]

FUNDAMENTAL ELEMENTS

The most common Web page elements are
- Page footers
- Body text
- Links
- Navigation systems
- Images
- Site IDs
- Forms

Less common are
- Videos
- Embedded programs (such as games)

Whether they help you find insurance quotes or entertain you with jokes, one thing that all Web pages have in common is their use of at least some basic Web site elements. Though it could be argued that the most basic elements of Web pages are text, image, sound, and so on, it turns out to be more beneficial to categorize Web site elements by their function. Navigation systems guide you through a site's content, forms gather necessary information, images communicate and stimulate, body text educates and engages, and page footers provide context and clarification. Lots of unique combinations of these common elements make the Web what it is today: useful and exciting.

Each fundamental element has its role within a Web page and in the context of the entire Web. When building Web pages, you need to consider the function of each element on the page and its resultant place in the page's visual hierarchy. Elements that provide mostly supportive information, such as page footers, should have minimal visual weight when compared to elements that provide valuable content and directly relevant information, such as body text. The role of each element determines the amount of visual weight (how much attention) it ought to have in comparison to the rest of the page.

It is important to note that the same types of elements could very well have different roles on different pages. For example, navigation elements on a content page should sit lower in the visual hierarchy than they do on a page consisting solely of destination choices (a navigation page). One page is set up to let you navigate, while the other is designed for accessing information. These distinct goals are why the element's role in relation to the page's main message (its story) casts the deciding vote on visual weight. Your primary means of visually communicating a page's story, the hierarchy, is most effective when every element knows its proper place and resultant visual weight (see Chapter 4).

In addition to maintaining an appropriate place in the page's visual hierarchy, each element needs to have a well thought out internal hierarchy. Within body text, should the page title have more visual weight than the copy or vice versa? Should the focus in navigation systems be on the labels or the divisions between them? Not only does the combined visual weight of each element need to reveal information about its role and importance within a Web page, but the element itself needs to communicate as well.

KNOW YOUR BASICS

While the differences between Web pages are as numerous as Web sites themselves, the distinctions between the elements that fill them are considerably fewer. Web conventions (discussed in Chapter 3) and the distinct nature of each Web site element result in a lot of shared characteristics. These commonalities are why most page footers look the same, are located in the same place on a Web page, and contain the same information.

The reasons the footer came into being (a need to provide sitewide supportive information on pages) influence how it appears on most Web pages. Because the footer fulfills the same role from site to site, it looks the same from site to site. Good news for Web surfers: After encountering several footers, they not only know what type of information they can expect when they see a footer, but they also have a good idea of where to look when they need that type of information.

But you may be left wondering, "How can I make a distinct site if every Web page element comes with its own set of constraints (positioning, content, and so on)?" Just as a sculptor cannot change the physical properties of marble, we cannot change the requirements and limitations of Web pages. Your audience needs a way to move from page to page. So unless your site consists of one page, you will have to make use of at least some links or navigation. Likewise, if you ever want to gather information from your audience, you might need to turn to forms. As a result, knowing the purpose and limitations of each Web page element does not limit you: It empowers you.

For the sculptor, knowing how marble responds to each chiseling tool lets him create smooth edges and crisp details. In other words, it provides him with the ability to create exactly what he wants. The same is true for anyone working with a particular medium. As a communication medium dependent on numerous technologies, the Web has its share of constraints. Being aware of them when you design Web pages gives you the ability to create not only effective but original solutions.

ELEMENTS AND PERSONALITY

Site elements can reinforce or establish the personality of a site in several ways. Even the amount of elements on a page can tell you something about the site's personality. Sites heavy on navigation tend to be information-rich and need multiple navigation options to get their audience to the content they seek. In contrast, sites with little navigation are frequently focused on entertaining their visitors with unexpected content or fixed sequences (such as the sequential presentation of a magazine story).

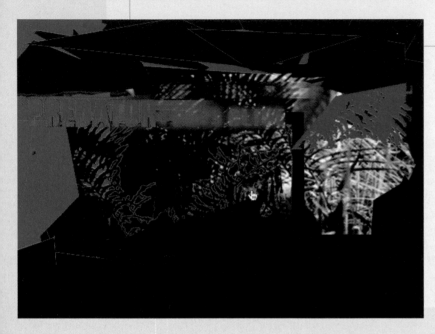

LESS NAV, MORE MOVIE

Looking for the navigation system in this site? Try following the occasional links given to you instead. This site for the film Predator takes you on an audio and visual ride through the film's themes and rarely lets you make a navigational choice of your own. The goal of the site (like the movie) is to entertain. What fun would it be if you knew what was going to happen next?

Contrast this site to the navigation-heavy Microsoft site (right) and you have a pretty good idea (from the amount and type of site elements present) which site is there to inform and which one is ready to entertain.

The visual presentation of site elements can also reinforce a sitewide personality. Common visual characteristics, such as color or type, between page elements can help unify a layout and establish a sense of place (See Chapter 4 and sidebar on the facing page).

The Web page elements of buyarock.com all work together to reinforce the personality of the site. In this example, the subnavigation system shows up within a book's pages and as arrows ready to flip pages. The images and body text also appear in the book, unifying the content in a fun and engaging interface.

Also note that the top-level navigation choices reflect the typeface found in the site's logo, maintaining a unified look and feel.

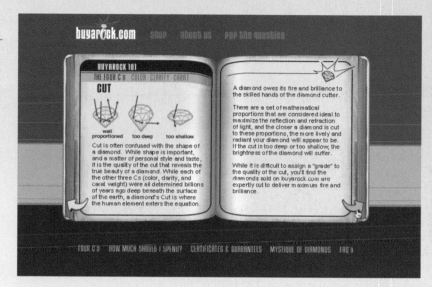

NAVIGATION SYSTEMS
[SECTION TITLE]

Navigation systems are at their best when they explain the structure of a Web site, provide an indication of where you are within that structure, and do not physically or visually overwhelm a page. I discussed many of the considerations necessary for effective navigation design in Chapter 2. After taking the issues presented there into account, you might have come up with possible navigation system ideas (in the form of navigation mockups). This section will look at how to apply visual communication and look-and-feel principles to your initial navigation system ideas.

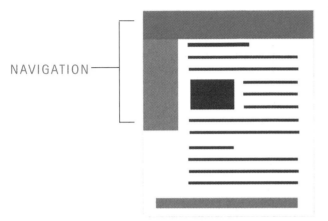

NAVIGATION

Visually organizing navigation choices not only tells your audience what types of behavior they can expect from each of their selections, it also helps to separate navigation from the rest of the page and explain the distinctions between different navigation options. An appropriate look and feel for your navigation reinforces your site's personality and can help reduce the visual contrast between navigation and the rest of a page.

BANDING TOGETHER

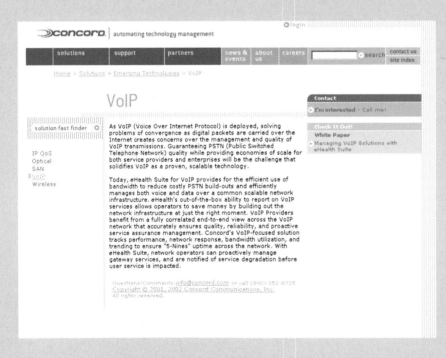

In this example from Concord.com, the band of blue helps to visually group the page's top-level navigation choices. This grouping not only distinguishes them from the rest of the page, but also associates them with a common function. The use of sitewide colors and fonts in the navigation bar allows it to "fit in" with the rest of the page and not distract from the content.

By managing the amount of visual contrast within navigation systems, you can successfully reduce the visual noise that might otherwise interfere with your audience's understanding. For example, when the borders or separators of navigation choices are given equal or greater visual

THE MINIMALIST BUTTON

Many early Web pages made obvious visual references to the kinds of three-dimensional buttons found in most computer programs. Because most people that used computers were familiar with these types of buttons, they had no problems understanding that labels with three-dimensional borders were clickable. (They even look like they can be pressed.) However, because screen real estate is at a premium, devoting lots of space to indicate buttons is troublesome. Also, thick three-dimensional borders are visually heavy and can distract from navigation labels and the rest of a page's content.

To the left is a typical example of the types of buttons found in most computer programs. The three-dimensional rendering of these buttons makes it clear that they are clickable.

This design "progression" of a simple navigation menu shows how "button" functionality can be alluded to with a minimum of distracting visual noise. The basic shape and relative size of buttons can be referenced with positioning and a common background color alone. The right-most example even eliminates the button references altogether and makes use of small arrowheads to indicate links.

weight than the choices themselves, the visual hierarchy is putting emphasis on the wrong content.

As an example, compare the two navigation bars below. Both make use of a common background color to visually group distinct navigation choices. And both reference the standard "button" shape of navigation choices with their approximate size and shape (see sidebar on previous page).

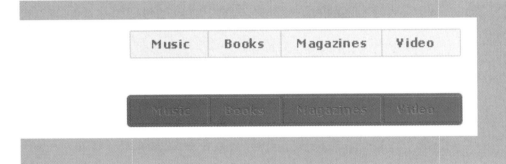

However, in the top-most example, the focus is on the labels of the navigation choices. The rest of the visual elements are reduced to the minimum amount necessary needed to visually separate the choices from each other and the rest of the page. Their common background, text, and border color visually group them as a single element and help to keep this new element distinct from the rest of the page's content. Also, the light color used in this navigation system probably keeps it from competing with the other page elements for attention (depending on what the rest of the page looks like, of course).

The second example, on the other hand, emphasizes the background color and border over the actual navigation choices. It is hard to concentrate on the labels, because the background color and the border continually compete for your attention. More likely than not, this navigation system would also heavily contrast with the rest of your page's elements, thereby forcing its way towards an undeserved place at the top of the page hierarchy.

Keeping contrast to just the amount necessary also applies to the You Are Here indicators that tell you your current location within a navigation menu. As you can see in the example below, a noticeable shift in background or text color is all that is needed to indicate your current location. The bottom-most example uses too much contrast and makes it difficult to focus on the rest of the navigation choices.

PROVIDING ALTERNATIVES

Your audience relies on your navigation system to empower them to freely move through your site in a manner of their choosing. As I mentioned in Chapter 2, different people use different methods to find their way. For this reason, you will often find sites with search boxes, navigation systems, site maps, embedded links, and more. Though all these navigation elements are intended to help you get to where you want to go, they sometimes actually hamper your progress. Too many choices can sometimes be just as detrimental as too few.

The 37signals site provides three possible ways to navigate their "signals" within an unobtrusive navigation system (small in size, positioned against the page edge). These options allow different audience members to interact with the content in a manner they find comfortable.

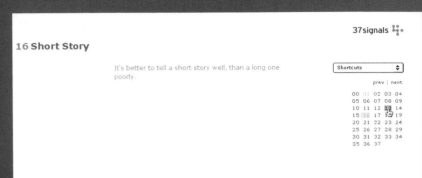

You can simply select a random or specific number to jump to a particular signal. Or you may navigate the signals in sequential form with the previous and next links. (Notice the subtle touch of yellow identifies these links as distinct form the numbers.) Your third option is to make use of the drop-down menu, which provides text descriptions of each signal. This menu allows you to quickly locate a particular signal or get a good overview of all 37 signals simultaneously.

The 37signals navigation is also a great reflection of the site's personality: simple and smart. No need for fancy graphics (or other forms of visual noise) here: only information that helps you to better understand the site's structure and your position within it.

Note that the "number" navigation makes use of saturated and unsaturated colors to indicate which signals you have already seen. Also, poised link colors (in this case, bright blue) provide indication to make certain you do not make an incorrect selection (as the numbers are quite close together).

Just about every book you will pick up has several methods for navigating its contents: table of contents, page numbers, chapter indicators, and an index. However, these navigation tools never distract from the book's content. The index and table of contents sit in familiar locations at the front and back of the book: there when you need them, but hidden when you don't. Page numbers and chapter indicators are restricted to the headers and footers of pages and often appear in smaller, light colored fonts, so as not to interfere with the body text. Likewise, the various navigation strategies you provide for your Web audience should "know their place."

KEEPING NAVIGATION IN ITS PLACE

The basic role of navigation is to get you to your destination and then quietly slip into the background so that you can do your work. (In fact, the best navigation systems are the ones that you barely notice. Using them is simple enough that you don't have to deliberately concentrate on "navigating.") That said, navigation systems should not altogether disappear from the page: They need to remain accessible and on call.

Positioning plays a big role in keeping navigation in check, yet available when needed. Most navigation systems hug the sides of a page: staying away from content, while still remaining accessible should the need arise. Hugging the page edges visually groups navigation with the page borders and separates it from the rest of the content. This deliberate placement allows navigation menus to effectively recede and clearly communicate their function.

The top and left-most edges of the page are the most frequent homes of navigation tools because pages expand from top to bottom and left to right. Were navigation positioned at the base of the page, the content above it might push the navigation off the screen and away from sight.

That said, there are often times when navigation systems are embedded within body text or images in addition to the edges of a page. In such

HOW 'BOUT A HUG?

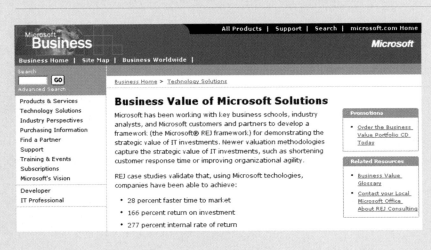

In this example from Microsoft.com, the navigation links "hug" three sides of the page layout. The use of shared background colors and fonts visually groups the navigation choices and effectively separates them from the body text of the page.

The two sets of links within the body text area are related resources and promotions tied to the body text content. Notice that they retain the same background colors found in the other navigation areas on the page. Though they are not positioned next to the other navigation links, they are still visually related to them (by color), telling the audience something about their role as navigation.

situations, it is especially important to make use of visual similarities between the distinct navigation areas to make it clear that they have the same function. Common background colors, type treatment, or visual elements are just a few ways that you can visually group distinct navigation systems on a page (see sidebar above).

BODY TEXT

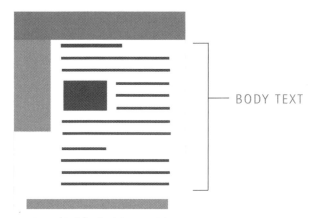

BODY TEXT

Because a lot of the information within Web sites is in written form, body text often ends up owning the bulk of a page's content. As a result, it frequently needs to become the focus of a page. Luckily, the similarities between the individual lines of body text result in it initially being perceived as one large visual group (see sidebar below). As a result, body text lays claim to lots of visual weight on the merits of size alone. Body text with lots of visual weight is good news because we want the content of our Web pages (often embedded within the body text) to be near the top of our page's visual hierarchy.

GRADUAL PERCEPTION

When you first notice a page layout, the visual similarities (color, typeface) and proximity of body text visually group it together creating the perception of one large visual element. Within this element, you again make use of the principles of visual perception to distinguish the unique portions of the body text (page title, subtitles, images). Finally, you're able to begin reading words when you perceive the distinct shapes formed by unique groups of letters (words).

BEING READABLE

In order for your audience to make use of your body text, it needs to be readable. Unlike printed materials (books, magazines, and so on), Web content is often difficult to read (especially for extended periods of time) because of poor resolution. Most books render type at 1,200 dots per inch (dpi), while your computer monitor is more likely to use 85 dpi[1]. For this reason, many people will print long Web pages, favoring the high resolution of print. The poor legibility of on screen text is also why I (and others) recommend limiting the amount of text on your Web pages to just the amount necessary (see Chapter 3). There's no need to make your audience wade through lots of difficult to read text if they don't need to.

Despite the limitations of screen resolution, you can employ a number of techniques to improve the legibility of body text. Proper selection of fonts and appropriate use of white space, line length, and color can improve the overall readability of Web typography in several ways.

Fonts: As I mentioned in Chapter 2, the differences between operating systems, Web browsers, and their individual settings can significantly alter the way your Web pages appear from computer to computer. These differences are readily evident in the presentation of fonts. The same typeface on a Windows machine will appear noticeably larger (with default browser settings) than on a Macintosh (Lynch & Horton, 1999). Also, different typefaces come standard with each operating system. Hence the reason why we always specify font "alternates" in all HTML FONT tags and CSS styles. Windows users see Arial, and Macintosh users (that do not have Arial) see Helvetica.

```
<FONT FACE="Verdana, Arial, Helvetica, sans-serif">Text</FONT>
P {font-family: Verdana, Arial, Helvetica, sans-serif;}
```

Though your choice of Web fonts is slim, you do have some choices (see sidebar). Keep in mind that fonts like Times or Arial, which are

[1] Patrick Lynch and Sarah Horton discuss considerations of Web typography in their informative book: *Web Style Guide: Basic Design Principles for Creating Web Sites* (Yale University Press, 1999).

very legible in printed work, do not work as well on screen. Often times, you might be better off using a font designed for on-screen reading such as Verdana or Georgia.

When you decide on a font for your body text, also keep your site's personality in mind. A sans-serif font like Verdana might accurately reflect the personality of a technology firm, but say the wrong thing to an audience of ballet dancers (see Chapter 5).

Font Sizes: In addition, you will have to make some decisions on font sizes as well. In order to sustain an appropriate visual hierarchy within your

Times New Roman, Times, serif
12 pt type, 16 pt line height

Arial, Helvetica, san-serif
12 pt type, 16 pt line height

Courier, Courier new, mono
12 pt type, 16 pt line height

Georgia, Times New Roman, Times, serif
12 pt type, 16 pt line height

Geneva, Arial, Helvetica, san-serif
12 pt type, 16 pt line height

Verdana, Arial, Helvetica, sans-serif
12 pt type, 16 pt line height

Microsoft Internet Explorer 5.1 - Macintosh

Times New Roman, Times, serif
12 pt type, 16 pt line height

Arial, Helvetica, san-serif
12 pt type, 16 pt line height

Courier, Courier new, mono
12 pt type, 16 pt line height

Georgia, Times New Roman, Times, serif
12 pt type, 16 pt line height

Geneva, Arial, Helvetica, san-serif
12 pt type, 16 pt line height

Verdana, Arial, Helvetica, sans-serif
12 pt type, 16 pt line height

Internet Explorer 5.5 - Windows

Times New Roman, Times, serif
12 pt type, 16 pt line height

Arial, Helvetica, san-serif
12 pt type, 16 pt line height

Courier, Courier new, mono
12 pt type, 16 pt line height

Georgia, Times New Roman, Times, serif
12 pt type, 16 pt line height

Geneva, Arial, Helvetica, san-serif
12 pt type, 16 pt line height

Verdana, Arial, Helvetica, sans-serif
12 pt type, 16 pt line height

Netscape Navigator 4.7 - Windows

Times New Roman, Times, serif
12 pt type, 16 pt line height

Arial, Helvetica, san-serif
12 pt type, 16 pt line height

Courier, Courier new, mono
12 pt type, 16 pt line height

Georgia, Times New Roman, Times, serif
12 pt type, 16 pt line height

Geneva, Arial, Helvetica, san-serif
12 pt type, 16 pt line height

Verdana, Arial, Helvetica, sans-serif
12 pt type, 16 pt line height

Netscape Navigator 4.6 - Macintosh

Without significant development efforts, your choice of available Web fonts (used to display HTML text) is limited to the fonts that ship with the most popular operating systems. The six most common font "suggestions" are shown in the two most popular Web browsers, Microsoft Internet Explorer and Netscape Navigator, on both Macintosh and Windows computers. Note the differences in sizes and spacing in each version.

body text, you will need a variety of text sizes. Your headlines, copy, captions, subheaders, footnotes, and more all rely on visual contrast (often achieved through differences in size) to communicate their relative importance to your audience.

THE RIGHT SIZE

Because of the differences in Web browsers and operating systems, many sites use distinct style sheets for each browser to ensure a consistent presentation and keep font scaling intact. A simple script like the one below (which checks for Internet Explorer) can detect which browser is being used and include the appropriate style sheet.

```
<SCRIPT LANGUAGE="Javascript">
if(navigator.appName == "Microsoft Internet Explorer")
{document.write('<link rel="stylesheet" href="css/ie.css" type="text/css"/>'
</SCRIPT>
```

Internet Explorer 5.1 on the Macintosh allows you to adjust the "text zoom" by percentages, changing the size of all fonts regardless of how they are specified in CSS. This example shows 100% and 120% zooms.

Netscape Navigator 4.7 on the Macintosh renders several font sizes smaller than Explorer and does not scale any type specified in pixels. This example shows the default font size in Navigator and the same fonts after selecting Increase Font Size several times.

Times New Roman, Times, serif
14 pixel type, 18 pixel line height

Times New Roman, Times, serif
12 pt type, 16 pt line height

Times New Roman, Times, serif
medium type, 1.5 multiple line height

Times New Roman, Times, serif
1.2 em, 1.4 em line height

Times New Roman, Times, serif
.4 cm, .5 cm line height

Times New Roman, Times, serif
100% type, 120% line height

Times New Roman, Times, serif
14 pixel type, 18 pixel line height

Times New Roman, Times, serif
12 pt type, 16 pt line height

Times New Roman, Times, serif
medium type, 1.5 multiple line height

Times New Roman, Times, serif
1.2 em, 1.4 em line height

Times New Roman, Times, serif
.4 cm, .5 cm line height

Times New Roman, Times, serif
100% type, 120% line height

Internet Explorer 5.5 on the Windows platform does not scale fonts specified in pixels, points, or centimeters in this example.

Times New Roman, Times, serif
14 pixel type, 18 pixel line height

Times New Roman, Times, serif
12 pt type, 16 pt line height

Times New Roman, Times, serif
medium type, 1.5 multiple line height

Times New Roman, Times, serif
1.2 em, 1.4 em line height

Times New Roman, Times, serif
.4 cm, .5 cm line height

Times New Roman, Times, serif
100% type, 120% line height

Times New Roman, Times, serif
14 pixel type, 18 pixel line height

Times New Roman, Times, serif
12 pt type, 16 pt line height

Times New Roman, Times, serif
medium type, 1.5 multiple line height

Times New Roman, Times, serif
1.2 em, 1.4 em line height

Times New Roman, Times, serif
.4 cm, .5 cm line height

Times New Roman, Times, serif
100% type, 120% line height

Netscape Navigator 4.7 on the Windows platform does not scale fonts specified as pixels. Notice the difference in .em specified fonts between the Windows and Macintosh versions of Navigator.

Cascading style sheets (CSS) are a great tool for maintaining sitewide type consistency, but fall short when faced with the differences between browsers and operating systems. Within CSS, you can specify font sizes as percentages, points, picas, inches, and more. In most situations, specifying font sizes means setting relative differences between fonts because individual users can adjust their personal font size preferences in their browser (see sidebar on preceding page). In most instances, relative font sizes are a good thing because they allow each person to set their preferences to a reading size they find comfortable.

However, you're likely to encounter situations when you want your fonts to remain a consistent size, especially, within navigation systems and forms where you want to maintain a stable interface. Providing relative font size suggestions within these Web page elements can significantly alter your layout when users adjust their font size preferences. A significant font size adjustment can turn important interface elements into

KEEP IT CLEAN

Here we see an example of when font sizes (adjusted by users) can get too big for their own good and destabilize an interface element. The resultant changes especially become a concern when you're creating Web services and applications, where a stable interface is necessary.

jumbled messes of type and color (see sidebar on left). In these cases, you might want to specify your fonts in pixels, which will keep the fonts from scaling, except in Microsoft Internet Explorer for the Macintosh or unless someone overrides page specific fonts in their browser's settings. Or better still, design pages to accommodate possible font scaling differences (see Chapter 8).

White Space: In addition to fonts, the amount of spacing you include within your body text can also increase readability. *Leading* (specified as line-height within CSS) is the vertical distance between one line of text and the one directly below it. Too little leading, and your lines of text bump up against each other; too much, and it is difficult to locate the next line while reading. A good general rule for Web page leading is to use a bit more leading than you might need in print. For example, if your text is set in 12 point type, try making the leading 16 points. Depending on how large your type is, you might want more or less leading.

Spacing between paragraphs also increases legibility on screen and helps your audience make distinctions between text blocks. You can make sure that appropriate spacing is present in your body text by remembering to close all your paragraph tags in your HTML code. Also remember to include some space for margins on either side of your body text. Margins visually separate your text from the rest of the page elements making it easier to focus on the content.

THE RIGHT LENGTH

Be careful not to make your body text lines too long if you want your site to be easily readable. Shorter columns of text, like the ones found in this book, are easier to manage because they fit into a comfortable eye span: about three inches (Lynch & Horton, 1999).

Color: Though most book layouts use black text on a white background to increase readability, this combination is sometimes troublesome online. The contrast between black on white on computer monitors is often exaggerated to a point that becomes uncomfortable for reading. As a result, you may want to include subtle hints of color within your body text that reflect your site's personality and simultaneously reduce the contrast between foreground and background.

LINKING WITHIN

Though links constitute the better part of most navigation systems, as distinct page elements they most often show up interspersed within body text. (They also commonly appear in footers, image captions, and more). Unlike navigation system links that need to "blend" in with their surroundings (see preceding section), hypertext links (hyperlinks for short) need to stand out from their surrounding body text.

Because I already spoke in depth about the design considerations of links in Chapter 3, I won't repeat myself here. However, recall that too many hypertext links within a block of text can be distracting for your reader. The use of links needs to be kept to just the amount needed to enrich your content with relevant information. Too many links will not only take attention away from your content, but they may end up disturbing your page's visual hierarchy as well by creating unnecessary visual noise on your page.

Here we have a <u>unvisited link</u> distinguished by a saturated contrasting color that helps your audience scan the page. In contrast, a <u>visited link</u> should use a less saturated form of the link color.

A poised link needs to "light up" and could use **background colors** or <u>underlining</u> to do so.

In Chapter 3, I mentioned that unvisited and visited links should be distinguished by differences in color saturation. The less saturated (duller) shade of the color gives a visited link a worn-out or used appearance.

The principle behind this perception is *natural mapping*. You can see natural mapping at work throughout your daily lives. When driving your car, you press the accelerator forward, and forward you go. On the elevator, the buttons for the top floors are above the bottoms for the lower floors. Natural mapping simply states that controls are easier to understand when they "map" to our expectations. In the elevator, we want to go up, so it makes sense for the upper floor buttons to be positioned above the ground floor buttons.

When compared to unvisited links, visited links are dull, and poised links are bright. The poised link color maps to our expectations of "active." (It lights up when on.) On the other hand, visited links have been seen before and lose some of their glimmer and, therefore, appear used.

IMAGES
[S E C T I O N   T I T L E]

Of all the site elements, images probably have the most diverse set of uses. They can appear in navigation systems, within forms, as links, and more. In this section, however, I am going to focus on the image as a distinct page element. Instead of talking about each time we make use of an IMG tag in a HTML document, I'll discuss how images can help with the visual organization and personality of a Web page.

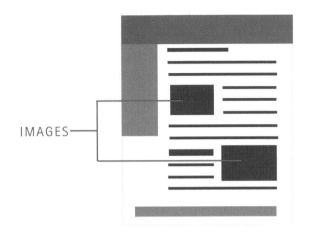

IMAGES

Because images tend to have a lot of variation in color, shape, and texture, they work well to capture our attention (see Chapter 4). The amount of detail present in images also helps to create articulate messages for your audience. It is often easier to communicate your ideas through an image, as anyone that has created a quick sketch on a restaurant napkin to make their point can verify. Not only do images communicate a great deal of information, they do so quickly. Therefore, images need to be used responsibly and not as arbitrary fillers of otherwise empty space.

ELICITING INTEREST

Whether it's to the constant parade of motion on TV or to your friend's recent vacation photos, we are all drawn to images. As we read the paper, we are captivated by images of truth, triumph, and tragedy that "take" us to another place. When reading a great novel, we continually "picture" the various scenes in our minds as we are drawn into the story. Taking advantage of this seductive power of images is a common way to create interest within page layouts.

Incorporating images within Web page content not only provides context for your prose, it also creates visual interest by breaking up the text with rich sensory experiences. Think how your experience reading about Egyptian camel herders' lives is enhanced by being able to "see" the desert as they do. Dark and murky photos of the Egyptian landscape provide a much more mysterious tone to the narrative than sunlit smiling faces of desert denizens. The experience is particularly memorable when the mood and tone set by the images is closely mirrored by the text. A dark and ominous tale is poorly served by happy-go-lucky images.

Because images play such a prominent (quick and effective) role in communicating personality, make sure that they are saying what you intend. At first glance, images can make a page layout seem exciting, fun, or serious. Before you draw your audience into one of these sensory experiences, think through it in terms of your site's overall message and personality and make sure that you're saying the right thing.

IMAGE INTEGRATION

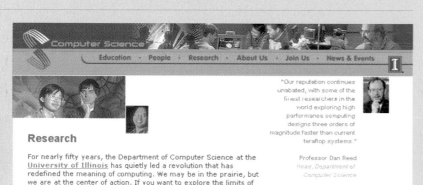

The images in this University of Illinois Computer Science (CS) Department layout serve two important purposes. The featured imagery (people and technology) is welcoming and exemplary of the cutting-edge research that characterizes the department. In other words, the images help the CS department tell its story by setting the tone for the page. We are on the cusp of computer technologies and very friendly to boot.

The placement of the images, on the other hand, helps to create visual interest in the composition. By echoing the blues found in the navigation bar, the images do not distract from the content: They complement it. Also note that their "step-ladder" positioning helps to lead your eye into the body text.

PART OF THE BIGGER PICTURE

As with all page elements, you need to keep in mind that each image you include within a page design is not an independent entity. Instead, it is part of the overall page hierarchy and the look and feel of the site. Because images are attractive, they can carry lots of visual weight even when used at a small size. The colors, patterns, and textures within each image can create a lot of contrast. As a result, be certain to offset the visual weight of images with other elements that keep your visual hierarchy intact.

DOMINANT IMAGES

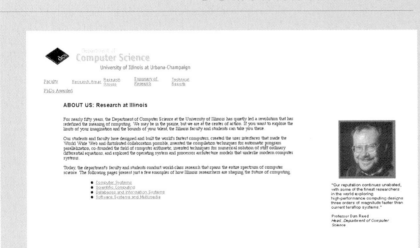

In this layout, the large size and detail of the image gives it more visual weight than the rest of the page elements. (The only thing keeping it in check is its placement against the right-most edge of the page.) Compare this layout to the redesign in the preceding sidebar and note how in the new version the images and navigation form a unified band that works together to ensure a smooth order in the visual hierarchy of the page.

You can also keep your images in check by "bringing them into" the layout. Effective image positioning (such as wrapping between text) can unite text and image in a symbiotic relationship. Close proximity of image and its related text visually groups the two, creating a single entity (or at least the perception of one; see Chapter 4).

Another way to create unity is to echo the visual elements found in other parts of the site within your images. By making use of common visual characteristics (color, shape, and so on), you can bring your images "closer" to the rest of the page layout. This technique reduces the amount of contrast between the image and the page and reinforces the personality of your site.

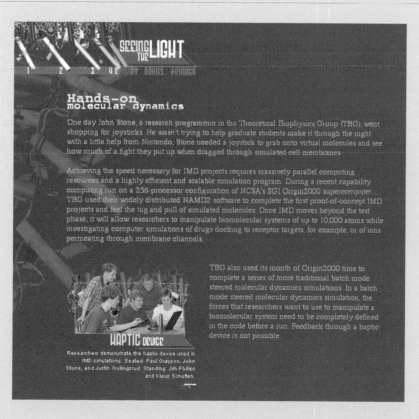

This online magazine layout repeats the visual elements of the article header within the background and caption images to create a more cohesive and engaging overall design that brings attention to the body text. The body text gets noticed more because of the visual similarities of the images and the sense of direction present in the background image.

It is also worth noticing that the title graphic "anchors" the navigation choices (see next sidebar).

You might also consider using images as "anchors" for your page layouts. Making use of a larger or visually complex image as the focal point of your page can create a center of interest to which your content can "cling." This technique is usually best suited for home pages without lots of body text. Two ways to make use of this method are the inclusion of a larger (but visually less complex) background image and the use of an attention-grabbing image to highlight important elements (see sidebar below).

ANCHORS AWAY

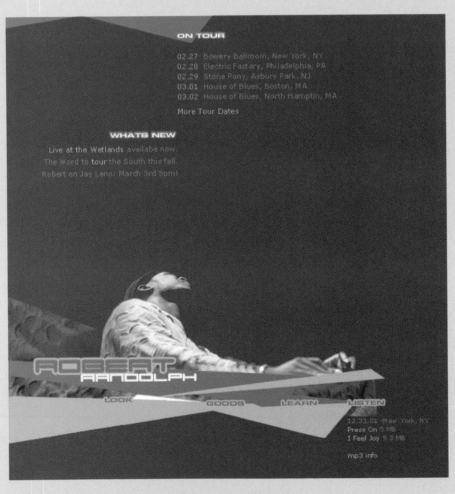

In this example, the unique shape and complex textures of the image make a great anchor for the navigation choices on the page. The image attracts the eye, thereby bringing attention to the navigation choices embedded within. Also note how the subtle reiteration of the dominant shapes in the main image is used to anchor the two content areas at the top of the page (which get noticed by the lack of image around them — white space)

KEEPING IT SMALL

Although images can provide all the benefits discussed in the preceding sections, they also currently come with some disadvantages. Of these, download time and accessibility provide the most immediate concern. Unlike text, images tend to be large in file size and consequently take a long time to download. A page filled with lots of images can make a Web site slow to snail's pace as it renders on your screen. This extra time becomes especially problematic for modem users (the current majority) with limited bandwidth.

As a result, whenever you choose to use images, make certain that you apply the techniques discussed in Chapter 3: compression, resizing, zoom-in views, and the use of IMG tag attributes, such as ALT and HEIGHT and WIDTH.

PAGE FOOTERS
[SECTION TITLE]

Footers are not unique to the Web; you frequently find them within books and even on TV. When flipping through TV channels, the little logos in the screen footer tell us what station is responsible for the content we are viewing. When we read a book, the footer reveals the source of quotations (footnotes) and tells us where we are within the book (page numbers, chapter names). This information most frequently appears at the bottom of the page. But regardless of the position (it could show up at the top), the information is presented similarly and serves the same purpose: revealing the origin of content.

FOOTER

By providing background information, the footer also provides you with a sense of trust. If you consider the Discovery channel a reliable source of quality programming, you may be inclined to believe the information presented on one of their shows. The role of the page footer on Web sites is rather similar. Because visitors can come to your page in any number of unique ways (even channel surfing), they need some form of general facts about the page content. Who is responsible for the content here? When was this page last updated? If it's clear that the content comes from a reputable source and was recently updated, trust is easier to come by.

WITHIN THE FOOTER

Though each Web site may include different information in their page footers, they generally use some combination of the following list.

Copyright & Privacy Information. Because the footer is low in the visual hierarchy, it's the perfect place to put your "fine print." Links to privacy information and terms of use let your audience know how they can interact with your site and reassure them that you respect their privacy. The copyright information, on the other hand, claims authorship of the page's content. This information also lets your audience know that you take responsibility for what they find within your site and helps to instill a sense of trust. (This trust is often reinforced with the inclusion of "security assurances" images from online quality assessment firms, also found in the page footer.)

fedex.com Terms of Use | Contact Us!
This site is protected by copyright and trademark laws under U.S. and International law. Review our privacy policy. All rights reserved.
© 1995-2001 FedEx

Contact Link: The contact information link is especially important because it shows that someone is responsible for the page's content and upkeep. With a contact link, your audience has a reliable means for sending you questions or feedback about the page.

Site ID: You can include a smaller scale version of your company logo or mark within the footer. This logo often serves as a link home and can help orientate your audience, especially if they followed an in-line link to your page and, as a result, missed the site ID at the top. Reiterating some of the visual elements of the site (such as the logo) also helps to provide a sense of continuance on the page: It seems related from top to bottom (more on this design consideration in the next section).

Credits: It is common to find site construction or content generation credits in a footnote. Usually, these credits appear only on certain pages (the home page, for example) and not on every page within the site.

Last Updated Information: It is often good practice to include an indication of when a page was last updated within the footer. This form of "dating" lets your audience know whether they're looking at recent or dated content.

Home • Search • About Us • Contact Us • Advertise with Us
©2001 Coyne & Blanchard, Inc. All Rights Reserved.

Relevant Links: Many page footers also include links to top-level navigation options. It is important that these links be well chosen and not simply a reiteration of other navigation elements present on the page. In the Design Interact example above, the types of links included are representative of the kinds of questions the audience might have when they arrive at the end of a page of content. After finishing an article, visitors may want to know more about the source, search for a similar article or idea they picked up in the article, or be impressed enough with the site's content to want to advertise there.

THE FOOTER AND THE PAGE

Remember that the main role of the page footer is supportive: It's there to answer questions about the rest of the page's content. The footer should never distract from the real content of the page. It should be

FOOTING THE NAV

As you surf the Web, you're likely to find sites that try to repeat their entire navigation system within the footer. The footer isn't a navigation tool. By using each Web site element as it was intended and expected, you will save your audience unnecessary confusion. Keep footer information in the footer. Every bit of text you add to the footer that doesn't belong there takes attention and valuable space away from the text that does. Fewer relevant materials will always be more effective than lots of unrelated ones.

found when it is needed, but remain unobtrusive until then. As a result, it's generally not a good idea to keep too much information in the footer. A few short sentences usually does the trick.

If you include too much information in the footer, you will end up unnecessarily increasing its visual weight. The footer should sit at the bottom of your page's visual hierarchy. It provides "additional" information and is relatively less effective in communicating a page's story when compared to other site elements. As a result, the footer should have less visual weight than the rest of the page elements, usually accomplished by:

> Using smaller and/or lighter text for the footer content.
>
> Separating the footer from the rest of the page with white space or a visual element, usually a horizontal line. (Make sure that the line has less visual weight than the footer itself!)
>
> Positioning the footer at the base of the page. (It is called the footer after all.)
>
> Using a band of color to minimize the contrast within the footer and have it act as a "unified band" distinct from the rest of the page.

Lastly, the visual treatment of the page footer can help to provide a sense of continuance to your pages. By reiterating a visual element or treatment found elsewhere on your page, the footer can help to "connect" your layout (see sidebar on next page).

AN ENLIGHTENED FOOTER

The footer on the Herman Miller site sits at the base of the page, is sufficiently separated from the rest of the page content with white space, appears in a lighter color, and consists of only one line of text. The combination of these techniques ensures that the footer remains the lowest item in the page's visual hierarchy.

A-BANDED FOOTER

The blue color band used to unify the footer contents on the Microsoft site not only keeps the footer content distinct from the main page elements, but it also helps to visually "complete" the page by reintroducing the visual elements (color, shape, and type treatment) found on the page header.

Though the Web is a highly interactive medium, the vast majority of online interactions simply consist of searching and browsing (following links, using navigation systems, scanning a page). When you need to move beyond these types of interactions, you will frequently turn to

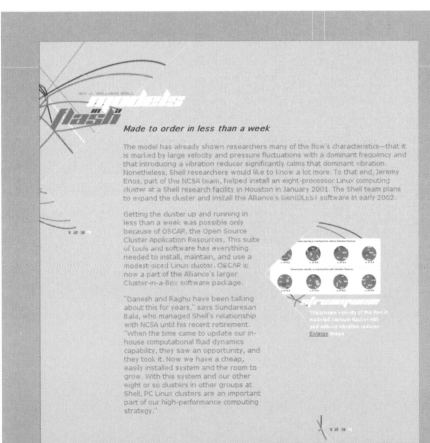

USING YOUR FOOTING

Outside of its role as a provider of background information, the footer can also assist in navigation and visual presentation. In this online magazine article, the footer reiterates the visual elements found in the page header and images, creating a unified visual presentation. It also repeats the article navigation links so that readers can continue on to the next page when they finish reading without scrolling back to the top of the page.

forms. Forms provide an effective means of gathering information from your audience and can be used to sign up for mailing lists, trade stocks, make online purchases, manage a bank account, and more.

Forms take on different responsibilities within each distinct Web-based service or application (see Chapter 8). When designing such interactions, a solid understanding of interface design guidelines, your audience, and their goals should help you make the right decisions. While each instance of form use may have a unique solution, the three lexicons of Web usability can help all forms communicate more effectively.

ASK THE RIGHT QUESTIONS

The primary role of all forms is to request information from your audience. Because you can collect audience input in numerous ways (see sidebar), you need to make sure that the forms you design clearly communicate what information is being requested and how it should be provided. In other words, you should ask the right questions.

For example, though you might initially think getting someone's phone number through an online form is a simple task, you actually need to consider several factors. First, you need to decide which interface element is right for the type of information you're collecting. In this case, it's pretty clear that a text box will work much better than drop-down menus, checkboxes, or radio buttons. The text box is compact and quick.

FORMING FORMS

Forms have several methods for collecting audience information. Text boxes, text areas, radio buttons, drop-down menus, and buttons each have their appropriate uses.

Text boxes: For collecting text information when the user's possible inputs are unknown.

Text areas: For when that text spans multiple lines.

Radio buttons: For selecting only one choice out of several provided options.

Drop-down menus: For selecting from several provided choices in a condensed format.

Checkboxes: For selecting several choices from those provided.

Buttons: For initiating actions, such as: submitting or resetting a form.

Submit

[1 ⬍][1 ⬍][1 ⬍] – [1 ⬍][1 ⬍][1 ⬍] – [1 ⬍][1 ⬍][1 ⬍][1 ⬍]

Phone Number

[   ][   ][   ]

Phone Number

[   ] ex: XXX-XXX-XXXX

Phone Number

[   ]

Phone Number

It only requires two mouse actions (click and release), whereas a drop-down version requires 30 (topmost image)!

Once you determine a text box is the best solution, you need to decide on formatting. Will the phone number be separated by dashes or spaces? Will it contain an area code? If you decide on numbers separated by dashes, make sure that your form explains this convention to your audience. The second solution (above) makes it clear through the relative size of each input field that only numbers are necessary and an area code is needed. However, this version requires your audience to skip between three input fields, thereby requiring extra keyboard or mouse actions. The third solution requires only one input field, but relies on a clarification label to let people know they need to input area code and number, separated by dashes.

The best solution might actually be the last one, which allows the input to arrive in any format and does some hidden data manipulation to get it into the format it needs. (For example, a simple script could add or remove spaces or dashes as necessary.) Notice that the size of the input field still communicates the amount of input needed (about ten digits for area code and number).

Even after these choices have been made, you're still not done. What if someone mistakenly omits a number or enters a letter instead? A well-designed form will also validate your audience's input and provide them with a descriptive error message (see Chapter 3) that indicates something is incomplete.

Lastly, you should examine the label you have chosen for your input element. Is phone number the most descriptive term, or does simply using phone work better? As a general rule, when deciding on labels, include only what is necessary for accurate understanding. Anything that does not help your audience understand your question is probably hindering it.

UNIQUE INPUT

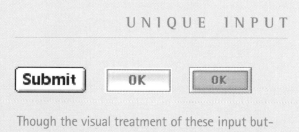

Though the visual treatment of these input buttons is different, they all maintain some visual affinities to the standard browser input element's visual presentation (most notably shape, size, and three-dimensional rendering).

This button from amazon.com not only retains the three-dimensional rendering, approximate size, and shape of the standard button (communicating its function), but it contains two significant visual presentation improvements. By placing two contrasting colors (see Chapter 5) next to each other, the text is given more visual weight than in the standard button (where it competes with the black border for attention). The addition of the arrowhead lets amazon.com's audience know more is ahead.

Though Cascading Style Sheets (CSS) allow you to alter the graphic presentation of basic form elements (not in all browsers, however), always make sure that they maintain enough common characteristics with the basic representations to be recognized. For example, replacing buttons with custom images is quite common. The images you use, however, should maintain some attributes of the three-dimensional styling that makes them look like buttons so that their role is clear to users.

MAKE CONSISTENT REQUESTS

Consistency is not just important when deciding on appropriate input elements, it also figures prominently into your form's presentation. Keeping the information requests in your forms consistent makes them easier to interpret and gives you the opportunity to highlight areas of higher importance or unique concern. For example, if all your input elements have a blue label, the one with a red label will visually contrast and therefore stand out. This difference becomes especially useful when someone has mistakenly missed a form's input field or made an error. The form can then be presented with the field in question highlighted.

In the before and after form redesign example (right), the original form did little to maintain consistency between its information requests. In the redesigned form:

> All the input labels have been consistently positioned to the left of the input field they correspond to, making it clear which labels go with which input element.

> All the form elements have been aligned, creating a clear sequence for the audience to follow.

> The size of the text boxes has been changed to reflect the amount of input needed.

> The proper input elements have been used (in this case, radio buttons for the yes/no question).

> The form section title and its input fields have been visually grouped with the use of related background colors.

> The date fields have been scripted to accept different formats, removing the need for the clarification labels.

Current Account Information

Account Number

Sub Account Number

Percentage to be placed on this account?

Proposed Start Date   MM-DD-YYYY

Proposed End Date   MM-DD-YYYY

Is this a budgeted account?

Current Account Information

Account #:

Sub Account #:

Percentage on this Account: %

Proposed Start Date:

Proposed End Date:

Is this a Budgeted Account? ◯ Yes ◉ No

CREATE A VISIBLE ORDER

Forms often consist of distinct (frequently sequential) information areas. For example, one portion of a form may ask for your shipping information, while another requests your credit card number. Sometimes it makes sense to divide these steps into separate forms. Other times, however, you prefer to have forms self-contained. Single-page forms keep related information adjacent in space: your billing and shipping information are, after all, part of the same order.

The simplest way to visually display such a sequence is through positioning. Presenting form elements from left to right (probably not practical in most Web pages, where horizontal scrolling is not common) or top to bottom makes the necessary sequence of steps clear to your audience. You can also provide macro (big picture) information about the form with the use of small multiples and visual hierarchy.

FOLLOW THE CART

In this form from amazon.com, small multiples (in the form of images) at the top of the page let you know where in the purchasing process you are, while simultaneously allowing you to jump back to any step in the process. The use of color tracks your progress and visual contrast (the more saturated text with a shopping cart stands out) provides orientation.

amazon.com

WELCOME   ADDRESS

Enter the shipping address for this order.
Enter the name and address where you'd like us to ship your order. Please also indicate whether your billing address is the same as the shipping address entered. When you're done, click the Continue button.

Full Name:
Address Line 1
(or company name):
Address Line 2
(optional):
City:
State/Province/Region:
ZIP/Postal Code:
Country: United States
Phone Number:
Is this address also your billing address? ● Yes
○ No (If not, we'll ask you for it in a moment.)

Continue ▶

Note: For APO or FPO addresses, please enter APO or FPO in the **City** field and one of the following two-letter codes in the **State** field: AE for Armed Forces Europe, Middle East, Africa, and Canada; AA for Armed Forces Americas; and AP for Armed Forces Pacific. Also make sure that you have selected United States in the **Country** field.

Visual hierarchy within forms and input elements can communicate the big picture (macro) and little details of forms. The big picture provides general and sequential information. In the amazon.com example above, the page title (in orange), the amazon.com logo, and the Continue button have more visual weight and communicate macro information (what is this page for and where to go next). Within the form labels, visual hierarchy helps to separate important information from clarifying text (as seen in the address line labels). In this manner, visual hierarchy allows you to better understand each form's intent.

HR Funding Source Change Form

Employment Information

Division: ADMIN ⇕

Group: [   ]

Social Security Number: [   ]

Employee Name: [   ] [   ]
First   Last

Annual Salary: [   ]

Position Type: Academic Professional/Faculty ⇕

Current Account Information

Account #: [   ]

Sub Account #: [   ]

Percentage on this Account: [   ] %

Proposed Start Date: [   ]

Proposed End Date: [   ]

Is this a Budgeted Account? ○ Yes
● No

Submit Information

Submit Form : [OK]

MACRO READING

In this example, color is used to provide a better sense of the distinct portions of the form (a macro view). A quick glance reveals how many steps are needed to complete the form. (Each light blue area requires distinct information.)

37 ml ℮
25 U.S.fl.oz.

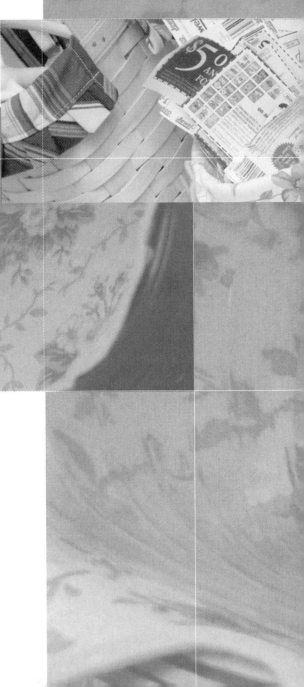

As the front door of your Web site, the home page has many important responsibilities. In addition to engaging and introducing your site to your audience, it needs to provide entry points to your content and reflect what is new or exciting within your site. That's quite a story to tell in 600 pixels of screen real estate! Luckily, the three lexicons of Web usability can help even the most cluttered home pages feel comfortable and coherent.

WHAT BELONGS AT HOME?
[SECTION TITLE]

Like the home you live in, home pages on the Web need to accommodate a wide variety of tasks. Your home is designed to make your daily tasks easy and efficient, and your Web site home page needs to be designed with the same objectives in mind. Before a house is built, careful consideration is given to how its owners will use it. Using the same logic, you need to lay the foundation for how your home page will be used. Then you can decide whether or not you need to put in that extra bedroom or set of links.

We can group the responsibilities of the home page into three categories: *introduction, entrance,* and *announcement.* Most likely, if something does not fit into one of these three categories, then it does not belong on the home page and is better off somewhere else (or nowhere else) in your site.

The *introduction* lets your audience know what your site is for and establishes an identity for the remainder of the site that the audience can rely on. An introduction is probably most useful for first-time visitors, but it can also quickly remind returning visitors of the unique features of your site.

WHAT MAKES UP A HOME PAGE?

Introduction
Describes the site
Establishes identity
Elements:
> Descriptive words
> Logo and tag line
> Short statement
> Visual presentation

Entrance
Entry to content
Explains what's inside
Elements:
> Navigation system
> Entries to services
> Search utilities

Announcement
Shows what's new
Encourages revisiting
Highlights content
Elements:
> Features, news
> Advertisements

The *entrance* provides just that — a doorway into your content. Most often, this doorway translates to having some portion of your navigation on the home page. But it could also include specific entrances to important services or features of your site. Members of your audience that have specific needs in mind will value a clear and easy path to the services and information that they seek. Those who are unsure about whether you have what they need will appreciate being able to see what you do or don't have to offer (see Chapter 2).

The *announcement* gives an indication of what is new or exciting on your site. The announcement portion of a Web site lets your audience know whether you have added items of interest and serves to highlight specials or promotions available from your company.

The example below shows the introduction, entrance, and announcement portions of the FedEx home page. Notice how all the page elements fit into one of the three categories.

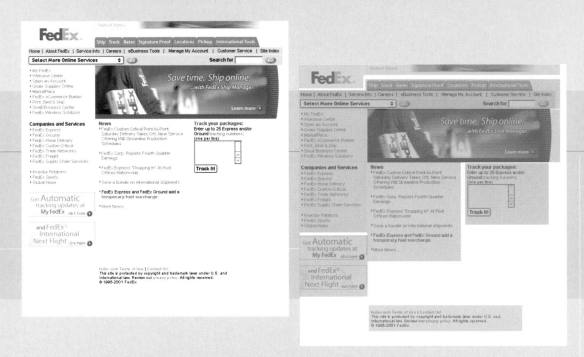

Introduction (orange highlight): The FedEx logo, color scheme, country indication, and footer information.

Entrance (purple highlight): The topmost navigation bar takes people to information related to their packages (likely the most common use of the site). The gray navigation below it consists of links to information about the FedEx corporation and the FedEx Web site. Its muted coloring gives it less visual weight than the more frequently used package navigation. Also note the Track your packages text box to the far right and the column of links on the far left.

Announcement (pink highlight): The large image serves to highlight Web site features, in this case, the ability to ship packages online. The column below the image displays recent news articles, and the animated images at bottom left highlight special company features.

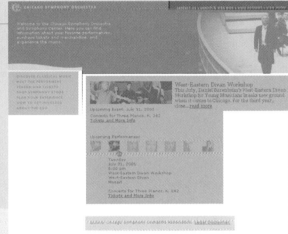

Introduction (orange highlight) - The Chicago Symphony Orchestra logo, color scheme, introductory paragraph, top image, and footer information make up the introduction to this home page. Introduction is given more space on this home page than in the FedEx example. The CSO site is far less service-oriented than FedEx and, as a result, can devote more screen real estate to visually appeal to its distinct audience.

Entrance (purple highlight): The two navigation areas allow CSO's audience to get more information about the organization and its services. Because the majority of visitors to CSO's site are interested in particular events and not general information, the entrance portion of this home page is minimal compared to the FedEx home page.

Announcement (pink highlight): The announcement portion of the CSO home page is emphasized by the use of images and white space. The white space around the announcement area helps to make the events stand out from the rest of the home page design. This use of visual organization is appropriate because more than likely visitors to CSO's home page are looking for upcoming event descriptions and information.

HOME'S CHANGING ROLE

Today's home pages do a lot more than they ever did in the past. Take a look at the evolution of the National Center for Supercomputing Applications' home page (we looked at it in the Introduction) over the years, and you can see more information and functionality appearing each year. What started off as a logo with a few links has become an information gateway for a wide range of visitors, each with their own agendas. (See the What's Inside section of this chapter.) As the content for home pages has increased, so has the need for the use of visual organization. Visual organization (Chapter 4) allows your audience to make sense of the large amounts of content needed on today's home pages.

1993

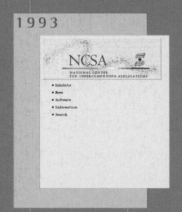

1994

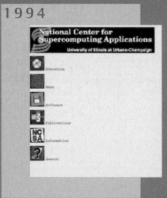

1995

1996

1997

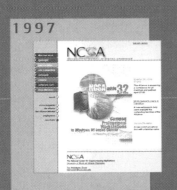

1998

1999

2001

EVERYONE WANTS TO BE AT HOME

On the Web, being at home means something different than spending time on the living room sofa. It means being seen. The home page is frequently the most visited and bookmarked page within a site. People coming to the site from personal referrals, TV and print ads, and external links are likely to encounter the home page first. As a result, items on the home page can get lots of exposure. So to get something noticed you should simply put it on the home page — right? Well, not exactly.

In this case, being selective is important. Although your site has many services to offer, it is wise to include only the most frequently utilized items on the home page, with separate links to some of the others. Likewise, you might have 50 news items, but including all of them might not be the best choice. The danger is ending up with a thoroughly cluttered and overwhelming home page. When you give your audience too many options, they won't know where to look or what to do. The first step to a successful home page design is to include only what is necessary and to forget about that extra end table.

BEFORE YOU PUT IT ON THE HOME PAGE...

Ask Yourself

Is this feature frequently used?

How important is this feature to the site's goals?

How important is this feature to the site's audience?

Is this feature's use clear, or does it require a lot of explanation?

TRAVEL CHOICES

The Expedia.com home page allows visitors to do a search for travel reservations. Having this functionality on the home page is appropriate because it's an entrance to Expedia's most frequently used services. Notice that the designers used icons to represent the available services. This technique not only allows visitors to understand what is available, but also takes up less valuable home page real estate. Also note that the flight search options are condensed — a link to more options is below.

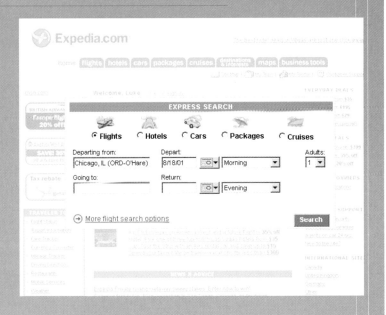

A SIMPLER HOME

In the two home page redesigns shown here, simplification reigns supreme. The Guru redesign (left) condenses four navigation choices into two easy-to-understand, consistently presented links.

The FedEx example reduces 21 choices to 14 and introduces additional visual distinctions (the log-in button and category labels) to distinguish between different types of entrance links.

A PLACE FOR COOKS

The Williams-Sonoma home page is a nice example of how designers can introduce many Web site features with relatively little screen real estate. The main activities available on the site are quite visible: shop, gift ideas, recipes, and wedding and gift registries.

Compare the Williams-Sonoma site to the Complements to the Chef site at the right. Though both sites cater to the cooking enthusiast, the Complements site has more information than is needed on its home page. Much of the site's home page content could easily reside a level or two deeper in the site.

HOUSE CLEANING

Elements that do not help your audience to understand your site's main message should not be placed on the home page. They take valuable space away from those elements which do help guide and teach your audience. Some examples of things to avoid include the following:

Most intro movies
Animated logos
Very large images
Splash pages

LEAVE IT IN THE GARAGE

Now truth be told, you might actually need that extra end table, so keeping it in the living room might not be such a bad idea after all. But putting a full size roller coaster next to that end table is by and large not a good idea. Most people recognize that placing a huge item of limited use inside their kitchen is not a good use of space. (It only gets in the way when you're trying to make dinner.) The same is true with huge useless items that appear on many home pages.

Giant spinning logos, blinking starbursts, and a whole slew of similar elements congest home pages on a regular basis. These elements do very little to enhance an audience's understanding of a Web site. How does a large animated logo help you find information about a particular product? Instead of making a purchase, you spend several minutes waiting for a larger than life identity to whiz by, just so you can click on it to enter the site.

The rule to abide by is if it doesn't help your audience to understand your site, it probably is hurting their ability to understand your site. In other words, if you have no better reason for including a home page element other than it "looks cool," you're better off leaving it in the garage and hoping someone buys it at your next yard sale.

A few years ago, the presence of Flash (Macromedia's vector-based Web content delivery platform) developed "intros" took over the Web. It seemed that every site you went to had a lengthy Flash animation to "introduce" you to the site. Most of these consisted of giant letters zooming in and out of corporate photos and rarely "introduced" viewers to more than a lengthy download time.

Luckily, many of these had Skip Intro buttons that allowed you to sidestep the movie and get into the site. After the initial novelty of these intros wore off, their unpopularity led to the popularity of a site called skipintro.com (now moved to www.skipintro.nl/). Even Macromedia, the developer of Flash software, poked fun at the irritating intros at their User Convention in New York in 2001. The photo above shows "Web superheroes" getting past a site's Flash intro.

FIRST IMPRESSIONS
[S E C T I O N   T I T L E]

There is something comforting about coming home. You know what to expect when you walk through the door. You have been there before, and it's familiar to you. Though your audience might never have been to your home page before, you want them to feel like they belong there. In order to create this feeling, you must really know your audience. If your home page does not say the right thing to your audience, they just need to hit the Back button, and they're gone. This possibility makes the introduction portion of your home page very important.

Your home page needs to introduce visitors to your organization and what makes you unique. Answer questions like "Who lives here?" and "What do they do?" You also need to consider the kind of personality your audience expects. Is your company's success based on your cutting-edge research in databases? Or are you a manufacturer of fine scented bath oils? From your home page design, your audience should be able to tell the difference.

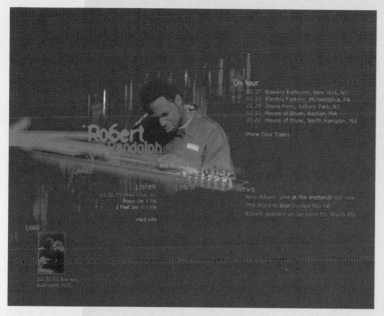

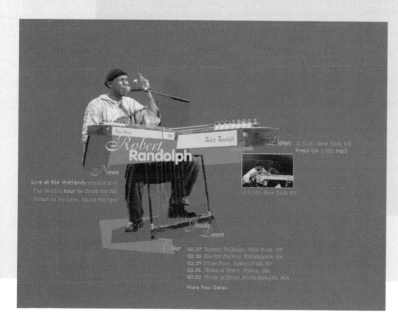

Compare the two designs for the Robert Randolph home page. Which one makes Robert's music seem like fun? Which one is more serious? Which one seems more approachable? The vibrant colors of the design on the bottom combined with the distinctive shapes used for the navigation links, and the energetic photos make for an uncommon layout. The choice of typefaces also contributes to a sense of playfulness and fun. The typefaces in the design at the top add a more serious touch to the site.

Images, colors, typefaces, and layout combine to give a design its distinct personality. Careful consideration of these elements can help you design a home page that sends the proper message to your audience. The first time your audience sees your home page, they will have an instinctive reaction to it. Funny, informative, luxurious... make sure it is the reaction you want.

One of the most important aspects of technical usability to consider when developing your home page is download time. (Well, truthfully, this depends on your audience. If they all surf the Web with a broadband connection, you have different constraints.) If you want to reach the majority of Web users, having a home page that loads quickly is important. What's even more valuable is having something worth downloading!

YOU NEVER GET A SECOND CHANCE

"You never get a second chance to make a first impression." From a technical usability standpoint, waiting several minutes as these large images download is a good way to make a poor first impression. To top it off, once these massive images download, a visitor must select their country of choice and repeat the waiting process anew. Notice only one image has an ALT tag: Welcome!

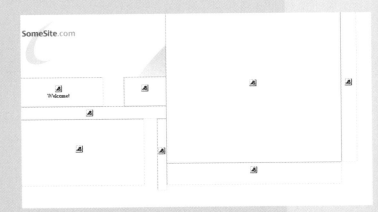

THE BIG PICTURE

Earlier in this chapter, I stated that it is probably a good idea to avoid using very large images on your home page. So why is Sapient doing it? The answer is simple: audience. Remember all design decisions should come from audience considerations. Sapient delivers high-end technology solutions to its Internet savvy clients. The majority of these clients have high-speed Internet connections, so downloading images is not a big problem. Also, Sapient's clients look to Sapient for innovative technology solutions. So it's very appropriate for Sapient's home page to do something distinct. It is Sapient's experience with the technological aspects of Web solutions that allows it to pull off this home page design. In other words, think through who your audience is before trying this at home.

WHAT'S INSIDE?
[S E C T I O N   T I T L E]

During a stroll of your favorite hometown mall, you might pass a few stores, occasionally glancing at the large window displays. The displays are there to give you a peek at the sorts of things you can expect to find once you enter the store. A quick look usually gives you a pretty good sense of what you can expect and whether or not it's of interest to you. Web sites unfortunately don't have large see-through windows (at least not yet!). But they do have home pages. And through the entrance portion of your home page, you can give your audience (the casual browser or the expert shopper) an awareness of what is inside the site. Often, you can do this by including your site's top-level navigation links and frequently used services on your home page.

CONTRACTING YOUR ENTRANCE

Giving your audience a sense of what is inside your site does not necessarily mean putting excessive links on the home page. On the Sapient home page, a small navigation box lets visitors know what the site has available for them. The four navigation options are very clear. A visitor can move their mouse over the particular section that interests them and see what content is in that section. This space-saving technique (see Chapter 2) eliminates the need for Sapient to include all 40 of its links on the home page and lets the audience choose the content that interests them.

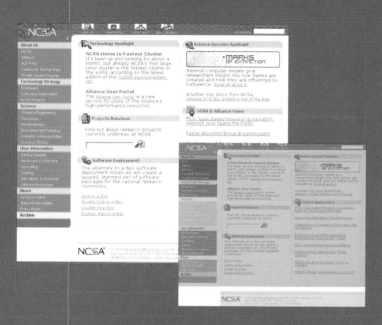

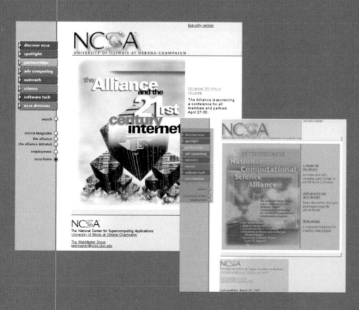

Compare the National Center for Supercomputing Applications (NCSA) home page from 1997 with the version from 2001. The colored images show the amount of screen real estate devoted to introduction (orange), announcement (pink), and entrance (blue). Prior to the redesign, NCSA received many complaints from users who "couldn't find" the content they were looking for. This was because the ~70,000 Web pages of content NCSA had were condensed into eight categories. NCSA's site is used by different types of visitors, each with their own agenda. In order to meet the expectations of a wide range of visitors, more room had to be devoted to entrance elements. The audience needed to see what was inside NCSA's site.

THE RIGHT AMOUNT OF CONTRAST

The 1997 version of the National Center for Supercomputing Applications (NCSA) home page had eight top-level navigation choices (the bright color bands on the left side of the screen). Because a diverse audience uses NCSA's site, the navigation needed to be expanded. (See sidebar on previous page.) Notice that the navigation bar on the left in the 2001 redesign of the NCSA home page no longer uses the bright colors found in the 1997 version. Instead, the entire navigation is composed of similar blue-green colors. This monochromatic color scheme results in less visual contrast within the navigation. Less contrast in the navigation allows the rest of the home page contents to be visible. In other words, the navigation does not distract from the rest of the home page because it blends together and acts as one unit: a blue-green band of color.

Let's see what would happen if the expanded navigation used the high contrast colors of the 1997 version. As you can see (below), focusing on the content to the right is very difficult.

CONTRASTING USES

The principles behind visual contrast can make a home page element stand out from the rest of the page (lots of visual weight). However, they can also be used to keep an element subdued so that it does not interfere with the rest of the page's content (little visual weight). Your audience's needs should determine how much visual weight each element should have.

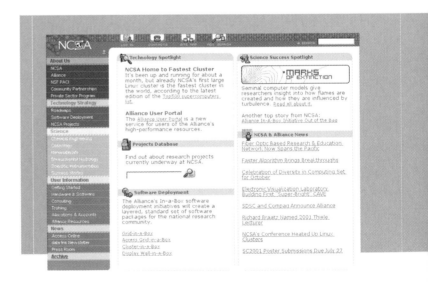

The intense colors interfere with the audience's ability to interact with the rest of the elements on the page. By reducing the contrast, you can make sure that the navigation does not distract from the rest of the page.

It's worth noting that although the contrast of the blue-green navigation bar is not a distraction from the rest of the home page, the navigation links within it still have enough contrast from their background color to be read and used.

THE LEAST AMOUNT NECESSARY

When making distinctions with visual contrast, use the least amount of contrast necessary. You don't need to go over the top with the amount of contrast you use. A little bit of contrast can go a long way.

Determining just the right amount of contrast necessary requires some work (you may have to try several options), but it's worth your while. You don't want your entrance elements to interfere with your audience's ability to interact with the rest of the page, but you also want your audience to be able to enter your site when they need to.

DON'T BOX YOURSELF IN

Because many home pages have a variety of content, many designers "box" the different sets of information into groups. This boxing is one use of visual groupings, which help the audience understand the similarities and differences between content on a home page. However, without proper consideration of visual contrast, theses boxes can go from helpful to harmful. The weather.com home page uses thick three-dimensional borders to group content. Notice that the layout seems rather crammed as a result.

Now observe the use of boxes on the Amazon.com home page. Instead of a thick three-dimensional line, Amazon.com uses the minimum amount of visual contrast necessary to visually group their content: a thin light line. The use of white space to separate the boxes combined with a thin light line separates the content much better than the thick three-dimensional lines. Though these differences may seem small, they play an important part in the bigger picture: a clear and understandable home page.

Cash for Content
The Amazon Honor System: it's time you got paid for your Web site.

Associates
Sell books, music, videos, and more from your Web site. Start earning today!

Special Features
• Buy or redeem a gift certificate
• Purchase Circles
• Amazon.com Anywhere
• Get info on new releases with Amazon.com Alerts

ENTRANCE HIERARCHY

In the FedEx Web site, the primary service that a visitor is likely to be interested in is sending or tracking a package. Therefore, it makes sense that the strongest visual elements on the page are related to these tasks. The first thing to catch your eye on the FedEx home page is the large vivid image. This image is half announcement, half entrance. It highlights the ability to ship packages online, probably one of the most common uses of the Web site. And if you didn't know you could ship online, now you do!

The second strongest visual element is probably the bright orange navigation. This bar contains links to package-related information, such as ship, track, and rates. So the two strongest visual elements map directly to the most commonly used features of the Web site. This design is a good use of visual hierarchy. Most of FedEx's audience comes expecting to find information on sending packages, and the home page design accommodates that need.

It is also worth noting that the text box in the lower right, which allows visitors to track their existing package orders with FedEx, is given visual emphasis not with strong colors, but with the presence of white space. Positioning this element in its own column and surrounding it by a large amount of white space gives it more visual weight than if it were surrounded by similar elements, such as the navigation links to the left.

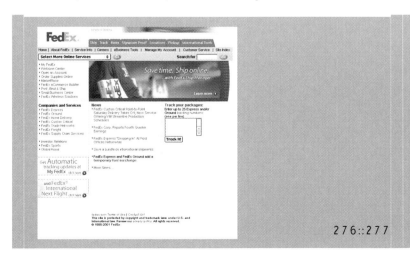

AN EVEN HIERARCHY

On the Microsoft home page, the most visual weight is given to the large bands of blue at the top and bottom of the page. Other than the announcement graphic in the center column, the remaining elements on the page have nearly equal visual weight. This homogenous visual hierarchy is probably intentional. Microsoft's audience comes to their site with differing needs and expectations. The situation is not as clear as it was with FedEx, where you knew most people came for information on packages. Microsoft's audience comes to download software, troubleshoot an operating system bug, find out about the corporation's educational policies, and more. Therefore, the goal of the home page is to help diverse users with varied needs get to information quickly and easily.

GROUPING ENTRANCES

On the Microsoft home page, the navigation items in the top and bottom blue bars consist of general categories of information, such as search, training, about, and contact us. Their similarity (in function) is emphasized by the use of a common background color. In other words, they have a visual relationship, which lets the audience understand they are likely to find related content (in this case general information links) within the two bars.

BACKGROUND RELATIONSHIPS

Using a common background color for several elements is a common way to emphasize that they are related because of subject matter, functionality, and so on.

Another use of visual groupings occurs in the leftmost column, which contains specific information links, such as the Office product family, information for Microsoft partners, and bCentral resources. This column is distinguished from the rest of the page with a light gray background color. (Note that the color is very light and, as a result, does not interfere with your ability to read the text. In fact, it makes the text easier to read by reducing the contrast between text and background — see Chapter 6.) This use of background color simultaneously separates the column from the rest of the page and helps to group the information within the column. Though the column contains three sections, the use of visual grouping lets the audience understand that they are related. To be exact, they are all specific links to information commonly sought on the Microsoft site.

The column also contains further categorization. A thin gray line and the bold font of the category titles help to visually separate the three categories (product families, information for, and resources). Here, you can see visual groupings working to separate information into logical categories. The repetition of the gray line and bold font makes it clear that you're dealing with three related but distinct categories.

You can see the same thing happening in the middle column. The four features in the column are visually represented in the same manner (light blue line, bold blue headline, and black explanation text). Therefore, once you understand that one of them is a highlighted feature of the Web site, you know the others are, too.

Boost team collaboration.
Just one of a dozen reasons why upgrading to Office XP makes sense.

You also know that the explanation of each feature appears in black text under the blue headline. Visual organization makes it clear.

In the rightmost column of the Microsoft home page, the headlines are not bold, but in the same blue color as the feature headlines, and with the same black text underneath them. The understanding gained from the features translates directly to these news items. In other words, you know the blue text is a headline you can click on for more information, and you know the black text below it further explains the headline.

• Get started on Visual
  Basic .NET
  with new Beta 2 code
  samples.

In this example, you can see how the visual treatment of one set of home page elements can in turn help your audience understand another set of elements, which are similar.

Visual organization principles can help your audience understand what to expect from the different types of entrances available on your home page. Your audience doesn't need to wonder what can be found within the site because visual organization makes it clear.

The mall's window displays we were admiring in the last section frequently get covered up with large SALE signs that advertise the store's latest specials or new arrivals. Sometimes, a window contains so many advertised specials, you can't even see inside! Like your favorite stores, Web sites also have changes they would like you to know about. But like too many SALE signs, the announcement portion of your home page shouldn't distract from the rest of the content. An excessive amount of announcements can lead to clutter and audience confusion.

Instead, think about limiting the amount of announcements on your page. A few well-placed features can often make more of an impact than lots of randomly inserted ones. This principle is especially true when visual hierarchy is used to guide your audience through the story your announcements tell. Each announcement has its place in the hierarchy: It is either just as or more important than the rest. Managing the distribution of visual weight on your home page helps put announcements in their place.

WORKING TOGETHER

The Apple home page has many announcements — 12, to be exact. Yet the page does not seem cluttered. In fact, it feels rather comfortable. This perception is made possible by the clear visual hierarchy on the page. The featured announcement is the one given the most visual emphasis. (In this case, it's the "Pro create" Ad.) Not only does the size of this image cause it to be very noticeable, the use of white space around the image also brings it to the forefront. This announcement is the one Apple wants to make sure that its audience notices first, and therefore it is at the top of the page's visual hierarchy.

TEAM WORK

When elements on a home page work together instead of competing for your audience's attention, they are more likely to be noticed by your audience.

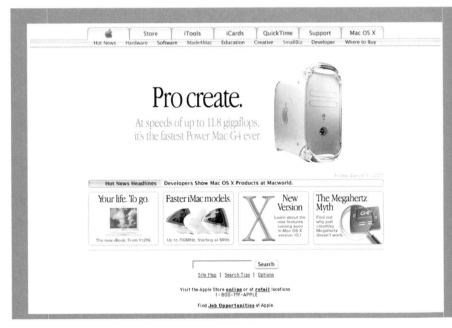

The row of four images below the featured announcement is the second item in the home page's visual hierarchy. These images are equally important to Apple's audience, and as a result, they are given equal visual weight and similar visual treatment. These four announcements do not compete with each other for their audience's attention: None of them tries to be louder than the others. Because they work together as a team to draw the audience's attention, they all get noticed more. Once your visitors focus on the full row, they can then examine each announcement in turn. This way, everyone gets noticed. Go team!

GETTING NOTICED

When you have a clear home page hierarchy, you automatically gain the ability to get things noticed. As your site changes (and it will), you will need to bring new content or features to your audience's attention. To give things more attention, just increase their visual weight. In other words, add more contrast. You can accomplish this task by adding or removing white space, adding motion (see sidebar on next page), increasing or decreasing the size of page elements, changing the colors, textures, shapes, and direction of elements, and more.

THERE IS NO I IN TEAM

This example is so stricken with "ad-fever" — that is, it's difficult to know where to look — there is no sense of visual hierarchy here. Instead, every element is competing for the audience's attention, and it's clearly not a team effort. The home page should work together to communicate the right message to your audience. On this page, everyone wants to be the star and, as a result, no one wins.

In the Design Interact site, the majority of the content consists of a featured company, a site of the week, and an interview with a designer in the field. This content changes frequently. Therefore, it's important for Design Interact's audience to see what has changed each time they revisit the home page.

Visual contrast helps make the changes apparent. The three featured areas contain vibrant colors and are larger than the rest of the elements on the page. The monochromatic color scheme (aqua-blue) used for the other interface elements gives the rest of the page a sense of unity. As a result, the three features stand out, and the rest of the page blends together and fades back. This treatment allows Design Interact's audience to quickly see what is new in the site from the home page.

NEWS IN MOTION

The Apple news ticker scrolls a total of six headlines. That's quite a lot of news for such a small area, so you might be wondering, "How is this tiny band supposed to get noticed by the audience?" Although the band is not large in size nor colorful, it still gets noticed— through the use of motion. The band is the only element on the home page to be animated. As a result, it catches the audience's attention. Keep in mind that the animation is not fast or annoying. Instead, it gently brings up an occasional news headline. The news band uses just enough motion to get noticed, yet not enough to distract.

	Saturday August 4, 2001
Hot News Headlines	
Hot News Headlines IDC Reports	Saturday August 4, 2001
Hot News Headlines IDC Reports That Apple	Saturday August 4, 2001
Hot News Headlines IDC Reports That Apple Leads K-12	Saturday August 4, 2001
Hot News Headlines IDC Reports That Apple Leads K-12 Education Market.	Saturday August 4, 2001

Whenever you increase the visual weight of any element on your home page, you need to be aware of how the rest of the visual hierarchy is affected. Often times, when you increase the visual weight of one element, you will have to decrease it for other elements. If not, you might end up with too many elements at an equal visual weight fighting for your audience's attention. Instead of giving your featured announcement more attention, you will have done just the opposite. Remember that a clear hierarchy can only be achieved with balance. We gauge the visual weight of an element based on what we see around it. (We only know what is big because we understand what is small.) In order for one element to come forward, others may need to retreat: all for the good of the big picture.

Though static Web pages continue to remain numerous and valuable, two increasingly popular trends allow Web designers to provide applicable content and compelling interactions for their audience. Dynamic publishing technologies make use of database connectivity to significantly reduce the amount of work needed to maintain current content. Web applications, on the other hand, introduce services beyond basic information retrieval that include sophisticated interactions and the ability to get work done. Both of these soon-to-be commonplace strategies require a distinct set of design considerations to effectively communicate. Dynamic content relies on a "templating" design approach, whereas Web applications are often independent of the browsing metaphor that is the cornerstone of effective Web surfing.

A WEB IN NEED

After the 2001 dot-com "shake-out" (and subsequent economic slump), lots of people came to realize that it's not that easy to make money online. Sure, you'll still see the occasional net-millionaire pop up, but if dot-com stock prices are any indication, the odds are not in your favor. (However, you can rest assured that knowing the three lexicons of Web usability can significantly improve your Web product and thereby increase your chances of success, but you already knew that. After all, you are reading this book.)

Lots of factors contribute to the problems that led to the fall of many a dot-com. Faulty business models and usability issues aside, a few causes are worth examining because they directly relate to the challenges of Web publishing and help explain the continually increasing popularity of dynamic content publishing and Web-based applications.

Dynamic content and Web applications emerged as solutions to (and natural outgrowths from) the difficulties faced by many Web companies. It quickly became apparent that static HTML pages were only effective to a certain point. As Web companies grew, that point became a series of stumbling blocks that confirmed a new approach had to be employed. In order to appreciate dynamic content and Web applications, it helps to look at some of these stumbling blocks and how they can be overcome.

THE DYNAMIC ADVANTAGE

The first few stumbling blocks we can look at are the challenges associated with maintaining useful content. In order for content to be useful, it needs to not only be informative but applicable as well. In many cases, being applicable includes being current (last week's weather probably won't help me today). I mentioned earlier in the book the multitude of "ghost sites" that still sit in cyberspace providing testament to the fact that consistently updating a site is not an easy task. First of all, it takes time. Second, it takes skills. If you have a site consisting mostly of static HTML pages, updating them requires generating new content, updating HTML code, uploading to a server, and more.

While it's true that many tools exist that can assist with this process, they still require some basic skills and an understanding of the Web development environment (what is a Web page, what is a Web server, what is HTML, and so on). They also require time to learn and utilize. A better solution is dynamic content publishing, which allows you to effectively separate content and formatting (most often through the use of databases and formatting templates).

With dynamic content publishing, the need to understand the Web environment is removed and up-to-date content can be automatically distributed to an entire site by just about anyone (including computers). This process eliminates the time needed for updates by trained personnel, thereby alleviating many of the costs associated with content delivery.

With dynamic content publishing, it's also possible to get closer to one of the original goals of the World Wide Web: the separation of content and formatting. The initial structure of HTML marked up content in an informative manner: paragraph tags marked body text, header tags indicated section headers, and so on. This system was designed to label each portion of a document's content by what it was, not how it should look. Within such a system, each computer that accessed an HTML document would display it in a way that made it clear what was a paragraph and what was a section header. This system effectively separated content and formatting by letting each machine display the page in an appropriate (but often unique) manner.

XML IS COMING

If you have been keeping up with Web technologies, you have no doubt heard about the Extensible Mark-up Language (XML) that promises to re-shape the very Web we weave. Sometimes called HTML on steroids, XML does a great job of separating content and formatting. In fact, it allows you to mark up content in a far more informative way than HTML ever could. For example, a simple XML page for a weather report might look like this one adapted from Simon St. Laurent's informative book, *XML: A Primer* (MIS Press, 1998). Notice that the tags describe the content they surround instead of simply specifying formatting.

```
<WEATHERREPORT>
<DATE>07-24-02</DATE>
<CITY>Champaign</CITY>
<STATE>IL</STATE>
<COUNTRY>USA</COUNTRY>
<HIGH SCALE="F">98</HIGH>
<LOW SCALE="F">82</LOW>
</WEATHERREPORT>
```

Once the Web became graphical and popular, however, HTML content and formatting merged. Designers used tables and headers to create effective layouts, not content distinctions. And additional tags were added by browser vendors, such as FONT (which has since been depreciated in HTML 4.0), to meet the presentation needs of corporations and individuals. Pretty soon most HTML code was written in an attempt to achieve a cohesive layout (formatting) instead of to make content distinctions.

Such HTML code carries several disadvantages with it. First, it often becomes rather complex. Second, it buries the content underneath piles of code making it difficult to update, especially at the sitewide level. By separating content (usually in databases) and formatting (usually in templates and style sheets), dynamic content publishing makes it easier to automatically update sites. For example, the same content database could be pooled and presented within distinct templates: one for older browsers, one for newer browsers, or one for my personal display preferences and one for yours. (I'll talk more about the power of templates later on in this chapter.)

Publishing content dynamically has the added benefit of customization. In other words, with an effective dynamic content publishing system, you can deliver applicable content to distinct visitors. As an example, amazon.com provides me with custom-tailored links to materials relevant to my interests (see sidebar). These links not only create a great marketing opportunity, they also help build long-lasting customer relationships by recognizing that each audience member is unique and has distinct interests.

MY VERY OWN CONTENT

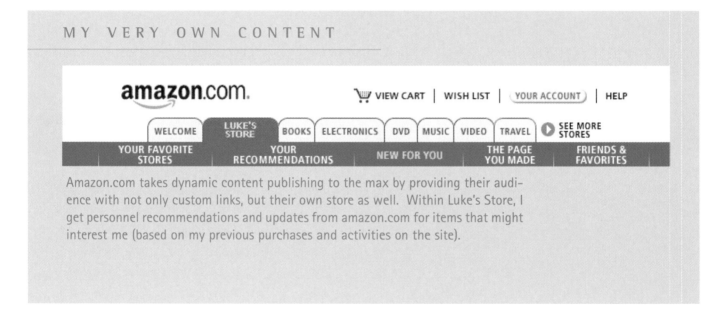

Amazon.com takes dynamic content publishing to the max by providing their audience with not only custom links, but their own store as well. Within Luke's Store, I get personnel recommendations and updates from amazon.com for items that might interest me (based on my previous purchases and activities on the site).

NO LONGER JUST BROWSING

The second set of stumbling blocks we can look at, before jumping into the specifics of dynamic content, originate from the nature of most Web interactions. The bulk of Web sites currently only provide information. While this information is extremely valuable and arguably what made the Web popular in the first place, it's rarely a sustainable source of income for Web entrepreneurs. With the tumbling cost of Web advertising, making a profit from delivering content alone is increasingly difficult. Instead, many organizations have turned to offering online services (in the form of Web applications) that provide valuable services for their customers.

It is worthwhile to point out here that there are many situations where solely delivering content can be a very profitable undertaking. As an example, a corporation that migrates the majority of its technical support documentation to the Web can save time and money. Likewise, any organization seeking to distribute information to a global audience has a relatively inexpensive means to do so through its Web presence. But for organizations and individuals seeking to make a living from publishing Web content, the current situation is discouraging.

Not only are advertisers offering less for ad space (and Web surfers more intent on ignoring the annoying banner ads that clutter their Web experience), but the difficulties with directly charging your audience for content are not easily remedied. The majority of the Web-scouring public firmly believe that the information they find online should be free. These expectations have been reinforced for years and arose from the original design and intent of the Web [1] (which initially served as a means to freely exchange information between researchers). In other words, don't look to get rich from subscription services to your content anytime soon.

[1] If you are interested in learning more about the original intentions behind the World Wide Web, pick up *Weaving the Web: The Original Intent and Ultimate Destiny of the World Wide Web* (Harper Business, 1999) by Tim Berners-Lee.

Instead, many Web business ventures have turned their sights to Web-based applications. Web applications can be loosely defined as serious software being delivered as a service online. The term "serious" is applied because Web applications do not include simple forms or basic applets that accomplish little beyond collecting information (Wroblewski & Rantanen, 2001). Web applications range from systems for taking university-level courses online (Unext's Cardean University) to team organization tools (Microsoft's SharePoint Team Services).

These applications provide value to Web audiences by allowing them to create, collaborate, collect, and more. As such, they form the basis for the next generation of Web use: a step beyond simple searching and browsing of Web pages. The benefits of Web services can be illustrated by the fact that many successful Web-only companies are service based: Ebay and Paypal, for example.

PROVIDING SERVICES

Microsoft's SharePoint Team Services Web application allows groups to coordinate events, share documents, and collaborate within a customized Web site. This example highlights the Events interface that allows members to create, modify, share, or delete team events. That's quite a few steps beyond what most Web sites can handle.

Web applications can also add value to the Web sites of "brick and mortar" companies as well. An online system for managing your checking account at a bank's site or an online exercise program at your health club's site are just a few possibilities.

DYNAMIC DESIGNS

Let's face it: The Web is a medium fraught with variables. We have seen how the differences in browsers, their settings, monitors, and operating systems can alter carefully constructed layouts, much to the frustration of designers. In fact, it often seems that the only constant in Web design is variation. This situation is the exact opposite found in many other communication mediums. For example, a printed poster not only maintains the exact colors and typefaces you chose, but it does so regardless of where the piece is viewed: at home or in China. (No wonder many designers coming from the print world end up fighting against the very nature of the Web.)

As we all know, it is much better to fight your battles with somebody than against them. This advice is especially good for Web design. Instead of fighting against the variable nature of Web pages by creating increasingly complex HTML code that is difficult to update (or resorting to massive amounts of images to maintain a consistent layout), try making variables your ally, not your enemy.

Dynamic content publishing mirrors the nature of the Web itself by making use of variables for content delivery. As a simple example, we can think of the current date as one variable and display only content that is up-to-date. Or we might consider each distinct visitor a variable and customize the content they see to their liking. The basic principle behind both of these scenarios is the same: Applicable content is automatically displayed based on the current situation (date or visitor). The key to this type of system is being able to distinguish between content and its formatting rules.

THINK IT THROUGH

Careful initial thought to how and where content can be applied within your site should always precede any dynamic publishing development efforts. This forethought is especially important because the initial construction of dynamic systems takes a lot of up-front work and can be expensive. After these systems are up and running, however, maintenance time and costs are significantly lower. If you find you must return to the construction phase to fix errors, odds are you will also return to spending lots of time and money.

GETTING TO CONTENT

The basic principle behind many forms of dynamic publishing is that data (content) sits in one location and the means for displaying it (formatting) sits in another. When it comes time to present content to your audience, you grab the appropriate data, run it through the "format ringer," — and presto, you have properly formatted, applicable content for your audience.

The diagram (right) details a rather basic dynamic content publishing system. When a visitor makes a page request, a Data Retriever script pulls the appropriate content from a database, sends it to a Code Generator script that wraps the content with the appropriate styles (from a series of templates), and sends it back to the browser as viewable HTML (or XML, SVG, and so on) code. All of this process happens on the server and is hidden from the Web user, who only sees the finished HTML page pop up in his browser.

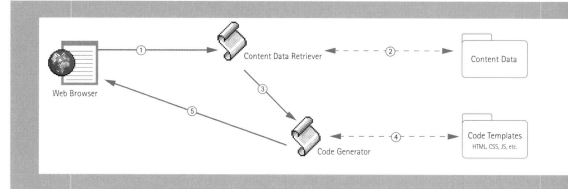

Though this schematic is simple, most dynamic content publishing systems are even easier to understand and implement. Dynamic systems like Microsoft's ASP (Active Server Pages), Macromedia's ColdFusion, PHP, and CGI/Perl allow you to simply create Web documents (which consist of HTML code and some scripting) that communicate with databases; The majority of each system's complexity is hidden from you.

The diagram below shows how ASP or CFML code embedded within in an HTML page sends a request to the server for content and displays the formatted end result to the user. The only things Web developers are responsible for are creating templates, setting up a database, and making sure that the system works (not too difficult of a task with ASP or ColdFusion).

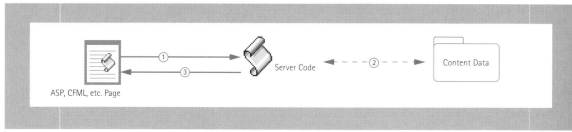

The good news for *content providers* (those responsible for creating content for the Web site) is that they never have to see HTML code again. They simply copy and paste their additions into a database (this could easily happen through a Web-accessible form or other convenient means), and it's online, saving time and keeping the site current and correct. (This ability means never having to wait all weekend for the Web programmer to return and fix a spelling error or incorrect date on your corporate site again).

We can also add a layer of complexity to dynamic publishing systems for the added benefit of user recognition and custom content delivery. The diagram below adds a database of User Information that could store user-specified settings or previous content interests such as recent purchases. This system would first consult the user database to see what content it should grab from the content database and then wrap it in the proper template (which could easily be custom tailored for the individual).

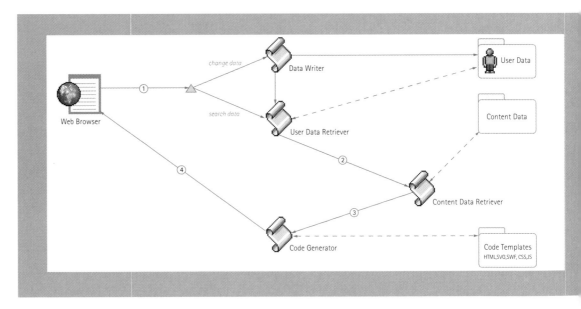

Delivering custom content for individuals has numerous advantages, including specific marketing opportunities, growth of customer relationships, interface simplification, and more.

TEMPLATE POWER

No dynamic content publishing system is complete without effective visual presentation templates. Templates take stark content and transform it into the usable Web pages that are the subject of this book. Templates can contain navigation systems, formatting rules, footers, and a whole lot more. As a result, they can ensure sitewide interface consistency, greatly ease the updating process, and help you make the most of your content.

In order to understand the power of templates, we can look at a Server Side Include (SSI) system for a relatively large site. The diagram below shows how the reused portions of a site (the top navigation bar and footer) can be divided into separate HTML files that "wrap" around any given content — essentially creating formatted pages on the fly.

In order to modify the navigation system, for example, only one include file (include-header.html) needs to be changed, and the entire site reflects the modification. That result is quite a savings in time: Just imagine sifting through hundreds of pages to make a small grammatical

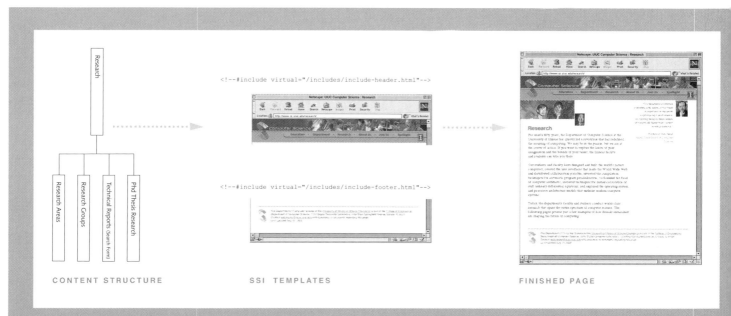

CONTENT STRUCTURE   SSI TEMPLATES   FINISHED PAGE

2 IS THE MAGIC NUMBER

Truthfully, when accommodating for browser variables, you only really "have" to consider two groups of two: preversion 4.0 browsers by both Netscape and Microsoft, and the differences between Netscape Navigator and Microsoft Internet Explorer. While other browsers and issues exist, your decision to devote development and design time to accommodating them should be based on your audience. (Use Web logs to see what kinds of browsers your audience brings to your site.)

change in the navigation bar. Though such tedious updates sound far-fetched today, not too long ago, the majority of Web page updates were still done by hand. (Well truthfully, most people charged with such a chore turned to scripts to solve the problem, but woe to the nonprogrammer with even 50 pages to update.)

This type of SSI system also helps to maintain sitewide consistency, regardless of where Web page content happens to originate. Anyone wishing to create a new page only has to add one line of server code to include an entire navigation system or set of formatting rules. For anyone charged with the upkeep of a large Web site, template systems are a valuable means of maintaining control over look and feel and interface consistency.

Templates can likewise assist with the variable display issues found in different browsers and operating systems. If a user comes to your site with an older browser, simply wrap the content you're presenting to them with a template designed to accommodate the lack of presentation features in preversion 4.0 Web browsers (most notably a lack of style sheet support). If they arrive with a newer browser, by all means use the template designed to take advantage of the latest browser features.

Relying on templates to accommodate browser and operating system variables eliminates the need to create two versions of your site (see Chapter 3). Simply wrap the appropriate template around your content. Your audience never has to know you have made any adjustments for their browser.

Within a more complex dynamic content publishing system (where content sits in a database), templates can assist in maximizing the potential of content. Applying portions of content in the right places can breathe new life and immediacy into your site (see sidebar at right).

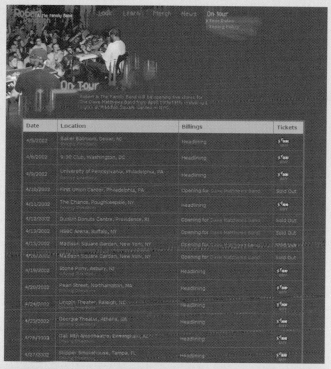

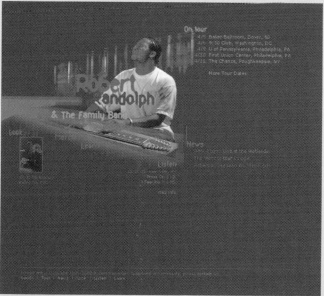

In the Robert Randolph site shown here, a database of tour dates is used to automatically keep both the home page and tour schedule page current. Though both pages use ASP code to access the same database, the home page only displays dates and location information for the current week's show. The tour page, on the other hand, shows all the information for each show, including billing, ticketing, and location information.

The inclusion of the most recent tour dates on the home page keeps the site's entrance current. You could even add some immediacy to other static pages, such as the biography page, with a small "Where is Robert now?" section that automatically displays the current tour date. This way, you can use the same data throughout the site to automatically create an active, up-to-date experience for users.

Templates themselves can also be dynamic (see sidebar below). For example, introducing variable recognition into your templates could allow your navigation system include file to automatically reflect a user's current location with a You Are Here indicator. Or, perhaps a variable within your template could alter a user specific preference such as color or text size.

TEMPLATE VARIABLES

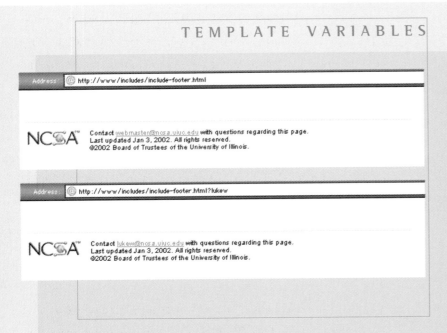

In this footer template, the contact link is dynamically inserted based on who is responsible for the page's content. If the URL has no query string (the variable following a question mark in the URL), the default Webmaster e-mail link is used (top image).

Otherwise, the page's owner can include a query string to alter the contact information (lukew in the example below).

This way, you can use the same footer include file throughout the site (maintaining consistency) with the proper contact information still included.

KNOW WHAT TO EXPECT

The key to designing effective templates comes from an understanding of the systems that deliver your content and an appreciation of "rule-based design." In other words, templates have to know what is coming and what to do with the content once it gets there.

Because content coming from databases is variable, it can't be specifically designed; instead, you are designing "rules" for how it will be presented to your audience. These rules need to be based on an understanding of the different parts of your content. You will need to think about the amount of content you expect: Will it disrupt the layout? Is it too much for one HTML page? You also need to consider the type of content you are dealing with: What kind of internal hierarchy does it need to communicate clearly? When is it most useful to your audience? Create flexible layouts that can deal with variable amounts of content.

GENERATION PLEX
[SECTION TITLE]

The instant popularity of the World Wide Web quickly resulted in a massive transfer of information-rich content to cyberspace. Corporations and individuals alike rushed to put up informative sites on everything from their current products to specialized hamster feeding techniques, and quite quickly, the information superhighway was born.

The general means of traversing this highway (your Web browser) works hard to make browsing and searching vast seas of information easy. All of a Web browser's interface elements are designed to get you to and from information: the Back, Forward, and Home buttons, the Address Bar, the Favorites menu, and so on (see Chapter 3). Heck, they even call it a "browser." However, as the Web continues to grow, new types of interactions are not only possible but unavoidable. As Donald Norman has pointed out, "Services, rather than browsing, are the future" of the Web (Norman, 2000).

The future of online interactions is in Web applications that allow you to do everything from organizing your book collection (www.spinfree.com/singlefile/) to exchanging currencies online (www.fxtrades.com). In other words, Web applications allow you to go beyond simple information browsing and provide a powerful means to get real work done. Such Web applications often include complex interactions with data and people that are poorly supported in a browser environment. (Your Web browser is optimized for information retrieval, not maintaining a checking account.) Understanding what makes Web applications distinct from Web sites allows you to design appropriate interfaces that effectively communicate and don't confuse your audience when they transition from your Web site to your Web-based services (which is a frequent occurrence, because most Web applications are embedded within larger Web sites).

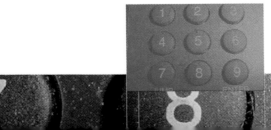

OUR COMPLEX NATURE

Web applications can best be thought of as half Web site, half client application (programs that run on your desktop). The majority of the technical Web usability guidelines I discuss in Chapter 3 are designed with Web sites in mind. (Visual communication and look and feel considerations, of course, apply to all forms of interface design.) These guidelines attempt to optimize Web pages within the browsing interface model that keeps the Web wired together. Web applications, however, contrast with Web pages in several ways.

Not only are most Web applications more interactive than standard Web sites (you are, after all, doing a lot more than just surfing), but the interactions you're likely to find within Web applications tend to be more complex. In addition, many of these interactions are unique, exhibiting dramatic differences in design and workflow. For example, the manner in which you maintain and work with your exercise data on one health club's site might be quite different at a competitor's site. On the other hand, following links on the two sites is likely to be quite similar.

Web applications are also likely to be used more intensively than regular Web sites. Because your audience wants the services your Web application offers them, they are more likely to spend extended periods of time learning and interacting with a Web application interface (Norman, 2000). The payoff is worth the investment of their time: They get things done (hopefully in an easy manner). The opposite is often true in Web pages, where your audience will move on if they cannot quickly make sense of your site (Nielsen, 2000). (Remember the short attentions spans I discussed in Chapter 3?)

Technical Web usability guidelines aim to optimize just this type of rapid information surfing. Page scanning, download time minimization, and more are intended to make browsing fast and effective. Web applications, on the other hand, may require some time to master. But the payoff is increased productivity and efficiency.

Client applications more closely mirror the kinds of interactions you are likely to find within Web applications. But trying to apply client application interface guidelines (such as those found in Apple, 1992) to Web

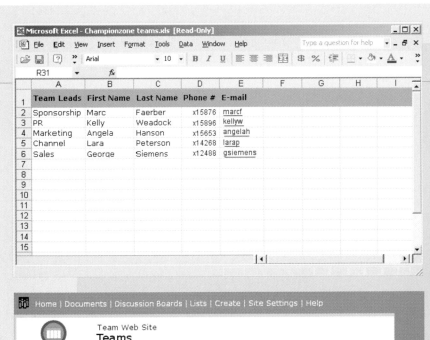

WEB VS. CLIENT

Here, we see the same spreadsheet within a common client application (Microsoft Excel 2000) and within a Web application (Microsoft SharePoint Team Services). Though these two interfaces share many similarities in, notice that the SharePoint example looks more like a Web page. This difference is because the limitations and conventions of the Web have been taken into consideration in its design.

applications is not the answer either. These guidelines do not address the most limiting and compelling factor of Web application design: the Web itself. Because Web services are accessed through a browser, your audience will instinctually perceive their use to be similar to a Web page. This perception especially becomes problematic when they attempt to utilize the Back button to undo actions or go for the browser's Save option to back up their work.

The limitations of the Web also pose unique problems for users. Downloading delays and connection errors need special accommodations, as does the limited amount of presentation control possible within HMTL layouts. (Remember the font sizing issues in chapter 6?)

Finally, many Web applications do not exist as stand-alone entities. Instead, they are an integral part of a corporation's unified Web presence. To maintain a consistent user experience from Web site to Web application, the visual presentation of a Web application needs to reflect the design and personality of its host site. This constraint is not typically found in client application design.

DOING OUR OWN THING

The same visual communication considerations we examined in Chapters 4 and 5 still hold ground in the more complex world of Web applications. But several technical Web usability guidelines (see Chapter 3) fall short when you're designing Web applications. The expectations and goals of your audience are quite different, in particular the limitations of attention and consistency with the browsing model of the Web. Not only are these design considerations no longer applicable, they could even be detrimental to Web application usability.

VISUALLY IT'S ALL THE SAME

Though Web applications incorporate more complex forms of interaction than most Web pages, the visual communication principles that allow them to effectively communicate with your audience remain the same. Note the use of visual hierarchy, grouping, contrast, indication, and consistency in this screen layout, and you will see how you can apply the lessons learned in Chapters 4 and 5 to just about any form of interaction the Web throws at you.

The first step to creating a Web application that effectively communicates is letting it speak its own language. Doing so often means separating it from the interaction model of the Web browser, accomplished by using full-screen mode or a new browser-less window (see sidebar at right). A devoted screen not only allows your audience to focus on the Web application's unique interface, it also maximizes the display area available for the application.

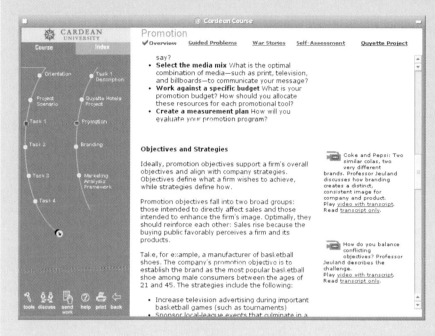

A common practice when presenting Web applications is making use of a new window without browser tools. Though this practice is not good for most Web pages, it is recommended for Web applications. The elimination of the browser's tools and menus allows users to focus on the interaction model present within the Web application (In this example, one of Cardean University's online courses). This practice removes distracting interface elements that lose their value.

For example, the Web browser's address bar is not necessary when interacting with a Web application. It is also no longer informative because most URLs created by Web applications provide no sense of orientation. (They generally consist of meaningless strings of characters.)

Second, the tools a Web application needs to effectively communicate are frequently more complex than those found on standard Web pages. Nonstandard interactions (see sidebar on the next page), frames, plug-in technologies (see sidebar 2), and more can increase Web application usability by adding functionality, alleviating Web page shortcomings, and allowing designers to make use of motion, sound, richer information displays, and three-dimensional interactions.

BEING NONSTANDARD

Avoiding nonstandard interactions within Web sites is generally a good idea. However, nonstandard interactions often come in handy in Web applications. In this example, a drag-and-drop approach to organizing content is utilized. Direct manipulation (used here) allows the audience to see the results of their actions as they are being performed. This way, the audience feels that they control the objects represented on the screen (a great use of feedback).

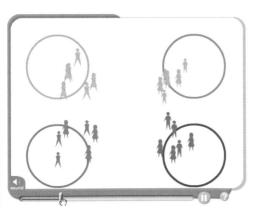

BEYOND HTML

Cardean University's online higher education classes make use of unique technologies to support richer forms of interaction and communication than those found in static HTML pages.

For example, Macromedia's Flash technology is used here to illustrate advanced concepts through motion. Also, Flash allows this information presentation to appear identically between different browsers and platforms. As a result, it's a great way to make sure that everybody gets the right message.

Standard Web page elements, such as links and form elements, however, are still used within most Web applications and should function consistently from Web site to Web application. This consistent approach allows your audience to transfer the skills they already have (from using the Web) and apply them to the unique interactions found in your Web applications.

EXPLAIN YOURSELF

While SharePoint makes use of common links (found on all Web sites) within its interface, it uses adjacent images (see Chapter 3) to distinguish between action links ("New Item", Export Event", and so on) and navigation links ("Go back to list" and the top navigation bar).

MORE TO COME

Web applications are still in their infancy. As a result, many of them are being solely assembled by developers without due consideration to how they visually communicate. We encountered the same situation in the early days of the Web. The focus was on the technology and not the user experience. As a result, many Web pages were confusing and cryptic. Avoiding this situation in the next generation of Web tools (Web applications) is dependent on proper use of visual communication principles to create Web services that say the right thing to their audience. Stay tuned.

CONCLUSION:

WHAT'S NEXT

The more things change, the more they stay the same.

Although the World Wide Web initially threatened to undermine this age-old kernel of truth through promises of "with the Web everything is different," time (and the recent dot-com downfall) once again proved otherwise. Though the Web is a unique communication medium, it is still subject to the same rules that govern business, perception, usability, and more.

The same holds true for the myriad technologies and mediums that promise to be "the next big thing." From smart rooms to information appliances, you can rest assured that your ability to understand your audience and their goals, to meet their expectations, and to communicate will enable you to design effective and appropriate solutions.

Whatever form the next big thing takes, the visual communication principles outlined in this book will still hold weight. The manner in which human beings make sense of visual information is not going to change. As a result, you can rely on visual hierarchy and contrast to work in the same way on information appliance interfaces as they do on traditional brochure designs.

In other words, the design methodology and communication skills presented in this book will outlive the Web and the technologies that come after it. As long as we're using our eyes to make sense of the world around us, visual communication will be there to provide meaning.

Admittedly, the Web still has a long life ahead of it, though it may not be in a form you will readily associate with the images in this book. The long-term trend you can count on is that the Web will progressively be hidden from view. That is, you won't have to know if the gas pump from which you receive traffic updates or the oven in your kitchen that quickly downloads a new recipe into its instruction set are both connected to the Web. Instead, you will go through your daily life making use of the information provided by the Web without knowing it is there. The days of typing "http://" will be distant memories, but the information online will be more useful than ever before.

This notion of a "hidden" Web mirrors some of the more tangible changes that are happening online right now. In particular, simplification, customization, service distribution, content separation, and new device applications promise to outline the course the Web will take in the next few years.

Simplification: This trend can and should be applied to all aspects of our lives, not just the Web. We are currently in a state of often overwhelming complexity. Each new product designed to "ease" our lives often just makes them more complicated. Our cell phones have more features than we can learn in a day. When deciding what to make for dinner, we have thousands of cookbooks and even more online recipes to choose from. Though these seem like inconsequential examples, the sum of thousands of these kinds of options adds to an awful lot of complexity to our lives.

We can see this same complexity on almost every Web site. Home pages are full of choices, too many choices. Not only do these options add clutter, they force us to relearn each time we visit a new site. (This is probably the reason many people return to the few sites they have taken the time to learn.) I believe in the near future you will see many sites re-evaluating what is needed for their sites to communicate and then making a determined effort to reduce the complexity of their interface: a simplification era, if you will.

This process is in keeping with the ideas behind a "hidden" Web — the complexity of the systems is invisible to you, and you are only asked to make a few simple choices from time to time.

Customization: Though we currently live in a world of mass marketing, the need to "tell" you what you want is slowly (very slowly) giving way to a new movement of actually letting you decide what you want. We can see this philosophy at work on Web sites with sophisticated customization features (see Chapter 8). These sites make use of your decisions and previous interests to provide you with timely and applicable choices. (Such selective presentations can also help simplify interfaces by providing only relevant options.)

Custom content delivery has the potential to be quite popular. As an example, I am an avid fan of avant-garde jazz music and would readily welcome advertisements (reflective of my particular tastes) from the labels that produce such records. On the other hand, I violently dislike the barrage of spy-camera and online casino site advertising that pollutes my Web browsing experience. The polite (catered to my tastes) content is more likely to generate a sale than ads, which only serve to annoy me.

Again, when a "hidden" Web arrives, customization will reflect where and how I access my content. From custom devices (a personal music player) to specific locations (a jazz record store for example), content applicable to my interests and lifestyle can be delivered with a much better degree of accuracy and therefore success.

I believe this trend will not only be restricted to the Web. As custom content delivery solutions become less expensive and easy to implement, traditional mediums, such as print, TV, and radio, will also cater more to individual tastes. Then again, I could just be a dreamer, but doesn't your "own" radio station sound cool?

Service distribution: I spent significant time in Chapter 8 detailing the rise of Web applications and how they promise to create a more useful Web for us all. For the foreseeable future, I believe such Web accessible services will form the bulk of new and successful Web ventures. (I see it on an almost monthly basis now.)

The ability to get things done on the Web will not only provide compelling reasons to be online, but it will probably foster new ways of working that redefine group dynamics and personal data interactions. Eventually, most software applications will be remotely accessible and kept out of sight on the "hidden" Web. (That's right, no need to ever install programs again.)

Content separation: Making the distinction between content and presentation is another trend I touched on in Chapter 8. However, the applications I outlined were rather basic. The real power of discrete content is evident when there are multiple means for accessing and applying it.

Shared banks of information can be pooled by various methods and published to any (or all) mediums (a Web site and a poster, for example). The common markup standards (currently taking shape with XML) will allow companies and individuals to locate and share information in ways previously unheard of. These systems will also ease the process of finding (or creating) multiple connections between content. These types of connections will allow information retrieval to be more intelligent and accurate.

No longer will you have to search with simple keywords, but instead you might search by concepts, the relationships between information, or in a manner specific to your unique needs.

New device applications: Although multiple devices for accessing the Web are already available now, many more are on the way. From traffic advisors and driving direction consoles in automobiles to communication devices that take over for e-mail and telephones, Web-ready devices will come in all shapes and sizes.

These "information appliances" will be designed with specific tasks (such as taking pictures with a digital camera) in mind, but also readily share their data with other smart devices. As a simple example, think of a digital camera that "talks" to your printer and creates a print of your vacation photos for your wall. Or better yet, the camera talks to a frame on your wall, which automatically updates the photo is displays. To take it another step further, that frame is plugged in to the "hidden" Web and automatically updates another frame at your parent's house with your most recent photos.

Fun stuff, to be sure.

WHAT'S NEXT FOR LUKE?

If you enjoyed this book (or at least found it somewhat useful) and are interested in seeing what I am currently up to, feel free to check up on my activities at www.lukew.com. As time permits, I try to continually update the site with samples of my current projects and ideas. See you in cyberspace.

PERMISSIONS

Web site	Permissions Text
37signals.com	Image courtesy of 37signals.com.
Adobe.com	©2002 Adobe Systems Incorporated. Used with express permission. All rights reserved. Adobe and Acrobat is/are either (a) registrered trademark(s) of Adobe Systems Incorporated in the United States and/or other countries.
Amazon.com	©2001 Amazon.com, Inc. All rights reserved.
Apple.com	Screen shots reprinted by permission from Apple Computer, Inc.
Bluenile.com	Copyright © 2002, Blue Nile, Inc. All rights reserved.
buyarock.com	buyarock.com ®
Cardean University	Cardean University images are reprinted with permission from Unext.com, LLC. ©Copyright 2002, All rights reserved.
Chicgao Symphony (cso.org)	©Chicago Symphony Orchestra Association.
Cintara.com	©Cintara Corporation.
Complementstothechef.com	Image courtesy of Complements to the Chef.
Concord.com	Copyright ©2001, 2002 Concord Communications Inc. All rights reserved. www.concord.com

COLOR THEORY

PANTONE Guide to Communicating with Color, Leatrice Eiseman, Grafix Press Ltd, 2000.

Designer's Guide to Color, James Stockton, Chronicle Books, 1984.

Creative Color: A dynamic approach for artists and designers, Faber Birren, Schiffer Publishing, Ltd., 1987.

Color and Culture: Practice and meaning from antiquity to abstraction, John Gage, Bulfinch Press, 1993.

EXPERIENCE DESIGN

Experience Design I, Nathan Shedorff, New Riders, 2001.

INFORMATION ARCHITECTURE

Information Architecture Design. Peter Morville & Samantha Bailey, User Interface Engineering, 2001.

Information Architecture for the World Wide Web, Peter Morville & Louis Rosenfeld, O'Reilly & Associates, 1998.

INFORMATION DESIGN

Visual Explanations, Edward Tufte, Graphics Press, 1997.

Envisioning Information, Edward Tufte, Graphics Press, 1990.

INTERFACE DESIGN

Macintosh Human Interface Guidelines, Apple Computer, Inc. Addison-Wesley Publishing Co., 1992.

Design Requirements for Hypermedia, Colleen Bushell, Virginia Commonwealth University, 1995).

About Face: The Essentials of User Interface Design, Alan Cooper, IDG Books Worldwide, Inc., 1995.

Inventing Interfaces: Tactics, Tricks, and Techniques for Breakthrough Innovations, Larry L. Constantine & Lucy A.D. Lockwood, User Interface Engineering, 2000).

Language and Communication: Essential Concepts for User Interface and Documentation Design, Agnes Kulkulska-Hulme, Oxford University Press, 1999.

The Humane Interface: New Directions for Designing Interactive Systems, Jef Raskin, Addison-Wesley Publishing Co., 2000.

Designing the Use Interface: Strategies for Effective Human-Computer Interaction, Ben Shneiderman, Addison-Wesley Publishing Co., 1998.

Tog on Interface, Bruce Tognazzini, Addison-Wesley Publishing Co., 1992.

Tog on Software Design, Bruce Tognazzini, Addison-Wesley Publishing Co., 1996.

Visual Design of the User Interface, Edward Tufte, IBM Corporation, 1989.

NAVIGATION

Inner Navigation: Why we Get Lost in the World and How We Find Our Way, Erik Jonsson, Scribner, 2002.

Planning During Map Learning: The Global Strategies of High and Low Spatial Individuals, Cathleen Stasz, Rand, 1980.

Performance Models for Spatial and Locational Cognition, Peter W. Thorndyke, Rand, 1980.

Plan Your Route: The New Approach to Map Reading, Victor Selwyn, David & Charles, 1987.

PSYCHOLOGY & HUMAN FACTORS

The Perception of Symbols on Screen and Methods of Retrieval From a Database, Mary Dyson, Hilary Box, & Michael Twyman, British Library Research and Development Department, 1994.

Theories of Personality Calvin Hall Springer and Lindzey Gardner, Wiley & Sons, 1970.

The Silent Language, Edward T. Hall, DoubleDay, 1959.

The Hidden Dimension, Edward T. Hall, DoubleDay, 1966.

: **bibliography** :

Designing with the Mind in Mind: Basic Phenomena in Human Memory and Problem Solving, Thomas Hewett, User Interface Engineering 2000.

How the Mind Works, Steven Pinker, Norton & Company, 1997.

Design of Everyday Things: The Psychology of Everyday Things, Donald Norman, Currency Doubleday, 1988.

The Invisible Computer: Why Good Products Can Fail, The Personal Computer Is So Complex, and Information Appliances Are the Solution, Donald Norman, MIT Press, 1999.

The Media Equation: How People Treat Computers, Television, and New Media Like Real People and Places, Byron Reeves & Clifford Nash, Cambridge University Press, 1996.

Consilience: The Unity of Knowledge, Edward O. Wilson, Vintage Books, 1999.

TYPOGRAPHY

Typography on the Web, Joseph T. Sinclair, AP Professional, 1999.

Type Rules! The designers guide to professional typography, Ilene Strizver, North Light Books, 2001.

WEB APPLICATIONS

The Rise of Weblications: Keynote address presented at the User Experience World Tour, D.A. Norman, November 17, 2000, Chicago, IL.

Design Guidelines for Web-based Applications, Proceedings of the 45th Annual Meeting of the Human Factors and Ergonomics Society (pp. 1191-1195), L. Wroblewski & E.M. Rantanen, Santa Monica, CA: HFES, 2001.

WEB PROGRAMMING

Javascript: The Definitive Guide, Third Edition, David Flanagan, O'Reilly & Associates, 1998.

Cascading Style Sheets: The Definitive Guide, Eric Meyer, O'Reilly & Associates, 2000.

HTML and XHTML: The Definitive Guide, Chuck Musciano & Bill Kennedy, O'Reilly & Associates, 2000.

XML: A Primer, Simon St. Laurent, MIS Press, 1998.

Beginning ASP 3.0. David Buser, John Kauffman, Juan T. Llibre, Brian Francis, David Sussman, Chris Ullman, & John Duckett, Wrox Press, 1999.

WEB DESIGN

Fresh Styles for Web Designers: Eye Candy From the Underground, Curt Cloninger, New Riders Publishing, 2002.

Patrick J. Lynch & Sarah Horton, Web Style Guide: Basic Principles for Creating Web Sites. Yale University Press, 1999.

The Art & Science of Web Design, Jeffery Veen, New Riders Publishing, 2001.

WORLD WIDE WEB HISTORY

Weaving the Web: The Original Destiny and Ultimate Destiny of the World Wide Web by its Inventor, Tim Berners-Lee, Harper Business, 1999.

WEB USABILITY

Developing Schemas for the Location of Common Web Objects. <u>Proceedings of the 45th Annual Meeting of the Human Factors and Ergonomics Society</u> (pp. 1161-1165), Michael L. Bernard, HFES, 2001.

Web Site Usability: A Designer's Guide, Jared M. Spool, Tara Scanlon, Will Schroeder, Carolyn Snyder, & Terri DeAngelo, Morgan Kaufmann Publishers, Inc., 1999.

Don't Make Me Think: A Common Sense Approach to Web Usability, Steven Krug, New Riders Publishing, 2000.

Designing Web Usability: The Practice of Simplicity, Jakob Nielsen, New Riders Publishing, 2000.

INDEX

INDEX

INDEX

INDEX